Faulkner's Inheritance
FAULKNER AND YOKNAPATAWPHA
2005

Faulkner's Inheritance

FAULKNER AND YOKNAPATAWPHA, 2005

EDITED BY
JOSEPH R. URGO
AND
ANN J. ABADIE

UNIVERSITY PRESS OF MISSISSIPPI
JACKSON

www.upress.state.ms.us

The University Press of Mississippi is a member of the Association of
American University Presses.

Copyright © 2007 by University Press of Mississippi
All rights reserved
Manufactured in the United States of America

First edition 2007

Library of Congress Cataloging-in-Publication Data

Faulkner and Yoknapatawpha Conference (32nd: 2005: University of Mississippi)
    Faulkner's inheritance/Faulkner and Yoknapatawpha, 2005; edited by Joseph R. Urgo
and Ann J. Abadie. — 1st ed.
    p. cm.
    A collection of essays examining the influences on Faulkner's fiction, including his own
family history, Jim Crow laws, contemporary fashion, popular culture, and literature.
    Includes bibliographical references and index.
    ISBN-13: 978-1-57806-953-8 (cloth: alk. paper)
    ISBN-10: 1-57806-953-X (cloth: alk. paper) 1.   Faulkner, William, 1897–1962—
Criticism and interpretation—Congresses. 2.   Faulkner, William, 1897–1962—
Family—Congresses. 3.   Southern States—In literature—Congresses. 4.   Race in
literature—Congresses. 5.   Popular culture in literature—Congresses. I.   Urgo,
Joseph R. II.   Abadie, Ann J. III.   Title.
    PS3511.A86Z78321178 2005
    813'. 52—dc22   2006029993

British Library Cataloging-in-Publication Data available

For Joseph Blotner,
Faulkner biographer and longtime friend
of the University of Mississippi
and the Faulkner and Yoknapatawpha Conference

Contents

Introduction

1

What Faulkner inherited, in terms of probate, was not much. The Falkner family was not a wealthy clan and, as families go, was in a period of social decline when baby William entered the world. What he inherited in terms of what came to him from his civilization, of what he assumed was his to shape and mold and to leave behind, was indeed much. Critical attention for the past seventy years or so has examined with increasing scrutiny the matters Faulkner seemed to feel, in his gut, were his to bequeath to future readers, and for them to contemplate and unravel: complex matters of race and gender, issues ranging from the esoteric to the mundane, from the spiritual crises of men and women in conflict with time and place to bickering arising out of petty jealousies and mean ambition. Faulkner threw it all to probate, for surviving generations to parse and parcel, as generations of critics deal successively with the texts and with their critical inheritance. What we as a civilization have inherited in Faulkner is a massive voice defining for us the agenda of our culture's most pressing inequities and most profound contradictions. Most ventures through probate in Faulkner lead to violent ends, a device of literary structure that inevitably makes such received issues press harder on collective consciousness, press very hard on our common sense of Faulkner's Inheritance.

The opening fragment to "Was" (the opening chapter in *Go Down, Moses*) is a kind of Faulknerian manifesto on the idea of inheritance and, specifically, the ways in which inheritance entangles with free will and chance. It serves well as an introduction to the essays in this volume, *Faulkner's Inheritance: Faulkner and Yoknapatawpha, 2005*. We are told that McCaslin Edmonds, the narrator of the tale that follows the opening fragment, is not the legal heir to the fortune he received in property and slaves from Isaac McCaslin's father. McCaslin Edmonds inherited what Isaac McCaslin refused, and because of this refusal, McCaslin Edmonds became, in the words of the fragment, "yet not withstanding the inheritor, and in his time the bequestor, of that which some had thought then and some still thought should have been Isaac's."[1] *Go Down, Moses*, Faulkner's epic novel of race relations, hinges ever so delicately, and ever so blunderingly, on matters of inheritance. Isaac McCaslin famously refuses his inheritance, in an effort to remove himself from received inequity, abuse, and scandal. His refusal is the delicate matter he bequeaths to his cousins. The Edmonds family, in turn, somewhat blunderingly inherits the refusal along with the refused inheritance, a situation not lost on the disinherited descendants of slaves who work for them. In the subsequent, guiding metaphor of "Was," it comes down, in the end, to handling the cards we are dealt. The complicating factor in the metaphor as it emerges in "Was" is that, despite the implication of fatality, when it comes to playing poker, no hand is ever dealt purely by chance.

Central to McCaslin Edmonds's memory in "Was" are two hands of cards, each resorted to at key junctures in the tale—moments of impasse, to be precise, when a postponed decision looms. The first hand is dealt after Hubert Beauchamp and Uncle Buck McCaslin have spent hours in an inconclusive pursuit of the runaway slave, Tomey's Turl, a failed hunt complicated by Uncle Buck's having placed himself in a compromising position with Hubert's sister, Sophonsiba. To settle matters that have become far too complicated for rational discussion (because they are marked at once by deep emotional fears and by conflicting interests in human property and real estate), the two men agree to let chance be the arbiter. "One hand" (20) is what Hubert calls for. Draw Poker is the men's choice of hands, a game calling for a modicum of skill, but primarily determined by chance if only one hand is played. The loser of the hand will win Sophonsiba (as sister or wife, either) and be compelled to purchase the two negro slaves whose desire to marry gave rise to the episode in the first place. However, while poker may be a game of chance, the method of play in "Was" is far from dependent on the luck of the draw.

The poker hand between Uncle Buck and Hubert McCaslin should have ended the matter except for one factor: Hubert cheated. In McCaslin Edmonds's telling:

> So Uncle Buck shuffled the cards and Mr. Hubert cut them. Then he took up the deck and dealt in turn until Uncle Buck and Mr. Hubert had five. And Uncle Buck looked at his hand a long time and then said two cards and he gave them to him, and Mr. Hubert looked at his hand quick and said one card and he gave it to him and Mr. Hubert flipped his discard onto the two which Uncle Buck had discarded and slid the new card into his hand and opened it out and looked at it quick again and closed it and looked at Uncle Buck and said, 'Well? Did you help them threes?' (21; emphasis added)

It is possible, of course, that what Hubert means by "Did you help them threes?" is did you help the three cards you kept when you discarded and received two more? To mean this clearly, though, Hubert would have had to have asked, "Did you help them three?" It's more plausible, then, that what he referred to was the three threes that Buck received when Hubert dealt the cards to him. And if Hubert knew that Buck held three threes, he would also know that "them threes" received no help from his next dealing. Hubert's control of the deck in turn makes his full house ("three kings and two fives" [21]) inevitable, but far from decisive.

When Uncle Buddy hears Cass Edmonds's account of the two men's interaction, he quickly travels to Hubert's property and immediately, after supper, sits down to play cards with Hubert himself—calling him, as it were, on the previous hand. Of course, neither man, acting as a gentleman, brings up the card hand played earlier that day. The tale's second poker hand begins as soon as the two men sit down at the card table. The man who is dealt the stronger hand will get most of what he wants; the loser will be saddled with things he does not want. And because he won the previous hand, even if he loses, Hubert will walk away with some wealth.[2] Realizing that Buddy is a more seasoned card player, Hubert suggests that Buddy shuffle the cards, Hubert cut them, and young McCaslin deal them. The offer seems generous, given McCaslin's allegiance to Buck and Buddy. As if to throw Hubert off guard, Buddy refuses this offer ("He's too young. I dont want him mixed up with any gambling" [22]). Hubert responds by calling for anyone outside who is capable of dealing cards, as if to acknowledge to Buddy that this will truly be a hand of chance. However, as made plain in the story's denouement, Hubert has fallen for Buddy's ruse, because just outside the door, waiting for his cue, is Tomey's Turl, the man whose fate lies in the outcome of the gamble. As the game of five-card stud comes to a finish, Buddy ups the stakes, confident of winning. At the moment of calling the bet, Hubert hesitates and, as if finally recalling what kind of game he initiated, he asks Buddy, "Who dealt these cards, Amodeus?" It is at that moment, when he sees that the dealer is Tomey's Turl, no impartial agent, that he folds.[3]

What, then, might it mean in a Faulknerian cosmos to consider the hand we are dealt? Nothing seems left to chance in "Was," and cheating appears to be an accepted method of play. Or perhaps it is not cheating we witness in "Was," but the interplay of free will within a universe of chance. "It's said that a man playing cards with Amodeus McCaslin aint gambling," admits Hubert Beauchamp (22). And neither was Uncle Buck gambling when he agreed to let a hand of poker with Hubert decide his fate. Moving back to the story's initial, and controlling, metaphor of inheritance, we may suspect that for Faulkner, inheritance is no passive act of receivership, but an active challenge by forces outside our influence to command the future. In this understanding, we may see the issue of inheritance as central to a Faulknerian conception of the complex interplay between received conditions and the human capacity to act, to redress the past, to affect the present, and, in one's turn, to bequeath to the future the products of one's own effort. "[A]nd in his time the bequestor," as Faulkner writes in the opening passage to *Go Down, Moses*: and in our time, the hand we are dealt, and the will we have to alter events, to determine the difference between cheating and fair play—these matters are ultimately questions of justice in Faulkner.

2

Leading the volume is Noel Polk, "Making 'Something Which Did Not Exist Before': What Faulkner Gave Himself," framing a comparison between the virtually blank landscape from which Willa Cather created her Nebraska and western plains aesthetic and the potentially overdetermined landscapes of Mississippi and the South inherited by Faulkner. Whereas Cather hands Jim Burden, in *My Ántonia*, "a land completely free of a history that would shape the way he could understand it," Faulkner bestows upon Quentin Compson, in *Absalom, Absalom!*, a body more properly understood as "a barracks filled with stubborn back-looking ghosts." Out of Faulkner's struggle with this inheritance comes the signature aesthetic of mistrust—mistrust of what Polk calls "the dictatorial logic of sequence," manifest in such narrative traits as the refusal to fill historical gaps, the creation of sequential and nominative inconsistencies, and the conjuring of the past as less linear than "evanescent, fragmentary, 'shadow, paradoxical,' and most often available only in traces." From this aesthetic response to overdetermination, Faulkner "allowed himself to know differently the world his predecessors had thought they knew, and so knew a different world."

The volume turns next to biography. Wealth is often inherited through marriage, and what Faulkner gained by his lifelong intellectual and emotional dialogue with Estelle Oldham is taken up by Judith Sensibar in "Estelle and William Faulkner's Imaginative Collaboration (c. 1919–1925)." Sensibar argues that Estelle's short career as writer influenced Faulkner profoundly, literally providing him "the means to find his own fiction writer's voice," and spurring his decision to abandon poetry for prose in the mid-1920s. A crucial point of intersection comes when Faulkner typed and revised Estelle's story, "A Crossing," elements of which would surface in many subsequent novels. This story led Faulkner "to see how to turn from the bookishly imitative and psychologically opaque figures in his poetry to the people and issues of his own generation and world." In short, Sensibar suggests, Estelle instructed the neophyte author William Faulkner "how to move from convention to invention in this crucial period of his aesthetic development." The essay revises our understanding of what Estelle brought to the marriage, and perhaps as well suggests why Faulkner, deep into its darkest days, felt so committed to sustaining it.

In "Atomic Faulkner," Priscilla Wald examines the world Faulkner inherited in the 1950s, the world into which he was propelled after the Nobel Prize, and the "public role he had neither expected, nor particularly coveted." Nonetheless, like a distant relative inheriting his estranged Uncle Sam's white elephant, Faulkner became one of the nation's earliest and most influential interpreters of the atomic era, defining its characteristic emotion of fear in 1950 with his famous phrasing of the era's persistent interrogative, "When will I be blown up?" Fear, then, became a motif in his public speeches, as the unlikely inheritor of Franklin Roosevelt's dismissal of the emotion (when he invoked the single most fearsome thing to be fear itself) insisted time and again that it was fear that enslaved citizens—fear of bombs, yes, but also fear of change, fear of the Other, fear of new ideas and new ways of social organization. "Nothing better represented that enslavement, nor posed a greater challenge to its opposition, than the inequity—and tragedy—of race relations in the South." Faulkner would contrast the fear shown by his contemporaries in the face of coming changes in the South to the courage of their ancestors in the face of momentous changes—a comparison that could lead some to suspect a reactionary perspective, revealing Faulkner's occasional (and, in Noel Polk's view, fundamental) departures from strictly rational thinking. The artist was at his best in the syntax of literary representation, and Wald concludes her essay with an illuminating study of Thomas Sutpen's motivation by the peculiarly American merging of fear and innocence, and "the racialized politics of fear" that pervades *Absalom, Absalom!*

Adam Gussow, in "Plaintive Reiterations and Meaningless Strains: Faulkner's Blues Understandings," offers what may well stand as the definitive positioning of Faulkner within local Mississippi blues culture. Debunking the "proximity effect," the linking of Faulkner and the blues from its depths in tourism to its higher forms in academia, Gussow offers a thoroughly positivist accounting of Faulkner's "blues education"—what he knew, and how he came to know it in places like Memphis, Clarksdale, and Oxford. With the facts in hand, Gussow engages those texts in which the blues inform Faulkner's meaning, including *Soldiers' Pay*, *Sartoris*, "That Evening Sun," and "Pantaloon in Black." Gussow's readings place Faulkner's texts within a nexus of blues lyric and structure, moving adeptly into biography and social history, evoking a set of richly nuanced strands of evocation. Gussow finds that Faulkner's understanding of the blues deepened over time and needs to be positioned parallel to more general trends in his intellectual development. "As Faulkner probes the emotional sources and signifying registers of black blues expression with increasing subtlety in the course of his career, he also finds more evidence for the inadequacy of white response," Gussow argues; "as his blues-literary art grows blacker, it also grows more pessimistic about the power of the blues to engender racial understanding."

Moving from the South to the northern metropolis, Jon Smith examines Faulkner's interaction with big city consumerism in "Faulkner, Metropolitan Fashion, and 'The South'" and finds cause to separate Faulkner from his well-known Fugitive contemporaries for his fascination with (for example) the New York City fashion world. "Faulkner is a good deal hipper than his critics have been," Smith asserts, and a lot more up-to-date in his dress and presentation than is revealed by popular images of him in tattered clothing. Smith's Faulkner is the Faulkner who enjoyed dressing up and looking good—one of many guises, but an important one in his multiple self-fashioning. A potentially dandified Faulkner is the one who wrote home in 1925 to rave over a sport jacket he'd seen in a shop window. His was a lifelong fascination with well-made things. Smith delves into the fashion aesthetic of *The Mansion*, and in particular the scene where Ratliff purchases exorbitantly expensive Allanovna neckties in the New York boutique, which he puts in productive juxtaposition to Mink's purchase of the "cooter" handgun in Memphis and Flem's installation of the hearthside footrest. As Smith examines Ratliff, he finds him moving steadily toward the confluence of fashion and modernism, seeing that the essence of modernist art (and fashion) is "experiential newness"; or, in Ratliff's words, "what you never expected to and hadn't ever imagined until that moment."

Returning to southern landscapes, Susan V. Donaldson places the psyche and fate of Joe Christmas within the context of one of Faulkner's more disturbing inheritances, that of a divided African American consciousness enforced by the brutalities of the Jim Crow South. "Faulkner's own angels of history survey the wreckage of a society all too confident in its categories of whiteness and blackness and in its power of surveillance and control," Donaldson explains, "and the steadiness of their gaze upon that wreckage interrogates and destabilizes the surveillance they fall under themselves as misfits, outcasts, and debris of a rigidly segregated society." Donaldson provides a deep reading of Joe Christmas, identifying him as one who sees himself "only through the eyes of a Jim Crow world that defines blackness as the negative of whiteness," and placing the image of his mutilated body within the macabre tradition of the lynching cabinet card, "those horrifying souvenirs that circulated in the heyday of lynching and segregation and that both reinforced and exposed the making and working of whiteness."

Martin Kreiswirth continues this volume's exploration of Faulkner's racial inheritance by examining the two novels that were originally titled "Dark House" (*Light in August* and *Absalom, Absalom!*), a place-holding title that in Kreiswirth's hands emerges as "an extraordinarily appropriate emblem of the racial uncanny." Building from Freud's theory of the uncanny, and its especial applicability to literary representation, and from commentary on the notion by Heidegger, Cixous, Wittgenstrein, Derrida, and others, Kreiswirth explores the *racial uncanny* "buried deep within the monomania of Rosa's narration, obliquely hinted at through the gentlemanly niceties of Mr. Compson's discourse, and only haltingly, but finally, exhibited through Quentin and Shreve's impossible imaginative recreation." And as well, in *Light in August*, "it underlies the inscrutability of Christmas's social re-presentation." Each novel through distinct forms of narration arrives at the critical juncture where "racial distinction is fundamentally baseless and nonexistent," so that it is "the impossibility of race itself that is the insuperable horror that Bon and Christmas display."

In "A Mammy Callie Legacy," Lael Gold traces the influence of the illiterate African American bible—the bible of an oral culture, whose scripture is received aurally, and not through reading—on Faulkner's aesthetics and literary production. Gold thus finds "two bibles" intersecting in Faulkner, the written and oral texts that he received from the two Mississippi traditions, one from white Oxford and the other, quite specifically, from the mouth of his black nursemaid, Mammy Callie. One result of this dual inheritance is the uncanny way in which the Bible "seems to hover over" novels such as *Absalom, Absalom!* and *If I Forget Thee, Jerusalem*, or the way oral and written bibles compete, in *Go Down, Moses*, for authority. Perhaps the most telling intersection is between Reverend Shegog's oral scripture, received by Dilsey in *The Sound and the Fury*, and the unread (and unreceived) Bible that Mrs. Compson demands she hand to her, immediately upon Dilsey's return. "This scene of habitual convalescence, of slackness of body and spirit, suggests once more the profound and personal engagement of those who experience the Bible via oral rather than written transmission. In Faulkner's imagination, this inheritance resulted in a profoundly dialogical comprehension—and aesthetic representation—of scripture."

We close the volume with an afterword by Faulkner's most recent biographer. Jay Parini, "In the House of Faulkner," ruminates on the biographer's task in sorting through inheritance and "of what *inheres*: in indwelling mystery of the *genius loci*." Major scenes in Faulkner's work have characters struggling with received knowledge and inherited circumstance—Parini considers Quentin Compson and Ike McCaslin, among others—revealing the very idea of "what *inheres*" as an animating force in Faulkner's imagination. Returning to the metaphor of the card game, we might think again about those narrative situations when Faulkner holds, when he discards, and when he calls—the habitual calling at moments of social and cultural crisis, for example, the insistence that all cards be shown, and the eruptions of violence and poignancy when his most reflective characters are faced with the hands dealt or acquired by Others.

Joseph R. Urgo
Hamilton College
Clinton, New York

NOTES

1. William Faulkner, *Novels, 1942–1954*, ed. Joseph Blotner and Noel Polk (New York: Library of America, 1994), 5. Subsequent references are made parenthetically.

2. Specifically, if Buddy wins, Buck does not have to marry Sophonsiba, but Buddy must still purchase Tennie as per the previous hand. If Hubert wins, Buck must marry Sophonsiba, as per the previous hand, but he gets no dowry from Hubert (22).

3. For another reading of the card games in "Was," one much more attendant to the very specific issues of race and property in the story, see Thadious M. Davis, *Games of Property: Law, Race, Gender, and Faulkner's* Go Down, Moses (Durham: Duke University Press, 2003), esp. 64–71.

A Note on the Conference

The Thirty-second Annual Faulkner and Yoknapatawpha Conference sponsored by the University of Mississippi in Oxford took place July 24–28, 2005, with more than two hundred of the author's admirers from around the world in attendance. Nine presentations at the conference are collected as essays in this volume. Brief mention is made here of other conference activities.

The conference began on Sunday with a reception at the University Museum and two lectures, followed by a buffet supper at historic Memory House. That evening, Oxford Mayor Richard Howorth welcomed participants to the conference, as did Joseph R. Urgo, chair of the University English Department. Charles Reagan Wilson, director of the Center for the Study of Southern Culture, presented the nineteenth annual Eudora Welty Awards in Creative Writing. Julie Armstrong, a student at St. Andrew's Episcopal School in Jackson, won first prize, $500, for her poem "The Day Edward G. Robinson and My Father Shared a Victory." Andrew Thomas, of Jackson Preparatory School in Jackson, won second prize, $250, for his story "I Dare You to Take Me Seriously." Frances Patterson of Tupelo, a member of the Center Advisory Committee, established and endowed the awards, which are selected through a competition held in high schools throughout Mississippi. Donald M. Kartiganer, director of the conference, announced the award of conference fellowships to three graduate students working in the area of Faulkner studies; the awards are sponsored by the William Faulkner Society, the *Faulkner Journal,* and donations in memory of John W. Hunt, Faulkner scholar and Emeritus Professor of Literature at Lehigh University. Professor Kartiganer then introduced Sam Apple, who read the winning entry—"The Administration and the Fury: If William Faulkner Were Writing on the Bush White House"—of the sixteenth annual Faux Faulkner Contest, sponsored by *Hemispheres* magazine of United Airlines, the University of Mississippi, and the Yoknapatawpha Press. The evening ended with local actors presenting *Voices from Yoknapatawpha,* readings from Faulkner's fiction selected and arranged by actor George Kehoe and Betty Hartington, wife of former conference director Evans Harrington.

Monday's program included three lectures and sessions during which Seth Berner, a book dealer from Portland, Maine, talked about "Collecting Faulkner" and James B. Carothers, Charles A. Peek, Terrell L. Tebbetts, and Theresa M. Towner discussed "Teaching Faulkner." Peter Brown,

Brittany Powell, and Matthew Sutton made presentations for the first of two panels sponsored by an anonymous gift made in honor of Joseph Blotner, Faulkner biographer and longtime friend of the University of Mississippi and the Faulkner and Yoknapatawpha Conference. The day's activities ended with Colby Kullman moderating the fifth Faulkner Fringe Festival, an open-mike evening at Southside Gallery on the Oxford Square.

Guided tours of North Mississippi and the Delta took place on Tuesday, as did an afternoon party at Tyler Place, hosted by Charles Noyes, Sarah and Allie Smith, and Colby Kullman. The day ended with Susan Donaldson's lecture. On Wednesday, after two lectures and a panel with presentations by Elizabeth Cornell, Jonathan Howland, and Reginald Martin, Elizabeth Nichols Shiver brought together current or former Oxford residents Harter Williams Crutcher, Carl S. Downing, Mildred Murray Douglass Hopkins, William Lewis Jr., and Dr. Ray J. Nichols to reminisce about Faulkner. Attendees then gathered for the annual picnic at Faulkner's home, Rowan Oak, and afterward enjoyed a reading by Michael Knight, 2005–2006 John and Renée Grisham Visiting Southern Writer at the University of Mississippi. Program events on Thursday were a lecture, two discussion sessions, and John Maxwell's performance of his acclaimed monologue "*Oh, Mr. Faulkner, Do You Write?*" The conference ended with a party at Off-Square Books.

Four exhibitions were available throughout the conference. The University's John Davis Williams Library sponsored an exhibition of William Faulkner's works and publications by his brother, John Faulkner; his great-grandfather, W. C. Falkner; and other members of the family. The University Museum exhibited more than forty etchings and lithographs artist Boyd Saunders created to illustrate *Spotted Horses, The Sound and the Fury, The Bear,* and other Faulkner books. *Whispering Pines,* a collection of twenty-seven color and black-and-white photographs by Mississippi photographer Birney Imes, was on exhibit at Barnard Observatory's Gammill Gallery. The University Press of Mississippi exhibited Faulkner books published by university presses throughout the United States.

The conference planners are grateful to all the individuals and organizations that support the Faulkner and Yoknapatawpha Conference annually. In addition to those mentioned above, we wish to thank Square Books, St. Peter's Episcopal Church, the City of Oxford, and the Oxford Tourism Council. Also, for use of *The Square,* by John McCrady (1911–1968), to illustrate this year's conference materials, we thank Mr. and Mrs. William Lewis and the Downtown Grill, Jeanne de la Houssaye, Blake Marshall, and the McCrady Estate.

Faulkner's Inheritance
FAULKNER AND YOKNAPATAWPHA
2005

Making "Something Which Did Not Exist Before": What Faulkner Gave Himself

For Joseph Blotner

NOEL POLK

In the opening pages of Willa Cather's *My Ántonia* Jim Burden describes his "interminable journey across the great midland plain of North America."[1] He's moving from his native Virginia to Nebraska to live with his grandparents, accompanied by a cowboy chaperone, Jake Marpole, who gives him a "Life of Jesse James," which, even while writing many years after the experience, Jim remembers as "one of the most satisfactory books I have ever read" (4)—a curious and revealing confession from a lawyer, classically trained in the writings of Virgil, whom he hopes to emulate: like Virgil, Jim wants "to be the first . . . to bring the Muse into [his own] country" (256). Getting closer to his destination, he does not "remember crossing the Missouri River, or anything about the long day's journey through Nebraska. Probably by that time I had crossed so many rivers that I was dull to them. The only thing very noticeable about Nebraska was that it was still, all day long, Nebraska." Arriving at Black Hawk, Jim stumbles from his sleep and from the train down into a world without form, and void, a "place where men were running about with lanterns. I couldn't see any town, or even distant lights; we were surrounded by utter darkness." Out of the "red glow of the [train's] fire-box" (5) emerge the Shimerda family, the emigrants from Bohemia whom the train's conductor had told him about, and Ántonia herself, who will become the beloved bête noir of his book—and of his entire life, as *My Ántonia* proves. She thus emerges out of a darkness, a void lighted only by the fiery glow of the modern, of a new-found national mobility: the trains that even then were already writing a national history across the American plains.

As he and Jake drive to his grandparents' ranch with Otto, who has met them at the train station, Jim tries to sleep but cannot because of the jolting; he gets up on his knees and looks out "over the side of the wagon":

> There seemed to be nothing to see; no fences, no creeks or trees, no hills or fields. If there was a road, I could not make it out in the faint starlight. There was nothing but land: not a country at all, but the material out of which countries are made. No, there was nothing but land—slightly undulating, I knew, because often our wheels ground against the brake as we went down into a

hollow and lurched up again on the other side. I had the feeling that the world
was left behind, that we had got over the edge of it, and were outside man's
jurisdiction. I had never before looked up at the sky when there was not a
familiar mountain ridge against it. But this was the complete dome of heaven,
all there was of it. I did not believe that my dead father and mother were watching me from up there; they would still be looking for me at the sheepfold down
by the creek, or along the white road that led to the mountain pastures. I had
left even their spirits behind me. The wagon jolted on, carrying me I knew not
whither. I don't think I was homesick. If we never arrived anywhere, it did not
matter. Between that earth and that sky I felt erased, blotted out. I did not say
my prayers that night: here, I felt, what would be would be. (70–8)

A couple of days later, on his grandparents' farm, Jim still finds very little
of interest in the landscape: "I wanted to walk straight on through the red
grass and over the edge of the world, which could not be very far away.
The light air about me told me that the world ended here: only the ground
and sun and sky were left, and if one went a little farther there would
be only sun and sky, and one would float off into them, like the tawny
hawks which sailed over our heads making slow shadows on the grass"
(16). Outside the contours of the familiar—outside, that is, the particulars
of time and place which make us who we are—Jim Burden feels "erased,"
nonexistent, undefined, and if he is not terrified he at least recognizes his
contingency in the new space as yet undefined by history. By not saying
his prayers, he recognizes also the helplessness even of God, the author
of purpose, in this land free of the secure and comforting confines of the
familiar, of causes and effects with which he had spent the formative years
of his childhood and which defined his world, and his self, for him.

Ántonia is herself part of this new world, though she is an emigrant to it
too, like Jim. The conductor of the train they have traveled on has talked to
Jim about the Shimerdas. He is a man "experienced and worldly . . . who
had been almost everywhere." As he begins to tell about the Shimerdas,
Jim notes that his "cuff-buttons were engraved with hieroglyphics, and
he was more inscribed than an Egyptian obelisk" (4). He thus juxtaposes
Ántonia with those ancient hieroglyphs, a language whose meanings
he cannot possibly understand. And when the conductor, teasing, asks
whether he doesn't think that Ántonia has "pretty brown eyes" (4), Jim
gets bashful, buries himself comfortably in his "Life of Jesse James," and
escapes into Jake's suggestion that "you were likely to get diseases from
foreigners" (5), a world he knows, a language and landscape he is comfortable with.

Ántonia thus first appears to Jim framed between two written texts, two
narrative possibilities for the writer-to-be to explore and perhaps exploit:
the esoteric, mysterious, and completely incomprehensible hieroglyphics

of the ancient world, and the completely known, clichéd, tawdry, romanticized, sentimentalized, and completely manufactured world of Jesse James that he knows so well doubtless from having read other such potboilers. We notice this the more because Cather's fictional introduction establishes her novel as Jim's written memoir of Ántonia and because, as just noted, several times in the text Jim declares his youthful desire to emulate Virgil by being the first to write about the country in which he was to grow up. Since he and Ántonia have arrived on the same train, and since the conductor has in effect turned her over to Jim's care, Jim may indeed be said to have brought the "Muse"—his Ántonia—to this country.

Further, Cather literally hands him a land completely free of a history that would shape the way he could understand it, a landscape that had never been described in books that taught him what to see and how to see it, and a character, a heroine, completely outside the range of his previous knowledge: a marvelous character he might have been able to see for what she is instead of what he needed her to be, instead of what the language of his understanding required her to be. What an astonishing gift to give a writer: a land almost completely free of previous eyes, a world completely free of previous commentary—a world, that is, completely free of previous and therefore defining representation and signification. Cather gives Jim the chance literally to start over, to see something new and to write about what his own eyes reveal to him, something not filtered through the writings or paintings of others. What Jim does with that astonishing gift is the subject of another paper; it is enough here for us simply to wonder at and admire the ingenuity and the audacity with which Cather plunks her narrator down into a brand new world beside a brand new character and says, "Here's your golden chance, big boy: now write. Let's see what you can do!"

Of course Nebraska has a history, as Jim Burden learns in school when he studies about Coronado's venture to the area immediately around Black Hawk. But it doesn't have what Eudora Welty called the "middle distance"[2] of history: that history of the immediately previous generations, perhaps the previous century, whose multiple intersecting and conflicting causes have engendered and continue to impose upon the present day the thousand-times multiplied effects of those causes.

Faulkner inherited this middle distance in spades, a rich history of War and Reconstruction, a landscape alive with rich resonant names—Bull Run, Manassas, Gettysburg, Vicksburg—and a galaxy of heroes with names equally resonant and powerful: Lee, Stonewall, Jeb Stuart. A powerful flood of history bore down on him from long before his birth to overdetermine him into a particular time and space, sat him astraddle a fiery historical comet that he was to ride until the end of this days. He had no such chance as Jim Burden had to start over; his muse had long preceded him to his country, had already been used—perhaps, he might well have thought, used up. Faulkner, like Quentin Compson, had "grown up with that [history]; the mere names were interchangeable and almost myriad. His childhood was full of them; his very body was an empty hall echoing with sonorous defeated names; he was not a being, an entity, he was a commonwealth. He was a barracks filled with stubborn back-looking ghosts"[3] of historical personages running riot, who had written their own stories across that landscape in heated blood and left it indelibly, inerasably, already narrated by and for their hapless descendants. And if that narrative was prewritten for Faulkner, how much more was the Southern landscape itself an established (or even corrected) text after Faulkner put his own imprimatur on it? No wonder Cormac McCarthy headed to the vast, presumably uncharted deserts of Mexico and Southwest Texas; no wonder Barry Hannah, Richard Ford, and other Southerners headed to the unnarrated Rocky Mountains of Montana and Idaho: precisely, I would bet, to escape the always already narrated South.

But I do not believe that Faulkner's description of his career in the Nobel Prize acceptance speech as a quest to "create out of the materials of the human spirit something which did not exist before"[4] is simply a metaphor to describe what he had already done; it is rather a recurring thematic throughout his career. He understood, of course, that there is no blank page, no starting over. He knew that even the "materials of the human spirit" were shaped by the same historical forces that set the materials of the mind and body in a particular time and place. So he spent a good deal of his fiction not so much trying to give himself a blank page but rather deflecting that blank page to his characters, pushing them ever backward into their lives toward their own imaginary blank pages, toward an originary moment where things began innocent of the influence of the already is: in effect, giving his characters what Cather had given Jim Burden. Joe Christmas's life story in *Light in August* begins in a patently Freudian trauma buried deep in his unconscious—a place where "memory believes before knowing remembers"[5] in an orphanage and specifically in a bathroom behind a curtain where he eats toothpaste while hearing Charley and the dietician have sex. But Joe's past is buried in a memory that he doesn't even have to remember consciously for it to affect him: it begins not in time lost because nothing escapes the unconscious, according to Freud, but in time unknown but knowable: time recoverable with the right psychotherapist. Faulkner already knows that he's after bigger game than the unconscious: he wants to go all the way back to those moments, as he puts it later in *Light in August*, hidden in the "old fetid caves where knowing began" (611).

Among his most powerful and memorable characters are those who resist with magnum force their own point in time and space in favor of another such point of their own choosing. These characters often seem so powerful and significant, so outside what we know as normal cause and effect, as to seem to have been before there was a blank page, even to have created themselves. The third day of *Mosquitoes* for example, begins as though "the first morning of Time might well be beyond this mist, and trumpets preliminary to a golden flourish; and held in suspension in it might be heard yet the voices of the Far Gods on the first morning saying, It is well: let there be light."[6] But barely an hour later Jenny and David stagger from their swim in Lake Pontchartrain into a world even before the "first morning of Time": "Trees heavy and ancient with moss loomed out of it hugely and grayly: the mist might have been a sluggish growth between and among them. No, this mist might have been the first prehistoric morning of time itself; it might have been the very substance in which the seed of the beginning of things fecundated; and these huge and silent trees might have been the first of living things, too recently born to know either fear or astonishment, dragging their sluggish umbilical cords from out the old miasmic womb of a nothingness latent and dreadful" (169). Old Ben, our favorite bear, is "so long unwifed and childless as to have become its own ungendered progenitor."[7] Roth Edmonds thinks as he looks at Lucas Beauchamp: "I am not only looking at a face older than mine and which has seen and winnowed more, but at a man most of whose blood was pure ten thousand years when my own anonymous beginnings became mixed enough to produce me" (*Go Down, Moses* 55). Lucas is "both heir and prototype"—that is, both originator and beneficiary— "simultaneously of all the geography and climate and biology which sired old Carothers and all the rest of us and our kind, myriad, countless, faceless, even nameless now except himself who fathered himself, intact and complete, contemptuous, as old Carothers must have been, of all blood black white yellow or red, including his own" (*Go Down, Moses* 91). In *Requiem for a Nun* Faulkner speaks of "maiden progenitresses" (645), and in *The Sound and the Fury* Quentin Compson famously claims he could be his own father's progenitor if he could just do something so horrible that it would remove him from time: "Say it to Father will you I will am my fathers Progenitive I invented him created I him Say it to him it will not be for he will say I was not and then you and I since philoprogenitive."[8]

Other important characters want to escape their time and place in history and start over: Quentin simply wants to go to hell and start over there. Sutpen desperately wants precisely the life that Isaac McCaslin just as desperately wants to give up. Flem Snopes calmly, methodically, resolves to be a city boy, and even Eula Varner, as Lorie Fulton has convincingly demonstrated,[9] uses Hoake McCarron and Flem Snopes to get herself out of Frenchman's Bend into Jefferson. And Temple Drake makes herself over into Mrs. Gowan Stevens to announce her own starting over after the disasters of *Sanctuary*.

Thomas Sutpen is not the first settler in north Mississippi, at least according to *Absalom*, but he and those settlers had a common idea, as we learn in *Requiem*. They all come to north Mississippi to escape their own history, precisely to begin over in this north Mississippi Eden. Faulkner couldn't be more specific. As Rosa Coldfield would have it, Sutpen speaks his domain, his new life, into existence: the "Be Sutpen's Hundred, like the oldentime Be Light" (6). He drags his mansion and even himself up naked out of the "absolute mud" that he and his Negro workers plaster themselves with as a defense against mosquitoes. But even that's not far enough back: When Quentin tries to tell Shreve that Sutpen was born in West Virginia, Shreve, the Canadian, who apparently knows more about Southern history than Quentin does, interrupts him to note that there was no West Virginia before secession because West Virginia had separated from Virginia over that issue. The mountaintop world Sutpen was born into is virtually, as Quentin describes it, without form and void, a place, for narrative purposes, outside of time and space (*Absalom* 183–84). It is precisely the chaotic nature of his background and his family life that propose to him his "design," a "design" that has less to do with building a dynasty and property than with imposing order on all that chaos which was his at birth. He wants to impose his own will on history and, by controlling the future, to control the past, to render it incapable of further harm.

Faulkner of course knew as well as Cather that you cannot wipe your own slate clean—you cannot start over from nothing—and he in fact made no pretense of erasing Freud, Einstein, James, Eliot, the Old South, War and Reconstruction, or anything else he found useful. He understood, as good historians do, that we, things, are always and inevitably descendants of what precedes—but of complicated combinations of things that precede. In his fictions he refused to treat the present moment as a logical and inevitable end result of a single stream of causes and effects, as Isaac McCaslin perceives his own life, his dramatic act of renunciation, as the single point toward which all of human history has been headed from the beginning and as Gavin Stevens does when he forces Tempe Drake Stevens to take responsibility for Nancy Mannigoe's murder of her baby.

That's perhaps why Faulkner's narratives do not narrate, but rather stop and spin and return, question, contradict, deny, and begin again. They live in and by a denial of sequence: they exist to deny logic and cohesion, from the fairly simple stream-of-conscious disruptions of *The Sound and the Fury* and *As I Lay Dying* and *Sanctuary* to the more ornate and convoluted antichronologies of *Absalom, Absalom!* and *Go Down, Moses*, and then on to the more pronounced, formalized, even stylized achronologies of *A Fable*. Throughout, Faulkner simply mistrusts the dictatorial logic of sequence: in some very important ways his work is an outright attack on sequence—history—as a source of truth or even cognition. *Absalom* is an elaborate attempt by several narrators to put in sequence a past that will not yield to sequence. Family genealogies appear to connect one generation with another, but hardly ever draw a clear and complete picture of a family's development: the missing father of Joe Christmas who may or may not have been black or Mexican; the gaps in Charles Bon's story: we never know for certain where he is born, who his father is, how he winds up in that unknown rural university in north Mississippi, where he meets Henry, and then his sister, who may or may not be his own half-siblings, and then Sutpen, who may or may not be his father; the tangled overlappings and fractures of the McCaslin family, black and white; the simple number of illegitimate or possibly illegitimate children throughout the oeuvre who may never know their own origins. Such historical gaps, writ large and small, are a methodological signature characteristic of his entire body of work: characters who reappear in successive books and stories but never precisely as they appeared before, bear new names, new ages, new relationships; related novels whose chronologies don't mesh keep us, and probably himself, from "knowing" them. Such gaps keep us from being certain of what we know. Faulkner simply refused to reread his own works, even when writing a sequel: he frequently couldn't remember scenes, names, characters: he knew them in their current moment, not their past ones.

We may extend these generalizations just a bit to think of this as a different kind of context for the constant disruptions of chronology not just in his individual works but in the work taken as a whole, which constitute a disruption and obviously deliberate frustration of readers' expectations. His ongoing and relentless attempts to redefine the novel are a monumental project also to renegotiate with his readers the terms under which we read fiction—and life. New readers who find themselves adrift and frustrated because cut off from their own expectations of novelistic knowing are exactly where Faulkner wants them to be, not just so they can relearn what a novel is and to operate independently of the novelistic tradition, but also and mainly so that they can learn by analogy to distrust the easy cultural bromides that make history—the way things are—such a politically powerful weapon in the hands of those whom Faulkner, for very good reasons, called "the lucky."

For his purposes, then, Faulkner wants the world always to "signify nothing," as the title to his fourth novel so famously suggests. The blank page he seeks is the world before it signified, but since he can't get there, he works to empower his readers, to create readers who can at very least make the effort to experience a world—his world, their own—as if for the first time: even to see a whale or a minnow in a fiction after 1851 as not necessarily a direct descendant of Melville's epic. These sorts of connections are the very stuff of our cognitive and interpretive processes, the stuff from which we create our individual and collective meanings. They are also—and again witness McCarthy in Mexico, Hannah and Ford in the Great Northwest—ropes that can strangle an artist looking for that blank page. Alas, as rich as they can be and often are, they can often strangle readers, too, those who do not understand how those connections strangle precisely because they provide cohesion, and therefore security, to our narratives. Faulkner works to destroy the generational connections that presume to connect everything with what precedes and so create a logic to our lives that our lives resist. He constantly attacks the cohesion that chronology and genealogy supply by showing us, if we will see, how fragile they are, how susceptible to manipulation and misinterpretation, and so how tenuously they supply us with the historical certainty, the stable world, that we cling to.

Faulkner's genealogies thus make the very idea of inheritance problematic by disconnecting one generation from another, by unsequencing sequence and laying inheritance itself open to question. Genealogies are culturally, historically, economically, and, most of all, legally essential instruments by which we document the passing of blood and of blood's corollary, property. His deconstruction of genealogy is therefore an attack upon the received order of things, a challenge to arbitrary structures of power and privilege that order our lives.

Perhaps Faulkner's most oft-quoted lines are in Gavin Stevens's powerful and appealing declaration to Temple Drake in *Requiem for a Nun* that "The past is never dead. It's not even past."[10] These pithy sentences have the ring of oracular truth, and generations of quoters have accepted them as a straightforward, accurate description of how the past works on the present in both Faulkner and in the modern South, of the past's formidable solidity and its inescapability—its looming "presentness." Yet the past in Faulkner is never solid, never substantial. It is always evanescent, fragmentary, "shadow, paradoxical," and most often available only in traces. Thus history exists only in its telling, a telling always prompted by a use to which the narrator wants to put that history. History always has a political purpose, and it seems clear, to me at least, that one of *Requiem's* purposes is precisely to question the truth content of Stevens's statement.

The prologues to the three acts of *Requiem* describe the powerful flood which drives the histories of Jefferson, Jackson, and Yoknapatawpha; it begins at the chance involvement of Jefferson's original settlers with a band of more or less drunken bandits who had strayed from the Natchez Trace into what the settlers had hoped would be an Edenic cocoon that would absolve them from the complicated worlds of the East Coast and the Natchez Trace, which had long since fallen from innocence into history. It is a history told forward, a construct of overlapping scenes on a stage, the last Indians disappearing from their brief time on stage, "like a float or a piece of stage property dragged rapidly into the wings across the very backdrop and amid the very bustle of the property-men setting up for the next scene and act before the curtains had even had time to fall; there was no time; the next act and scene itself clearing its own stage without waiting for property-men; or rather, not even bothering to clear the stage but commencing the new act and scene right in the midst of the phantoms, the fading wraiths of that old time which had been exhausted, used up, *to be no more and never return*" (622, my emphasis). It is a virtually seamless narrative that records how each successive stage of history gives way to the next, yielding to it then fading under the obliterating waves of each succeeding new. In *Requiem's* prologues, however, the past is not pregnant with the future, not a cause waiting to produce an effect: the future is an actual aggression not so much upon the past as upon the previous. Nor does the past stand there solidly, resisting the aggression. Nor is it really even past but merely a series of present moments punily giving way to the successive waves of the future either but of a succession of other present moments. Faulkner's metaphor for this succession is footprints:

> the fitted shoes which Doctor Habersham and Louis Grenier had brought from the Atlantic seaboard, the cavalry boots in which Alec Holston had ridden behind Francis Marion, and . . . the moccasins, the deerhide sandals of the forest, worn not by the Indians but by white men, the pioneers, the long hunters, as though they had not only vanquished the wilderness but had even stepped into the very footgear of them they dispossessed . . .; the red men and white and black—the pioneers, the hunters, the forest men with rifles, who made the same light rapid soundless toed-in almost heel-less prints as the red men they dispossessed and who in fact dispossessed the red men for that reason: not because of the grooved barrel but because they could enter the red man's milieu and make the same footprints that he made; the husbandman printing deep the hard heels of his brogans because of the weight he bore on his shoulders; axe and saw and plow-stock, who dispossessed the forest man for the

obverse reason; because with his saw and axe he simply removed, obliterated, the milieu in which alone the forest man could exist; . . . and now indeed the last moccasin print vanished from that dusty widening, the last toed-in heel-less light soft quick long-striding print pointing west for an instant, then trodden from the sight and memory of man by a heavy leather heel engaged not in the traffic of endurance and hardihood and survival, but in money. (619–21)

Vanquished. Dispossessed. Obliterated. The operative word throughout these prologues is "then," not "because." As E. M. Forster suggests, it's not a plot if the queen dies and then the king dies; it's a plot only if the king dies because the queen dies.

Of course there are traces of this history, reminders of these successive moments, as archaeology demonstrates, but what is left of all this obliteration are fragments—memories, shards of pottery, arrowheads, the leftover and incidental—that may or may not be related temporally to each other, and which therefore can at best give us only a partial, incomplete, and still photograph of any present moment, much less a comprehensive motion picture video which would link any of the shards to any kind of narrative cause and effect. Recovered, these shards and fragments are like thousands of separate pointillist dabs or electronic pixels, if you will, which if you back away from them may indeed seem to form a complete picture, but which, viewed up close, become just a jumble of unconnected dots with lots of space between.

Overseeing all this flux is the Jefferson courthouse and jail, housed in the same ramshackle structure which is in one sense the still point of Faulkner's chaotic turning world, though it too is subject to modification by chance, by the incidental and the irrational, by bandits, war, successive layers of whitewash and even by successive layers of Gavin Stevens's hogwash:

And so, being older than all, it had seen all: the mutation and the change: and, in that sense, had recorded them (indeed, as Gavin Stevens, the town lawyer and the county amateur Cincinnatus, was wont to say, if you would peruse in unbroken—ay, overlapping—continuity the history of a community, look not in the church registers and the courthouse records, but beneath the successive layers of calsomine and creosote and whitewash on the walls of the jail, since only in that forcible carceration does man find the idleness in which to compose, in the gross and simple terms of his gross and simple lusts and yearnings, the gross and simple recapitulations of his gross and simple heart); invisible and impacted, not only beneath the annual inside creosote-and-whitewash of bullpen and cell, but on the blind outside walls too, first the simple mud-chinked log ones and then the symmetric brick, not only the scrawled illiterate repetitive unimaginative doggerel and the perspectiveless almost prehistoric sexual picture-writing, but the images, the panorama not only of the town but of its days and years until a century and better had been accomplished, filled not only with its mutation and change from a halting-place: to a community: to a settlement: to a village: to a town, but with the shapes and motions, the gestures of passion and hope and travail and endurance, of the men and women and children in their successive overlapping generations long after the subject which had reflected the images were vanished and replaced and again replaced, as when you stand say alone in a dim and empty room and believe, hypnotised beneath the vast weight of man's incredible and enduring *Was*, that perhaps by turning your head aside you will see from the corner of your eye the turn of a moving limb—a gleam of crinoline, a laced wrist, perhaps even a Cavalier plume—who knows? provided there is will enough, perhaps even the face itself three hundred years after it was dust—the eyes, two jellied tears filled with arrogance and pride and satiety and knowledge of anguish and fore-knowledge of death, saying no to death across twelve generations, asking still the old same unanswerable question three centuries after that which reflected them had learned that the answer didn't matter, or—better still—had forgotten the asking of it—in the shadowy fathomless dreamlike depths of an old mirror which has looked at too much too long; (616–17)

I've read this passage for nearly forty years now, always with an increasing sense of awe at its beauty and its power—and its persuasiveness. But it is a passage at odds with the rest of the prologues in that it situates the jail as an unmoving observer of historical flux, a building, an institution, committed to the view that though the external, the ephemeral, changes, some truths about human nature do not. The jail appears here initially as a rhetorical construct of Gavin Stevens, Temple Drake's judge, jury, and prosecuting attorney in the dramatic portions; even the part of the passage following the parenthesis carries Stevens's image to a rapturous conclusion. A romantic and a sentimentalist, Stevens anchors history, continuity, in a single reality—human folly, basic human character—a single cause which produces all the effects: the wickedness caused by mankind's "gross and simple" appetites. History is for him an "unbroken—ay, overlapping—continuity," a single stream filled of course with "mutation and change," but still an "unbroken" stream that he can therefore trace all the way back to the cave dwellers: the "scrawled illiterate repetitive unimaginative doggerel and the perspectiveless almost prehistoric sexual picture-writing." No doubt there were and still are plenty of graffiti of this sort in jails everywhere, in schools and churches too; but the image insults the cave-dwelling artists of Dordogne and other sites which preserve their work; the comment is a patronizing, even contemptuous reduction to graffiti of the achievements of those who covered their blank walls with magnificent, even stunning representations of the life of their own time. From his vantage of privilege—he would be one of the "lucky" ones—Stevens smugly reduces nearly all of human life to a single low common denominator. He has his reasons: a man or a woman with a gross and simple heart is easier to understand than one with a more complicated understanding of her or his experience.

The jail/courthouse complex in Jefferson represents for Stevens his low opinion of most human beings; romanticize it though he might, it is a still point that he does not want to see turn, a point of certainty around which all the chaos of historical change swirls without changing its basic nature. *Requiem's* dramatic portions, which Stevens dominates, take place largely in government buildings—the courthouse, the state capitol, the jail—synonymous with because existing in the service of the law. The law for Stevens, and perhaps for Faulkner, though for different reasons, is nothing if not the minutely detailed record in volume after volume of cause and effect written and explained in precise, well-documented terms that demonstrate how law repeats by precedence: one legal decision is based in a previous one, all the way back to Blackstone and Coke upon Littleton. Law is the concretized record of inheritance, a detailed description of possession, the graven tablets of order and cohesion. It is therefore the comfort and sustenance of privilege, of the established order.

Stevens believes that the tragedy in his own family, the scandal that Temple Drake represents and Nancy Mannigoe's murder of Temple's baby, has a single cause rooted in Temple's unchanging character. He insists that though she has tried to whitewash her life by superficialities like a husband and a new name and a home on the right street, she is still the same Temple Drake who got off the train in Taylor and caused all the problems. He thus writes Temple's history backward, or rather forces her to write it backward, forces her to admit that the past is never dead, that that historical Temple, the one who spent the time in the Memphis brothel, had caused Nancy to kill her baby. He forces her to construct a single Temple Drake from present to past, so as to make her baby's death a predictable, even inevitable, outcome of her actions as a young woman. Temple, resisting him, tries to testify that there were plenty of contingencies at every point in her story, lots of tributary causes that affected the course of her life. She tells the governor: "I'm trying to tell you about one Temple Drake, and our Uncle Gavin is showing you another one. So already you've got two different people begging for the same clemency; if everybody concerned keeps on splitting up into two people, you won't even know who to pardon, will you?" (578). Stevens, who sees only one Temple, calmly insists: "It was as though she realised for the first time that you—everyone—must, or anyway, may have to, pay for your past; that past is something like a promissory note with a trick clause in it which, as long as nothing goes wrong, can be manumitted in an orderly manner, but which fate or luck or chance, can foreclose on you without warning" (582). There is no blank page for Stevens, never was. For him, in this a very good Puritan, history was always already written upon the gross and simple human heart.

Jim Burden botches his chance to draw Ántonia as she is, as he experiences her. Given a blank page, and even offered two possible rhetorical modes to use to write about it—the ancient hieroglyphics and the popular language of his "Life of Jesse James"—he yet chooses a third, a language which during his childhood with Ántonia he doesn't even know he knows. He chooses the language of the patriarch of all patriarchs, Virgil:

> Ántonia had always been one to leave images in the mind that did not fade—that grew stronger with time. In my memory there was a succession of such pictures, fixed there like the old woodcuts of one's first primer. . . . She lent herself to immemorial human attitudes which we recognize by instinct as universal and true. I had not been mistaken. She was a battered woman now, not a lovely girl; but she still had that something which fires the imagination, could still stop one's breath for a moment by a look or gesture that somehow revealed the meaning in common things. . . . She was a rich mine of life, like the founders of early races. (342)

In order to contain Ántonia, he must "fix" her in a series of gestures: a woodcut, an "immemorial human attitude," an "image in the mind that does not fade." Jim has to see, to locate, to impose "meaning in common things"—that is, in a common, a received meaning already at work in the culture to describe extraordinary women, not a brand new one that is worthy of her. He claims that Ántonia's hand on the crab tree and her look up at the apple as making him "feel the goodness of planting and tending and harvesting at last"—things that he moved to the city to keep from having to do. Jim is sentimentalizing: he doesn't feel Ántonia's goodness, her humanness, except as a literary conceit and as a memory constructed from what he has read since experiencing her. He didn't feel this way when he was living as her friend in Nebraska; and though he could weep buckets over a Lincoln production of the highly sentimental *Camille*, he has less than a spoonful of sympathy for Ántonia's plight as a pregnant and abandoned woman. Planting and tending and harvesting had made her, by his own admission, a "battered woman," had defeminized but not desexed her. Seeing her so unfeminine at the end of his book, as he begins his peroration, Jim imposes a classical western conceit on her: she ain't beautiful or busty, but by God she has what it takes to be a woman: just look at those kids! She was, he concludes, "a rich mine of life, like the founders of early races." But we are bound to ask, Which ones? Aeneas? There's no good answer to the question; Jim's assertion of her universality is as much a cliché of the classical praise of women as "The Life of Jesse James" is of popular fiction of the time. In his paean to Ántonia, Jim is in excess, an excess Gavin Stevens might have liked, to make of Ántonia an icon, a literary sign, one link in a chain of significations that creates an Ántonia different from the one he had to abandon but now can safely reclaim, and, by making her universal, he can divest her of her threatening sexual nature, even while admiring her for her children: a rich mine of life indeed, and can atone for his own terrifying and almost certainly Oedipal attraction to her. For all his writing, for all his confidence, Ántonia remains as incomprehensible to Jim as those hieroglyphs on the conductor's coat, and the language he uses to describe her is his own cultural equivalent of that in the "Life of Jesse James."

What did Faulkner give himself? How did he start over, not having Jim Burden's blank page? Perhaps in a real sense he did have a blank page, to the extent that he inherited from Freud and Einstein and deSaussure, among many others, a world in which all previous epistemologies and all assumptions about language had been swept away, leaving him free to do what Jim Burden could not do: to see the world with his own eyes and to designify it so that he could make it resignify. He allowed himself to know differently the world his predecessors had thought they knew, and so knew a different world.

That different world was not a blank landscape, but thanks to Einstein and Freud he allowed himself to see a page full and even overfull of newness, a page teeming with possibility, and he approached that fullness with an extraordinary language that strained gloriously, extravagantly, to push further and deeper into the margins of the sayable. He gave himself not at all a static page that lets us read laterally from one word to the next in order to accumulate information, but a dynamic page that forces us to read in more than one direction—to hold several different suspended narratives in our heads, to register simultaneously multiple layers of consciousness, to read around behind above below the words, even to read the gaps: to read all the text doesn't say as well as multiple versions of what it does say. He gave himself pages virtually three-dimensional, pages concave and convex, pages overfull with multiple layers upon layers of signification, language so new and alive and responsive that it practically jumps off the page at us, no matter how many times we read it—as though he tumbled all of everything he knew and wanted to say onto the printed line: he frequently said he wanted to put it all between one cap and one period, and it got pretty crowded in there.

One other thing he gave himself was the present moment. I do not mean a stable inflexible moment that we can call *now* because of course there truly is no *now* in our experience: by the time we say now we are already talking about a *now* subsequent to the one we were trying to name and so capture. The present moment he gave himself is a moment perpetually in motion, never fixed and stable. Unlike other novelists concerned with history, he gave himself that shifting present moment whatever era he was writing about. In any era, the present moment, constantly shifting, is wholly combustible and so does not allow for a past that is fixed and permanent either, never a past that proceeds from a single cause to a single effect: never a past that allows itself to be completely recovered and known: never a past that can be truly inherited.

Finally, Faulkner gave himself courage, no small thing: the courage to fail, as he often put it, the courage to befuddle and confuse and even alienate readers and publishers; the courage to risk excess, to enter a zone where, contra Hemingway, less is not more and even more is barely enough; and he gave himself the sheer dumb stubborn discipline to keep at it day after day even when his books hardly sold at all, because only in the constant act of writing could he hope to capture, to reach, his own necessary originary moment: that founding moment when he could drag his pages, one by one, "out of the soundless Nothing and clap them down like cards upon a table beneath the up-palm immobile and pontific," creating himself and his world, "the Be Yoknapatawpha like the oldentime Be light" (*Absalom* 4).

NOTES

1. *My Ántonia*, ed. Charles Mignon with Kari Ronning (1918; Lincoln: University of Nebraska Press, 1994), 3.

2. "The House of Willa Cather," in *The Eye of the Story* (New York: Random House, 1978), 45.

3. *Absalom, Absalom!*, in *William Faulkner: Novels 1936–1940*, ed. Joseph L. Blotner and Noel Polk (1936; New York: Library of America, 1990), 9.

4. "Address upon Receiving the Nobel Prize for Literature," in *Essays, Speeches, and Public Letters*, ed. James B. Meriwether (New York: Random House, 1966), 119.

5. *Light in August*, in *William Faulkner: Novels 1930–1935*, ed. Joseph L. Blotner and Noel Polk (1932; New York: Library of America, 1985), 487.

6. *Mosquitoes* (1927; New York: Liveright. 1997), 164.

7. *Go Down, Moses*, in *William Faulkner: Novels 1942–1954*, ed. Joseph L. Blotner and Noel Polk (1942; New York: Library of America, 1994), 154.

8. *The Sound and the Fury*, New, Corrected Edition (1929; New York: Random House, 1981), 122.

9. Lorie Fulton, "He's a Bitch: Gender and Nature in *The Hamlet*," forthcoming in *Mississippi Quarterly*.

10. *Requiem for a Nun*, in *William Faulkner: Novels 1930–1935*, ed. Joseph L. Blotner and Noel Polk (1951; New York: Library of America, 1994), 535.

Estelle and William Faulkner's Imaginative Collaboration (c. 1919–1925)

Judith L. Sensibar

This essay is drawn from my forthcoming book. It is about William Faulkner and three of the most important women in his life: Caroline Barr and Maud Falkner, who cared for him from his birth until their deaths in 1940 and 1960 respectively, and his wife, Estelle Oldham, whom he'd played with since early childhood and who lived with him from 1929 until his death in 1962. Its focus is the writer's relationships with these three complex, talented, and articulate women and the roles family and societal relationships play in the development of Faulkner's creative imagination. It is the first and only study to include serious biographical profiles of Faulkner's mother, his wife, and Caroline Barr.

Faulkner haunts and is haunted by his culture. This haunting is the subject of his art. Yet in literary and biographical studies, a huge area of this cultural terrain is blank. This is not surprising because, like Freud's "dark continent," its inhabitants were women. In Faulkner's art, racial, family, and erotic relationships are central. Yet in Faulkner biography, caricatures of these women and the artist's relationships with them substitute for the archival and documentary research that leads to something approaching historical and psychological accuracy.

Though the subject of my book is difficult, its premise is simple. Faulkner writes about Southern families locked in mortal conflict over the legacy of slavery that haunts their lives. Callie Barr, who was a slave, and Maud Falkner, whose family owned slaves, first taught little "Willie" that legacy, one that informs the thematics and poetics of his art. But consideration of his earliest and lifelong attachments to this racially mixed triad of highly imaginative, independent, and iconoclastic women on his artistic vision is absent from our reading of his work. In the era of cultural studies, global studies, feminist and poststructural theory, where contexts and interactions over time and space are deemed essential to our readings of all texts, a large piece of the world of Faulkner's history and memory is missing. My book reconstructs that history and shows how such knowledge revises our readings—in elemental ways—of Faulkner's life and art.

This essay is based on some chapters from Estelle Faulkner's section of my book.

"You may not be a poetess but you're a darn good literary critic," said the fourteen-year-old Billy Falkner to Estelle Oldham when she caught him trying to palm off verses from the Song of Solomon as his own during one of their frequent after-school meetings in the comfortable back reading room of Oxford's combination jewelry and bookstore.[1] John Faulkner, whose memoir is not sympathetic to Estelle, still claims her continuous intellectual and emotional connection to his brother as primary: "With her listening, Bill found (that) he could talk."[2] Yet, almost no one writing about Faulkner has suggested that such listening and talking, such a marriage of minds within their lifelong relationship, was crucial to Faulkner's creativity.[3]

Like Callie Barr and Maud's, Estelle and Faulkner's intertwined life poses hard biographical problems. What access does one have to the inner landscapes of two alcoholics, both children of addicted fathers and grandfathers? The disease itself is all about opacity and emotional unavailability. While most families have secrets, the culture of an alcoholic home is unique, for secrecy and denial dominate its atmosphere. Because written source materials are scarce, as with Maud and Callie, I have drawn on public documents, oral history, and interviews with those who knew Faulkner and Estelle to portray their intertwined life. As with Maud and Callie, few people, including Faulkner's authorized biographer, interviewed Estelle at any length or in any depth. Neither Faulkner nor Estelle kept diaries or journals. Very few intimate or personally revealing letters survive. There are no known letters at all from Estelle to Faulkner. Those from Faulkner to her date from the 1930s and '40s. Written from New York or Hollywood, they are, like his earlier letters to Maud, descriptive, rather than analytical or contemplative, their subject external not internal reality. As with Maud, he writes Estelle about his work.[4] The few intimate and loving sentences that he included in his letters from these years were deleted from his *Selected Letters,* published five years after Estelle's death and fifteen years after his own.[5]

Yet, there is at least one set of documents whose presence and content require fresh scrutiny of the prevailing Faulkner-Estelle narrative. Sometime between 1921 and 1924, the same years Faulkner was still struggling to find his voice as a poet, Estelle began writing fiction. She wrote a novel (now destroyed), which Faulkner typed and thought good enough to send to his publisher. She wrote at least three short stories that are extant, and other stories that Faulkner revised and published as his own. Her stories, in part, an ongoing and long-term imaginative dialogue with and critique of Faulkner's poetry, reveal her as a competent writer and observer of the contemporary scene, and, as Billy Faulkner noted, a pretty good literary critic. They also show her exploring themes and psychological terrain (absent or deeply masked in Faulkner's poetry) that in 1925, beginning with his first novel, became vital to his fiction. Finally, in one instance explicitly, they tell us much about how Estelle's authorial "I" saw girls and women like herself and the various relationships and communities that composed her worlds. These ranged from a six- or seven-year-old girl's conflicts over Southern history and codes of conduct, to racially inflected, gender-bending seductions played out in the unremittingly hierarchical colonial communities in Honolulu and then Shanghai where she had lived with her first husband. She was especially interested in power plays within (always) racialized erotic relationships and the fluidity of sexual desire and identity.

My narrative of Estelle and Faulkner shows that Estelle *as writer* was crucial to Faulkner's creative development. Coming to him when it did, at the end of 1924, her fiction literally gave him the means to find his *own* fiction writer's voice. For all of these reasons and in violation of the rules of normal biography, I foreground Estelle's stories—that is, her own writer's voice(s)—in my narrative of Faulkner and Estelle. This essay discusses one of her stories in the context of their relationship, their literary dialogue and collaboration, and of Faulkner's imaginative development.

Hyperbolic sentimentalizing of Faulkner's "love" and "respect" for Maud Falkner and Callie Barr and equally hyperbolic accounts of Estelle and Faulkner's "doomed" marriage compose the principal narrative threads of the writer's relations with Maud, Caroline, and Estelle in prior Faulkner biographies. "Doom" is the dominant descriptive term.[6] They only share their addiction.[7] While Faulkner and Estelle were alcoholics, this disease hardly defined their relationship. The sensitivity of their writing indicates that both had a visceral and intellectual understanding of the complex role alcohol played in their own families and in Southern culture at large. Its ubiquitous and always threatening presence haunts both Estelle's and Faulkner's fiction.

Also present in Estelle's and, later, Faulkner's fiction are the little girls or young women who don't play by the rules. In life and in her art, Estelle gave Faulkner models and tropes for his own rebellious and courageous little girls and young women. More overtly than either Callie or Maud, Estelle broke the rules. Like two of her fictional heroines, she tried "to speak in my own words." Her life and writing helped Faulkner find his voice. The challenge of writing Estelle's biography is to free hers.

Her fiction also shows Estelle using storytelling to claim subjectivity. She created a fictional "I" or series of masquerades to speak of matters that were otherwise off-limits to a proper Southern Lady. She needed these disguises to enter a space that, in her mind, was male-defined and dominated. Whether her fictional voices were also authentic is of less interest than to ask what were they attempting? What masquerades was Estelle performing with them? What price did she pay and how do the ways in which her masquerade is sexualized and racialized embody that price? Finally, why was Faulkner so drawn to Estelle's fictional "I"? The answers are crucial to understanding the shared and entangled space that all three women—Callie, Maud, and Estelle—filled in Faulkner's imaginative vision and why that vision yearned for both the presence and absence of all three.

If Estelle's stories were, in part, a response to Faulkner's writing, what had he written by 1924? In December 1918, when he returned from Canada to Oxford, Estelle was still in Hawaii with her first husband, Cornell Franklin. Manuscript evidence suggests that he worked on poems for his first commercially published book, *The Marble Faun*, during that winter and spring, and continued to do so during and after Estelle's first visit home. His final dating of the sequence—"April, May, June 1919"—linked its completion with Estelle's coming. Manuscript evidence from poetry written during and after her visit home and inscriptions and poems Faulkner wrote in several books he lent or gave to Estelle, probably before she returned to Hawaii, also suggest that he was deeply affected by this visit and her subsequent four-month visit in 1921.[8]

The explicit sensuality and sexuality of *The Marionettes* (1920) and its explicit denial in *The Marble Faun* (1918–1924) contrast sharply, suggesting the deep level of conflict Faulkner was then experiencing in his closest relationships. *The Marionettes* is filled with Estelle's presence or, rather, the presence of her absence embodied in Faulkner's text and illustrations—iconic fragments of her clothing, which include a single dancing slipper and a Chinese brocade stole (Figure 1). Furthermore, as I have noted elsewhere, Faulkner has drawn the virgin, Marietta, as a mirror image of contemporaneous photographs of Estelle (Figures 2–5).[9]

In part, *The Marionettes* is his thinly disguised attempt to come to terms with his own feelings about Estelle's marriage and motherhood. In this strange transparently autobiographical dream play the author manipulates his characters rather than adopting a persona like the Marble Faun who is manipulated. These characters are consciously patterned after puppets; their movements and costumes are highly stylized. But one has only to recall Faulkner's jazzy collagelike dance scenes in *Soldiers' Pay* or Red, Popeye's, and Temple Drake's or Joe Christmas and Joanna Burden's carefully choreographed dances of hatred and desire to recognize the incipient power of this early vision. Like their fictional offspring, Faulkner's first

Figure 1: Pierrot "in a drunken sleep" beside Marietta's slipper. "Flung across the chair back is a scarf of black and gold Chinese brocade" (TM 2, 3). *The Marionettes*, MSS 6271-aj, Special Collections, University of Virginia Library.

marionettes possess recognizably human forms whose actions he alone controls. The similarity of the settings in *The Marionettes* and *The Marble Faun*, as well as the similarity of Pierrot's physical state to the Marble Faun's (both are immobilized and "dreaming"), suggests that the Faun's lamented "impotence," his inability to "sing," may also be sexual. Using language to connect Pierrot's malaise with the Faun's, Faulkner hints that he (as author) is not capable of fuller imaginative exploration until he has understood the immense and enduring value to his creative imagination of allowing himself the guilty pleasure of experiencing Estelle as someone else's wife and mother.

As we know, myriad factors, among them his vast reading, his early training from his grandmother and mother in the visual arts, his family and regional history, helped shape Faulkner's imagination. Many of us, including myself, have written about how Faulkner's experiences with his male relations, friends, and mentors inform his first two novels. So also did Estelle Franklin's troubling, exciting, and almost continual presence in Oxford during all but three or four months of the five years preceding her marriage to Faulkner (early December 1924 to June 20, 1929). Integral to this presence were her sexually and racially unsettling stories,

Figure 2: The virgin Marietta watched over by Pierrot's "moon-mad" mother and other figures. *The Marionettes*, MSS 6271-aj, Special Collections, University of Virginia Library.

which he first read in longhand and probably began typing for her in the weeks before he began writing his first novel.[10]

Some time after the Franklins' arrival in Shanghai on New Year's Eve 1921 and before December 1924 when Estelle returned to Oxford (she hoped for good), she had written either all or part of her novel and drafts of at least three short stories. Two of the three extant stories that Estelle wrote while living in Shanghai were embedded in her colonial experiences there and in the Hawaiian Territories. These two, "A Crossing" and "Star Spangled Banner Stuff," are more surely crafted than the more discursive and overtly autobiographical "Dr. Wohlenski," but they share many of the same concerns with it and with her later stateside stories that Faulkner chose to rework and make his own. All explore a female pro-tagonist's difficulties with her family's and community's codes of conduct concerning how girls and women are defined and what they can say, think, feel, and do. They are especially concerned with power relations between generations and races and are complicated by a resistance to the dominant construction of human sexuality as strictly heterosexual and securely gen-dered masculine or feminine. Her interest in exploring homoerotic and bisexual desire may stem as much from personal experiences in Oxford

Figure 3: Estelle Oldham
Franklin, c.1920. Photograph
courtesy of Jill Faulkner
Summers.

and abroad as from the fiction and the "new" psychology she was reading and reading about. In Oxford's tight community, as elsewhere, homosexuality and lesbianism, like that other taboo, miscegeny, were hardly
unknowns. And, as articles and book reviews in both the Shanghai and
Honolulu newspapers show, public fascination with Freud and Freudian
theory was ubiquitous. From 1918 to 1924 Estelle was reading these
papers. She even played a lead role in Susan Glaspell's then very popular
Freudian farce, *Suppressed Desires*.

Estelle's shipboard romance, "A Crossing," is an excellent introduction to Estelle and Faulkner's imaginative collaboration, which had begun
again that summer of 1919 or perhaps even earlier, once Estelle was married to Cornell.[11] This story also seems very much part of their literary
dialogue that they started in childhood and continued during her first
marriage.

Edna Earl Tomlinson, her story's virginal heroine, hails from the modern Midwest rather than a Wildean, Beardsleyesque dreamscape, but
her family background, its "wild blood," and the cloistered, puritani-
cal upbringing against which she rebels replicate that of Faulkner's virgin, Marietta, in *The Marionettes*. However, while Marietta's seduction
by Pierrot's Shade is firmly heterosexual, Edna Earl's sexual initiation
is both miscegenous and homoerotic, subjects Faulkner had not begun
to touch in 1920–21 or even by 1924. Drunkenness plays a significant

Figure 4: Pierrot's Shade and Marietta. *The Marionettes*, MSS 6271-aj, Special Collections, University of Virginia Library.

role in both Faulkner's play and Estelle's story, but Faulkner operates within the parameters of the decadent, symbolist genre he's imitating. Estelle's more adventurous psychological approach anticipates addiction's complex thematic and tropic presence in the novels Faulkner will write once he embraces prose. Perhaps most importantly for Faulkner, Estelle's imagination expresses itself in a kind of breezy and contemporary sounding prose; she writes about a clearly identifiable now.

These and other factors make "A Crossing" much more than a thinly disguised account of Estelle's personal problems. Like her first marriage, which, on its surface, appeared to fulfill her parents', her friends', and her own ideal of a perfect match, her story initially appears to consist of elements that mark it as a typical imperial or colonial romance.[12] She was familiar with this genre since such romances were published regularly in the English-language Honolulu and Shanghai papers. Set in her own present, it's an adventure, an initiation or spiritual quest tale in which Edna Earl Tomlinson, a beautiful, innocent, golden-haired American missionary steams off on a ship bound from San Francisco to the mysterious, decadent, and "heathen" "orient" (AC 4). As in the typical colonial romance, her first civilizing mission is to redeem "natives."

Figure 5: Estelle Oldham Franklin holding her son, Malcolm Franklin (c. 1927). Courtesy of Jill Faulkner Summers.

Coding her Marietta-like character as a fictive self and invoking one of the South's most famous fictional heroines (herself a fiction writer), she also gives Edna Earl her own father's middle name, and her own gray, tear-filled eyes and long slim legs (AC 12, 16). Through the pure and impure (sexual) mother-figures in her story, Estelle's authorial "I" explores her feelings about race and sex and weighs the benefits and costs of asserting desire in a culture where women's sexual desire is always figured as "black."[13]

On board, Edna Earl meets such Colonial Romance's perfect mate, a young minister who falls instantly in love with her. Although she cares nothing for him, he triumphs despite a series of interventions by a pair of foreign, exotic, and sexually predatory surrogate parents: Mme. Tingot, an elegant dressmaker, and her estranged husband, Ahmed Sassoon, a pianist manqué who abandoned his music to pursue material riches. This olive-skinned gem merchant, referred to as "the Levantine," mesmerizes Edna Earl with his burning "oriental eyes" (19, 18). He is not the only lure. Within the first seven pages we also learn that Madame has a reputation for seducing young girls and that her still devoted ex-husband is as unmoored to any sexual binary as his ex-wife. Edna Earl is attracted to the femininity and the foreignness characterizing *both* ex-partners. Thus racialized, the Sassoons seem designed to be another of Estelle's always ambivalent fictional representations and projections of a black maternal imaginary.[14] Each wants Edna Earl for sexual pleasure and material gain. Both want to use her as a mannequin (marionette?) to display and market their wares on shipboard. The naive virgin is seduced as easily as Faulkner's Marietta and for some of the same reasons. Like Marietta, Edna Earl is inherently attracted to "darkness." She, too, has inherited "wild blood"—only hers is from her loving, promiscuous, and beautiful paternal Aunt Marcy and her father, rather than the loose-living mother in Faulkner's play.

Because Estelle's story is, in part, a dialogue with Bill, it abounds with more substantive evocations of *The Marionettes*, which she revises in ways that foreshadow later Faulkner novels. Like Marietta and like Caddy's illegitimate daughter, Quentin, Edna Earl has been allowed minimal contact with her ostracized relative—an economically independent and openly sexual woman. As the story reveals, Aunt Marcy, like Pierrot's Shade, is her niece's forbidden self, the self Edna Earl's mother attempted to erase by changing her name. When Madame Tingot enters Edna Earl's life, she feels her aunt has been restored to her: "You remind me of Aunt Marcy. . . . She is the most wonderful aunt in the world" (AC 12). Mme. Tingot's sensuality and independence are what make her so appealing. She is Edna Earl's replacement "wild" woman, another blackened mother surrogate who offers her all the sensual physical pleasuring and material delights her mother denied her. Mme. Tingot and the feminized, orientalized Sassoon appeal to Edna Earl, as "white" images of a black maternal imaginary. As Sassoon observes, they are outlaws who tempt Edna Earl to enjoy her body, to revel in her "bad blood," and to explore other taboo territory that her own bigoted and hypocritical culture has tried to repress.

Like Marietta's, Edna Earl's "proper" female relations have cloistered her all her life, stuffed her head with religion, and forbidden her to learn to dance. But in Estelle's story, as it does in Faulkner's poetry and *The Marionettes* and will in his later fiction (see, for example, *Soldiers' Pay* and *Sanctuary*), dance signals illicit (racialized) sexual foreplay that is almost always under surveillance. Edna Earl, like Marietta, is thus ripe for ruin. The two "foreigners" waste no time in luring the simply dressed girl with their "caressing" bodies and voices and with offers of material goods. Here, too, Estelle's story responds to and revises Faulkner's play. There the virgin Marietta is drawn as a slim-hipped and plainly clad maiden. Once she's been seduced, Faulkner draws her as a bejeweled Wildean voluptuary. Faulkner's is simply an image. In contrast, Estelle's story gives her a motivation and narrative. Like Pierrot, Edna Earl drinks herself into a stupor. Whereas Pierrot's drunkenness is willed, hers is coerced. Madame Tingot plies her with booze without her knowledge. The "forgetting" it causes her terrifies rather than soothes. Estelle's treatment here of liquor as a drug given to gain control over and then exploit a naïve and ignorant young person suggests thematics that Faulkner will not attempt until he starts writing his own fiction.

Most importantly, "A Crossing" is a modern-day story of multiple crossings. Beginning with its opening paragraph, the boundaries defining gender and sexual preference appear permeable and subject to reinterpretation. The battle between "correct" and unruly sex is foregrounded. As her ship sets sail, Edna Earl's "exquisite profile" is the object of the predatory gazes of both the estranged and "strange" but fascinating couple and the very proper young minister. All three want to possess Edna Earl because they view her as a commodity that will sate their own erotic desires and enhance the value of the goods each is selling. Such a plot— the marketing of *white* women in these ways—on its own distinguishes this story from its contemporaneous Colonial Romance counterparts. Of equal interest is that "A Crossing" focuses on unorthodox and thus disturbing gender categories. Both themes are highly unconventional and both will become preoccupations of Faulkner's novels from *Soldiers' Pay* to *Absalom, Absalom!* and beyond.

Besides being innocent, Edna Earl is very much a creation of her strict mother's psychosexual and social obsessions and her Mrs. Oldham-like concern with protecting the family's "good name." Like Faulkner's Marietta, she has been subjected to a joyless and repressive Calvinist upbringing and has lived by a set of rigidly defined religious, racial, social, and sexual laws and hierarchies. But the foreign couple's dangerous allure and Madame's champagne change everything. Edna Earl's own unruly desires surface when she is drugged by drink and then tempted by the erotic mystery and the exotic treasures of this sexually irresolute pair. At the same time, the proper young minister wants to marry her so she can help him peddle Christianity to the Chinese.

Estelle's social critique in "A Crossing" enriches the factual documentation concerning her first marriage and provides solid evidence of her continuing intellectual and emotional attraction to Faulkner. It also gives insight concerning her acute perception of the societal pressures influencing her parents who wished her to make a marriage that fulfilled their own very conventional dreams. Finally, this story reveals Estelle's ambivalence through her analysis of the roles played by young girls and women like herself in the neo-colonial world of the Jim Crow South as well as the colonial cultures of the Hawaiian Territories and Shanghai's International Settlement.[15] As a colonial antiromance, "A Crossing" challenges the role romance fantasies play in Western imperialist endeavors.

It also suggests the nature and degree of Estelle's involvement with and collaboration in Bill Faulkner's imaginative life while confirming its author's active and questioning mind and her ability to give pleasing formal shape to her fantasies. In many ways, "A Crossing" is her response to and revision of much of Faulkner's early work. Many of the same tensions are present in both but are differently treated. Bill's dream play *The Marionettes* suggests his thinly disguised concerns about the nature of his own erotic desires and about the related issue of the relationship of his alcoholism to his sexuality and creativity. The play is also his imaginative response in 1920 to his triangulated relationship with his mother, Maud, and his abjured "black mother," Caroline Barr, now concentrated in one woman and manifested in his forbidden desire for the married Estelle. In "A Crossing" Estelle addresses such miscegenous and sexually fluid desires directly through Edna Earl's relationship with the Sassoons.

How did Estelle's and Faulkner's imaginative dialogue proceed? I suspect that in 1924, when he first read her revisionist response to his dream play and her Shanghai story, he offered to type her work. As he typed her manuscripts he continued their dialogue, first by inserting slight but telltale changes in phrasing in Estelle's portrayals of her characters, and second by shifting into prose himself and transforming the essence of her stories and others she either would write or had written into the "youngly glamorous" and "trashily smart," sexually volatile flapper worlds—the girls, boys, and boy-girls—who inhabit his earliest published novels, *Soldiers' Pay* and *Mosquitoes*.[16]

Imaginative collaboration takes many forms of which revision as part of a dialogue is only one. The language of a "A Crossing" provides evidence of an even more intimate level of dialogue, "a marriage of speaking and hearing . . . in order to overpass to love," as Faulkner describes the story that Quentin and Shreve coauthor in *Absalom, Absalom!* Faulkner's marks are on "A Crossing": self-consciously awkward grammatical inversions prescient of phrasing in his earliest novels and, occasionally, descriptions of Edna Earl, especially her looks or the ways in which her body registers her feelings, seem partly Faulknerian. As it will be so often in Faulkner's novels, voyeurism, masking, or illusion, disruption of sexual binaries, and psychological mirroring and doubling are "A Crossing's" opening and sustaining themes.

Assuming Faulkner did revise parts of "A Crossing," what it taught him as he mingled and merged his own phrases with Estelle's well-constructed narrative was to begin to see how to turn from the bookishly imitative and psychologically opaque figures in his poetry to the people and issues of his own generation and world. The here-and-now physical and emotional geography of Estelle's stories suggested specific interior and exterior landscapes that were the antithesis of the undifferentiated dream spaces of *The Marionettes* and his poetry. As he physically and emotionally immersed himself in her fiction, reading and then typing her sentences and paragraphs, he saw in its challenges to racial and sexual fixity how to move from fragmented lyrics governed by the heterosexual imperative to modernist narratives that often explored its alternatives. The results of this collaboration are immediately evident in Faulkner's first two novels, where traces of "A Crossing" compose many of the scenes and emotionally charged "crossings" of adolescent girls and young women. All of the troubled and troubling psychosocial and sexual preoccupations of the young women in *Soldiers' Pay*—Emmy, Margaret Powers, and Cecily—begin in Estelle's Edna Earl. Faulkner continues exploring such themes in *Mosquitoes*.[17]

One example of the direct and unmediated homage *Mosquitoes* pays to "A Crossing" occurs when the world-weary, upper-class, bisexual Margaret lures the naive servant girl, Emmy, into a prolonged, prone embrace with promises of empathic listening, care, and her own cast-off, beautiful clothes. Faulkner's scene is sophisticated work in which a heated homoerotic scene plays out against the counterpoint of Emmy's tearful recitation of a traditional heterosexual narrative of seduction and betrayal.[18] But the psychological and narrative impulse began, I suggest, with his experience of writing what became—in a matter of weeks—his newly transformed authorial "I" into Estelle's "A Crossing," especially into the scenes like the ones in Edna Earl's cabin where Madame Tingot becomes simultaneously the girl's "mammy" and lover (AC 10–13). Like Mrs. Powers in *Soldiers' Pay*, whom she anticipates, she is "that black woman" (SP 142).

Their family curse of "wild blood" causes the fictional parents or parent surrogates in *The Marionettes* and "A Crossing" to wall off their adolescent virgins from the world. But these adolescents' inexperience cannot account for the awkward mix of voyeuristic eroticism and sexual anesthesia that suffuses *The Marionettes*, "A Crossing," Estelle's other stories, and Faulkner's first two novels. There may well be a connection between this anesthesia and the amount of alcohol their characters drink, particularly in Faulkner's play and "A Crossing." Both writers explore the effect of drinking on their characters' responsibility for their choices, and its ability to provide escape, distort perception, and deaden or mask severe emotional pain. In her fiction, Estelle focuses on the use of alcohol as a means of social control, whereas Faulkner veils his personal relation to the subject by explaining its presence in *The Marionettes* as part of the decadent symbolist convention in which he was writing. Both writers make the causal relationships between alcoholism and masquerade, and alcoholism and moral and emotional anesthesia and debauchery, central to their fictional worlds. Yet unlike Faulkner's emotionally evasive poetry, Estelle's fiction dealt with the pain and shame associated with intimate and forbidden subjects—namely sex, race, and the always attendant alcoholism.

Alone in Shanghai in the early twenties, Estelle had dared write about this space well known to him but heretofore silenced in his writing. In her responsive yet revisionist stories that were her side of their literary dialogue, Faulkner recognized the vast imaginative potential of such tropes. She showed him how to move from convention to invention. In later novels, most extensively in *The Sound and the Fury*, *Sanctuary*, and *Absalom, Absalom!*, Faulkner will expand on the trope of the use of alcohol to coerce, subjugate, and psychologically and sexually abuse children in families where it pervades almost every relationship white children have with their adult relatives or white surrogate parents. It is an essential ingredient of white boys' brutal initiation into racism. As in their lives, this heritage became very much a part of their fictional dialogue and, later, of Faulkner's mature artistic vision.

Faulkner writes about the terrors, not the joys, of booze. He uses different aspects of alcoholic addiction as metaphors for total psychic dislocation. He also uses them to articulate compulsively self-destructive behavior whose root cause is a desire to repress unbearable and often unspeakably shameful racial and sexual pain, confusion, and desire. But Estelle explored these fears first in "A Crossing" and the two other stories she brought to Oxford in 1924. In "A Crossing," alcohol becomes a metaphor for the essential bigotry and misogyny of Edna Earl's colonial world and what it breeds.

On the ship that is emblematic of this world, she is faced with a selection of bad choices. Whether she chooses to be the Sassoons' mannequin or the wife of a dull and preachy colonial missionary, she will still be objectified, commodified, and silenced. She will never get to grow up. This colonial scene at this particular moment in American expansionism is the context in which Estelle sets Edna Earl's progress toward alcoholism, marriage, and silence. It describes her colonization and exploitation. Unlike the Faulkner of *The Marionettes* but very much anticipating the Faulkner of *Sanctuary*, Estelle looks here at this process through the mind of an adolescent girl. She was writing partly from self-observation. But her larger field of vision reached back to at least 1914 to include Bill's and Phil Stone's preoccupations with drinking, being drunk, and all the symbolic baggage alcohol carried in a Southern town. Alcohol's effects and her feelings about its effect on her authorial self are recorded in "A Crossing." Estelle's heroine claims that her personal salvation lies in her ability to speak for herself and to imagine her own narrative.

The problem is that, like Temple Drake at Miss Reba's whorehouse in *Sanctuary*, Edna Earl has nowhere to go. Given her upbringing and her lack of education and economic resources, her choices are either to do the missionary work for which she has been trained since childhood or become the Sassoons' drugged sex slave and private mannequin. The latter appears as, by far, the more interesting choice.

As in Faulkner's later fiction, Estelle's "A Crossing" and Bill's *The Marionettes* police and punish unruly women. Dancing in both serves as a prelude to and euphemism for illicit sexual play. Both Bill's and Estelle's virgins have grown up in homes where they are forbidden to dance. When they do "dance," they are punished. Both narratives end with the maiden's literal or spiritual death. *The Marionettes* and many of Faulkner's early poems, like "A Dead Dancer," repeat this formula. In "A Crossing," Estelle takes a fresh approach to the same subjects as she imagines a scene in which a female dancer is being looked at *and* looking. Forbidden to dance and so not knowing how when given the opportunity, Edna Earl turns *not dancing* into a tool for seducing others. But her guilt at her ingenuity overwhelms her. Thus her sin of omission, her *not dancing*, is far "worse" because "You were aware of being more beautiful *still* than the other women were in motion, and so you told the truth and said you couldn't dance. Then you lay in a long chair, your beautiful body mocking all the other bodies of women. And they hated you, lying there so wholly enticing, declaring you couldn't dance" (AC 15, my italics).

By transforming the still figure's gender from the drunken and immobilized Pierrot in *The Marionettes* to her own tipsy Edna Earl, Estelle also fictionalizes a familiar scene from Faulkner's and her shared adolescence, those dances in the university gym or at the Oldhams' home in Oxford. There, she had been the dancer who gazed hopelessly upon the still, the silent, beautiful, and probably inebriated Bill as he sat motionless on the sidelines, refusing to dance. She said that although he'd never ask "to escort me because he didn't care for dancing and really couldn't," he "would be there, impeccably dressed," which she loved and which "attracted" her to him. She thought "he was the first boy in Oxford to own a set of tails," which his grandfather "probably had made for him in Memphis, as Mr. Murry would have none of that kind of nonsense." At these dances Billy "would stand on the sidelines. Occasionally he'd ask me to dance or cut in, pushing me around for a few minutes until someone else cut in," and occasionally she'd sit out a dance with him.[19] Here, in "A Crossing," Estelle's authorial voice, in a wishful role reversal, imagines herself as Bill. In this reversal—Edna Earl as watcher—she performs an imaginatively bold move as, for a moment, just for the length of a sentence, she puts Edna Earl in charge of desire.

In "A Crossing," Mme. Tingot is the only woman who circumvents the system for more than a moment. She successfully uses her creativity—her dress designing—to be economically independent and she violates with impunity the heterosexual imperative. It is unclear, then, why Estelle first allows her to succeed but then lets her husband win her back with a ruby. Both "A Crossing" and *The Marionettes* raise questions relevant to the future of Estelle and Bill's relationship in 1924. Questions in "A Crossing" are can a woman leave her marriage to pursue a career and other women and not be outlawed? Does a daughter who has been rigorously trained to uphold her parents' and her culture's often stultifying values have a chance of becoming a person in her own right, of speaking in a different voice, "my own words"? What are the costs of abandoning one's art for material gain? Can a man be an artist without being feminized; can a woman be one without being masculinized? Or, will the culture marginalize all difference by charging it with sexual deviancy? What is the cost of allowing oneself to be silenced? "A Crossing" is about two women who try to speak for themselves. Edna Earl and Mme. Tingot, ultimately fail. What about the real Estelle?

We will never know for sure the source of these imaginative germs in "A Crossing" that come to fruition in Faulkner's novels. That they are present in all of Estelle's extant stories and brought together, reconstituted, and transformed in Faulkner's fiction argues for their origins in Estelle's modest and forgotten tales. More importantly, their presence in Estelle's stories suggests a shared store of imaginative material and an ongoing dialogue about writing.

NOTES

1. Joseph Blotner, *Faulkner: A Biography* (New York: Random House, 1974), 142.

2. John Faulkner, *My Brother Bill: An Affectionate Reminiscence* (New York: Trident Press, 1963), 122.

3. Exceptions are myself and Thomas C. Moser, who expanded on my arguments in *The Origins of Faulkner's Art* (1984) and my later essays in "Faulkner's Muse: Speculations on the Genesis of *The Sound and The Fury*," *Critical Reconstructions: The Relationship of Fiction and Life*, ed. Robert M. Polhemus and Roger B. Henkle (Palo Alto: Stanford University Press, 1994).

4. William Faulkner to Estelle Oldham Faulkner (Santa Monica, Calif.) 21 July 1934, in *Selected Letters of William Faulkner*, ed. Joseph Blotner (New York: Random House, 1977). Hereafter cited as SL.

5. SL. See the Faulkner Collection, Alderman Library, University of Virginia, for the uncensored versions of these letters.

6. Some of the more recent assessments of the Faulkners' marriage are as follows: "That early relationship . . . helped create their doomed marriage—doomed before they married." Frederick Karl, *William Faulkner: American Writer* (New York: Weidenfeld and Nicolson, 1989), 257; "During their honeymoon when she fearlessly and absentmindedly entered the tragic and mundane daily life that was to be hers, his wife attempted suicide." Edouard Glissant, *Faulkner, Mississippi* (Chicago: University of Chicago Press, 2000), 36; "(Faulkner) must have seen he was stepping into a doomed

relationship, one based on a fantasy of home and hearth, but he could not stop himself."
Jay Parini, *One Matchless Time: A Life of William Faulkner* (New York: Harper Collins,
2004), 130.

7. "As a couple, the Faulkners would begin the only habit they would ever really share:
drinking themselves into a deadly stupor." Glissant, 36.

8. For my account of his writing in this period (*The Marble Faun*, *The Marionettes*,
etc.) and its implications and revelations about his state of mind and creative process, see
The Origins of Faulkner's Art (Austin: University of Texas Press, 1984), 24–28.

9. See "Pop Culture Invades Jefferson: Faulkner's Real and Imaginary Photos of
Desire," in *Faulkner and Popular Culture, Faulkner and Yoknapatawpha, 1988*, ed. Doreen
Fowler and Ann J. Abadie (Jackson: University Press of Mississippi, 1990), 110–41; and
"Faulkner's Fictional Photographs: Beyond Patriarchy," in *Out of Bounds: Male Writers
and Feminist Inquiry*, ed. Laura Claridge and Elizabeth Langland (Amherst: University of
Massachusetts Press, 1990), 290–315.

10. See the two extant typescript versions of "A Crossing" (hereafter AC) in Jill Faulkner
Summers, Archive and Special Collections, Alderman Library, University of Virginia.

11. "A Crossing" (AC in text) exists in two versions. All quotations are from the later
version. On the earlier version, in the upper left-hand corner, Estelle's byline is typed as
"Estelle Oldham-Franklin." "Franklin" has been cancelled in black ink, probably during
the Franklins' divorce proceedings but perhaps earlier. On the later version Estelle's byline
appears simply as "E.O./Oxford, Mississippi."

12. There is confusion over the terms for identifying this genre or these "narratives
of empire" or "colonialism," as Sara Suleri calls them interchangeably in arguing that "the
conventions of romance control the literatures of Anglo-Indian colonization." *The Rhetoric
of English India* (Chicago: University of Chicago Press, 1992), 7, 11. Jenny Sharpe and
John McClure prefer the term "imperial romance." John McClure, *Late Imperial Romance*
(London: Verso, 1994) and Jenny Sharpe, *Allegories of Empire: The Figure of the Woman in
the Colonial Text* (Minneapolis: University of Minnesota Press, 1993).

13. Much has been written on this subject and Faulkner's fiction. Among the best treat-
ments are, for example, Minrose Gwin, *Black and White Women of the Old South* (1985)
and *The Feminine and Faulkner: Reading beyond Sexual Difference* (1990); Diane Roberts,
Faulkner and Southern Womanhood (1994) and *The Myth of Aunt Jemima* (1994). See also
Grace Elizabeth Hale's *Making Whiteness: The Culture of Segregation in the South* (1998)
for an excellent historical account of this phenomenon.

14. For a fuller explanation and analysis of Faulkner's fascination with what I call the
black maternal imaginary, see Sensibar, "Who Wears the Mask?: Memory, Desire, and
Race in *Go Down, Moses*," in *New Essays on "Go Down, Moses*," ed. Linda Wagner-Martin
(Cambridge: Cambridge University Press, 1996), 101–28.

15. She makes these parallels explicit in another story, "Selvage." This story was hers
originally. Then in 1928–1929 Faulkner and she collaborated on a version that he submitted
to *Scribner's* under their joint byline. It was rejected and Faulkner later may or may not have
made further revisions. He changed its title to "Elly," and then published it as his own.

16. Faulkner's characterizations of his first and second novels respectively in his response
to Horace Liveright's letter rejecting *Flags in The Dust*. WF to HL [mid- or late February,
1928], SL 40.

17. For a thorough analysis of the "gender trouble" in *Mosquitoes*, see Minrose Gwin's
"Did Ernest Like Gordon? Faulkner's *Mosquitoes* and the Bite of 'Gender Trouble,'" in
Faulkner and Gender, Faulkner and Yoknapatawpha, 1994, ed. Donald Kartiganer and Ann
J. Abadie (Jackson: University Press of Mississippi, 1996), 120–44.

18. *Soldiers' Pay*, 122–29.

19. Estelle Faulkner, notes from interview with Joseph Blotner, 9 December 1964,
Blotner papers, Southeast Missouri State University.

Atomic Faulkner

Priscilla Wald

The world that William Faulkner addressed from Stockholm, Sweden, on 10 December 1950, when he accepted the Nobel Prize for Literature, was only beginning to learn what it would mean to live with the technologies of modern warfare, from gas chambers to atomic weapons, and Faulkner centered his remarks on that challenge. The prize had propelled him into a public role he had neither expected, nor particularly coveted. He had, in fact, practically to be dragged to the event by his friends and family. But the speech he gave shows that he had entered fully into the occasion, and he used it as an opportunity to caution writers to beware of what he considered their greatest obstacle: apocalyptic fear.

"Our tragedy today," he lamented, "is a general and universal physical fear so long sustained by now that we can even bear it."[1] Habituation to this fear, he believed, would mean the destruction of art. "There are no longer problems of the spirit," he complained, and in their place "there is only the question: When will I be blown up?" Obscuring all else, that question makes the young writer of his day forget "the problems of the human heart in conflict with itself which alone can make good writing because only that is worth writing about, worth the agony and the sweat" (119). The aspiring writer "must teach himself that the basest of all things is to be afraid; and, teaching himself that, forget it forever, leaving no room in his workshop for anything but the old verities and truths of the heart, the old universal truths lacking which any story is ephemeral and doomed—love and honor and pity and pride and compassion and sacrifice" (120).

In what was perhaps the most memorable line of the speech, Faulkner worked to make art out of the image of apocalypse and to capture the indomitable spirit that art expresses: "It is easy enough to say that man is immortal simply because he will endure," he intoned, "that when the last ding-dong of doom has clanged and faded from the last worthless rock hanging tideless in the last red and dying evening, that even then there will still be one more sound: that of his puny inexhaustible voice still talking" (120). Art was about more than survival, and even the inexhaustible voice was not sufficiently triumphant. Faulkner probably surprised his audience when he followed the image with a simple assertion: "I refuse

35

to accept this" (120). Man, he insisted, "will not merely endure: he will prevail. He is immortal, not because he alone among creatures has an inexhaustible voice, but because he has a soul, a spirit capable of compassion and sacrifice and endurance" (120). For Faulkner, the art of the South spoke in that inexhaustible voice.

Fear remained a recurrent theme throughout the public addresses, lectures, and essays of his last decade, but with his return to the South, both literally and as a topic, the atomic threat became increasingly nuanced. Five months after Stockholm, back in Mississippi, he assured his daughter's high school graduating class that there was a fate much worse than nuclear annihilation. What threatened them was neither "the atom bomb, nor even fear of it, because," he explained, "if the bomb fell on Oxford tonight, all it could do would be to kill us, which is nothing, since in doing that, it will have robbed itself of its only power over us: which is fear of it, the being afraid of it."[2] Their danger, rather, came from fear itself, from "the forces in the world . . . which are trying to use man's fear to rob him of his individuality, his soul, trying to use man's fear to reduce him to an unthinking mass by fear and bribery" (123). He understood those forces as a Cold Warrior would: atomic culture was the scene of a contest between the champions of liberty and the forces of enslavement. His analyses of U.S. politics and atomic culture were in that sense more representative than insightful. But he was, as generations of Faulkner scholars have noted, a remarkably acute observer of the South, and when he turned to the subject of his life's passion, he struggled to articulate the insights he had come to in his fiction as a political analysis. While his analysis never equaled his storytelling, a canny and prescient anatomy of the politics of fear emerges from the whole body of work that is relevant not only to the U.S. atomic culture of the 1950s, but also to the present moment.

The Postapocalyptic South

In the South of his fiction, Faulkner had already identified a postapocalyptic culture, and in his public addresses he offered in its post–Civil War struggle a prototype for addressing the dilemmas of the nuclear age. Southern art, in particular, could show the world what it meant to be postapocalyptic: not merely to survive, but to flourish. In the middle of the decade, he would tell the youth of Japan "that Americans from [his] part of America at least [could] understand the feeling of the Japanese young people of today that the future offers him nothing but hopelessness, with nothing anymore to hold to or believe in."[3] The South could "reassure them," he contended, "that man is tough, that nothing, nothing—war, grief, hopelessness, despair—can last as long as man himself can last" (83). And to demonstrate the resilience of the human spirit was "the only reason for art— . . . the strongest and most durable force man has invented or discovered with which to record the history of his invincible durability and courage beneath disaster, and to postulate the validity of his hope" (83). Asserting that "war and disaster" are what "remind man most that he needs a record of his endurance and toughness" (83), he pointed to the "good writing" to have emerged from the South in the years following its destruction, evidence of both the (apocalyptic) devastation of Southern culture and the triumph of the human spirit as well as a reminder that the pervasive fears of atomic culture had much deeper roots than atomic warfare. The demise of the South was not the result of nuclear weapons, but of a social system that could not sustain its inherent contradictions. As the decade progressed, his focus on the South broadened his public analysis of the politics of fear, chronicling its role in the inequities of contemporary race relations and the consequent erosion, as he understood it, of "the American Dream."

The American Dream: What Happened to It? was the proposed title of a book that Faulkner began to write (but never finished) during the decade. Fear is the titular subject of one of the two published essays that he intended to be chapters of that book. There is no mention of the atomic bomb in "On Fear: Deep South in Labor: Mississippi," which appeared in *Harper's* in 1956. The "fear" in this essay is the fear that informs race prejudice and causes Southern whites to oppose equal social, educational, and economic opportunities for black Americans. They are benighted in their opposition, he argues, since racial equality is no longer a choice, but a reality that must be accepted.

The essay is a Cold War jeremiad in which the racial inequality that continues to characterize the South constitutes, for him, the greatest challenge to the American Dream and, most urgently, to the very freedom that is at its core. Decolonization has left a global power "vacuum," and "people who believe in freedom" are at war with the forces that offer an "equality in slavedom."[4] America could only win this "war" by practicing liberty and equality. "If we who are still free want to continue so," he writes, "all of us who are still free had better confederate and confederate fast with all others who still have a choice to be free—confederate not as black people nor white people nor blue or pink or green people, but as people who still are free, with all other people who are still free; confederate together and stick together too, if we want a world or even a part of a world in which individual man can be free, to continue to endure" (102–3). Abraham Lincoln had famously warned that the Union could not long endure half-slave and half-free, and Faulkner's invocation summons the image of a world poised at a familiar historical junction with a chance to rewrite the familiar story; he positions the South uniquely in this dramatic moment.

Faulkner was first and foremost a writer and was especially deliberate in his choice of words. The choice and repetition of the word "confederate" (four times in one sentence) was surely no accident. With it, Faulkner placed the South at the visionary center of world peace and the triumph of democracy—not because the Confederacy had been right all along, but precisely because it had not, because, in fact, it had been (rightfully) defeated. Situating race relations in the South at the heart of global as well as national politics, he gave his beloved region the opportunity for political redemption. "Confederate," in this sentence, is a verb, and it names a deliberate activity. The fallen Confederacy can redeem itself only through its active conversion of its own shameful past into the lesson through which the American Dream can be renovated and globalized. It can fashion an America that is feared worldwide not because of domination, but because it demonstrates the practice of freedom. The art of the South offered intrinsic proof of the transformation of the South into a symbol of the endurance and prevalence of the human spirit. The challenge was for the South to live up to its art, but it could only do so if the current generation of white Southerners could overcome their own crippling fear not only of black America, but also of freedom itself.

The essay manifests both confusion about the exact nature of that fear and Faulkner's own underlying anxieties about Communism and decolonization, which he sees as connected. The threat of an ideology of Communist enslavement Soviet-style bleeds into the reminder that "the mass myriads of all people on earth" (105) are not white. "On Fear" begins with the local and familiar observation that fear is the tragic fact that underlies white Southern racism: some white Southerners, "people who otherwise are rational, cultured, gentle, generous and kindly" (95), oppose all efforts at integration and other social and political reforms that would benefit their black neighbors because they fear that the gains of their neighbors would translate into their own losses. Although he insists on the economic dimension of the fear, Faulkner is more interested in its cultural implications. The source of white Southern fear as he understands it is the insight to which the efforts to address the black economic underclass have led: the obsolescence of the white Southern economic system, established as it is on "the artificial inequality of man" (96). He is especially dismayed by this white Southern racism because it evinces the cowardice of an unthinking attachment to the antiquated forms of the past that keeps a generation from accepting the challenges of the present. The white Southerners whom he condemns in the essay refuse to acknowledge that their economic system has shifted from a local to a national base, and their fear has a "tawdry quality" (95) for Faulkner because he understands it as not only an obstacle to, but also the fear of, freedom.

Faulkner condemns his compatriots' racism, but his strangest expression of shame is for their lack of confidence in the power of their own tradition. "What are we Mississippians afraid of?" he asks, after recounting the recent incident of Emmett Till's murder. "Why do we have so low an opinion of ourselves that we are afraid of people who by all our standards are our inferiors?—economically . . . educationally . . . politically. . . . Why do we have so low an opinion of our blood and traditions to fear that, as soon as the Negro enters our house by the front door, he will propose marriage to our daughter and she will immediately accept him?" (100). In what appears to be an odd juxtaposition, he chastises his generation for falling away from the fearlessness of the ancestors to whose legacy they seek to cling: "our ancestors were not afraid like this—our grandfathers who fought at First and Second Manassas and Sharpsburg and Shiloh and Franklin and Chickagmauga and Chancellorsville and the Wilderness; let alone those who survived that and had the additional and even greater courage and endurance to resist and survive Reconstruction, and so preserved to us something of our present heritage. Why are we, descendants of that blood and inheritors of that courage, afraid? What are we afraid of? What has happened to us in only a hundred years?" (101). Surely the ancestors, too, were fighting for a way of life, which, premised on the inequality of Africans and their descendants, was no less racist than the one that the white Southerners he decries are fighting to uphold.

The point of this invocation, it seems, is to distinguish between the "tawdry" nature of the white Southerners' fear and the courage of their ancestors, who went to war for their beliefs rather than to the courts because of their fears. Willing to be historical actors, the grandfathers fought heroically for a way of life that proved insupportable, and the contemporary generation that clings to its form foregoes the opportunity to enter into history in its own right. Equality is a political rather than social (or moral) issue for Faulkner. His repetition of the verb "confederate" could well suggest that the freedom and equality he advocates need not be—and perhaps ought not to be—premised on social commingling.[5] But the preservation of a system must come from its worth and not from fear. The entrance into history must entail more than the effort merely to preserve the past.

With this distinction, Faulkner reclaims the legacy of his grandfathers and once again puts the postapocalyptic South in the service of Cold War America. The "labor" of his title shifts from a socioeconomic reference to an invocation of rebirth ("The South in Labor"), as he slides the allusion to enslavement from the obsolete socioeconomic system of the South to the effect of Soviet ideology. Only the American dream, which he defines as the ideal of universal personal liberty and equality, can stand against the forces that will enslave the world. Describing the power vacuum left as colonies threw off the yokes of their oppressors, Faulkner glosses over the role of the United States in that oppression. It is part of a misguided past, a deviation from the global liberation at the heart of the American Dream. He incorporates his slaveholding forefathers—and the tragic Southern past—into this vision through his invocation of postapocalyptic art, while lamenting the fear that is causing white Southerners to miss the opportunity for heroic redemption.

In the half decade between his Nobel speech and "On Fear," Faulkner had shifted his attention from the dramatic collective and global fear of nuclear annihilation to the more mundane fear of displacement, of falling out of history, and of the freedom that comes with such unmooring that he believed underwrote his compatriots' white supremacy. In the arc traced by his speeches and essays from nuclear annihilation to the more "tawdry" fear of a loss of status, Faulkner anticipates the political analysis offered by Corey Robin in 2004, *Fear: The History of a Political Idea*. Like Faulkner, Robin distinguishes between the expressed fear of a dramatic common threat or enemy (such as the fear of terrorism) and a less visible, more "quotidian" fear that grows out of and reinforces internal social and economic hierarchies. The threat that produces the second kind of fear can take a range of forms, from the fear of violence to one's person, property, or family to the fear of a loss of a good, including (as in McCarthyism) one's career or livelihood, and it underwrites an investment in the status quo. While not characteristically understood in broad political terms if it is perceived at all, such fear "is so closely linked to society's various hierarchies—and to the rule and submission such hierarchies entail—that it qualifies as a basic mode of social and political control. . . . For all our talk today of the fear of terrorism, or, before that, of communism," Robin argues, "the most important form of fear is that which ordinary Americans have of their superiors, who sponsor and benefit from the inequities of everyday life. This kind of fear is repressive, constraining the actions of the less powerful, enabling the actions of the more powerful. It ensures that the less powerful abide by the express or implied wishes of their supervisors, or merely do nothing to challenge or undermine the existing distribution of power. Such fears are critical to power holders, enabling them to pursue their agendas with a freer hand, ensuring that they will enjoy their position for some time to come."[6]

Robin calls "this unspectacular, quotidian fear . . . the American way of repression" (20), and he argues that it is important to recognize the most familiar and ordinary spaces in which we live—the home, the classroom, the workplace—as sites in which the fear that is produced is political and is therefore in the service of social and economic hierarchies rather than an "inscrutable emotion from the psychological and cultural depths" (24). The fear intrinsic to political power taints all relations. The empowered are themselves motivated by a fear of the disenfranchised, who embody what the empowered fear most: the loss of their power.

What Robin calls the politics of fear would certainly not be within the lexicon of a Cold Warrior in the 1950s, and Faulkner was more impassioned than incisive as a political analyst. But the fear that interested him was distinctly a fear of dispossession, and his concerns as a novelist led him to explore the nature and personal experience of that dispossession. As the South's most determined chronicler, moreover, he offered insight into the distinctive racialization of this fear in the United States, an aspect that is noticeably missing from Robin's analysis. It is not surprising that the particular challenges and anxieties of atomic culture led Faulkner back to the themes of his greatest fiction, for, as he consistently pointed out, the anxieties were not new with the threat of nuclear annihilation.

The Politics of Fear

Strikingly, Faulkner poses the question of the white Mississippians' fear through the image of a front door, for it is with a forbidden front door that he had most perceptively addressed it in his fiction. The person at the fictional front door is neither black, nor a man, but Thomas Sutpen, the white "boy-symbol," as Grandfather Compson calls him in *Absalom, Absalom!*, and the center of Faulkner's most astute analysis of the politics of fear.

Absalom, Absalom! revolves around multiple narrators' efforts to understand the rise and fall of the House of Sutpen, which is founded on an outrage. The story of that outrage is the one event narrated by Sutpen, albeit indirectly. The tale is itself a legacy, told to Grandfather Compson, who tells it to his son, who in turn passes it on to his son, until Quentin, speaking in the voice of the postapocalyptic South, finally tells it to his Canadian roommate, Shrevlin McCannon, in their Harvard dormitory room on a cold winter night. Standing at the front door of a plantation manor house, Thomas Sutpen experiences the terrible fear of dispossession, and it propels him into a course of self-destruction through which Faulkner anatomizes the fall of the South.

Sutpen belongs to the heroic generation of the grandfathers, but he was not born into the ideal of white Southern manhood that he would come to inhabit, albeit ambiguously. In fact, his account of his early years reads almost like a slave narrative. He has no memory of his birth date and only a hazy memory of his boyhood in the Appalachian mountains, where neither land, nor time was divided up and catalogued, so there was neither property, nor history, as he would come to understand those terms. But he was not enslaved, and in this frontier culture were neither black people, nor distinctions among white people, only natives and settlers. His mother's death constituted his earliest memory, as it prompted the remainder of his family to tumble down the mountain and make their way to Tidewater, Virginia, or, as he would put it, to fall into the world. His story underscores the lack of a context for identity as well as the distinction between the complete absence of conventional measurements of temporality and property in the mountains and the specific exclusion of people like Sutpen's family from those terms in a society in which they are paramount.

Sutpen learns to see fully into the terms of identity in a well-known moment: entrusted by his father with a message for the master of the plantation on which he works, he is sent to the back entrance of the house by the enslaved man who answers the door. The event gives him a context to understand—and therefore fully perceive—what he had seen without noticing before. He experiences Du Boisian double consciousness, the "sense of always looking at one's self through the eyes of others, of measuring one's soul by the tape of a world that looks on in amused contempt and pity"—the *sense*, that is, of literally perceiving what someone else is seeing.[7] The experience gives him a clear view of racism, which he understands, in visual terms, as "a certain flat level silent way his older sisters and the other white women of their kind had of looking at niggers, not with fear or dread but with a kind of speculative antagonism not because of any known fact or reason but inherited by both white and black, the sense, effluvium of it passing between the white women in the doors of the sagging cabins and the niggers in the road and which was not quite explainable by the fact that the niggers had better clothes, and which the niggers did not return as antagonism or in any sense of dare or taunt but through the very fact that they were apparently oblivious of it, too oblivious of it."[8] Sutpen sees into, and through, the mechanism of racism, which is "inherited" through the senses. He sees the power of one group of (rich) white people to shape the sensory experience not just of the enslaved, the human beings they own, but of everyone. In the apparent—which is to say, performed—obliviousness of the slaves he sees the manifestation of the pernicious denial of humanity to the enslaved blacks and the impoverished whites by the master class. It is a profound insight; Sutpen learns in the instantaneous lesson of his own dehumanization—or, rather, humanization as "white trash"—to see through the violence to its source.

Sutpen is exceptional. His father and the other men do not share his insight. Sutpen recalls his father's proud account, one night, of having beaten one of the master's slaves and recognizes that his father could not see the source of his hatred and did not know that when he attacked the enslaved man he was striking impotently at the nameless (enslaving) force that prompted him, when drunk, "to break out into harsh recapitulation of his own worth, the respect which his own physical prowess commanded from his fellows" (186). There is no explanation for Sutpen's deeper insight, but the visual emphasis of his discovery underscores his own potential as a visionary. In the brief moment at the door, Sutpen consciously inhabits the gaze of his nemesis. He "looked out from whatever place he (the man) happened to be at the moment, at the boy outside the barred door in his patched garments and splayed bare feet, looking through and beyond the boy, he himself seeing his own father and sisters and brothers as the owner, the rich man . . . must have been seeing them all the time—as the cattle, creatures heavy and without grace, brutely evacuated into a world without hope or purpose for them, who would in turn spawn with brutish and vicious prolixity, populate, double treble and compound, fill space and earth with a race whose future would be a succession of cut-down and patched and made-over garments" (190).

He returns home to a gruesomely clear-sighted vision of his family's impoverished dwelling and "his sister pumping rhythmic up and down above a washtub in the yard, her back toward him, shapeless in a calico dress and a pair of the old man's shoes unlaced and flapping about her bare ankles and broad in the beam as a cow, the very labor she was doing brutish and stupidly out of all proportion to its reward: the very primary essence of labor, toil, reduced to its crude absolute which only a beast could and would endure" (191). He sees, that is, her exclusion from the terms of white femininity (hence, from full humanity) as defined by the master class and accepted, like the inherited racism, uncritically. The sexual description of his sister's work underscores her role in the brutish labor of the uninterrupted reproduction of poverty. Hopeless and purposeless, the "race" she reproduces is indistinguishable from cattle—or chattel. The illusion of the distinction, moreover, itself reproduces the power of the master.

Sutpen flees in horror, but the worst part of the experience comes later, with his explosive realization of the complete irrelevance of his existence. Even the message he was to deliver to the plantation owner was irrelevant: "*He never gave me a chance to say it and Pap never asked me if I told him or not and so he cant even know that Pap sent him any message and so whether he got it or not cant even matter, not even to Pap; . . . I not only wasn't doing any good to him by telling it or any harm to him by not telling it, there aint any good or harm either in the living world that I can do to him"* (192). What he understands is that, like the enslaved (and in the words of Orlando Patterson), he is *socially dead*, animated only by the will and in the terms of the master. Patterson roots social death in the "natal alienation" of the enslaved, their prohibition, that is, from freely integrating "the experience of their ancestors into their lives," from informing "their understanding of social reality with the inherited meanings of their natural forebears," and from anchoring "the living present in any conscious community of memory."[9] They are thus denied the basic attributes of human beings. At the front door of the aptly named Pettibone, Sutpen experiences himself in those terms.

With his ability to see through the dynamics of power, Sutpen is on the brink of rejecting the premises of his social order, of realizing the revolutionary potential of a visionary. But he decides instead to wage his battle in the terms of that order, believing that to combat them "you got to have what they have that made them do what they did. You got to have land and niggers and a fine house to combat them with" (192). Grandfather Compson puts it in the language of compulsion when he explains that Sutpen had suddenly "'discovered, not what he wanted to do but what he just had to do, had to do it whether he wanted to or not, because if he did not do it he knew that he could never live with himself for the rest of his life, never live with what all the men and women that had died to make him had left inside of him for him to pass on, with all the dead ones waiting and watching to see if he was going to do it right, fix things right so that he would be able to look in the face not only the old dead ones but all the living ones that would come after him when he would be one of the dead. And that at the very moment when he discovered what it was, he found out that this was the last thing in the world he was equipped to do because he not only had not known that he would have to do this, he did not even know that it existed to be wanted, to need to be done, until he was almost fourteen years old'" (178–79). The terms that he understands as the prerequisite for social existence are history and genealogy, and he learns what they are: the power to tell a story in the present that will construct a past—hence, a social existence—not only for the sake of his descendants, but for his ancestors who survive (and prevail) only through that story. From his account, Sutpen seems never before to have thought about ancestors; it is a term that he learns when he experiences the consequence of their absence. Through genealogy—through, that is, building the House of Sutpen—he will claim humanity not only for himself, but for his progenitors and his heirs. Genealogy—the terms of inheritance of the name that signals the law of the father—is the sole protection against social death, the mechanism of which, as Patterson notes, is the exclusion from history and genealogy. The language of ancestry, of course, ironically binds him to the terms of his exclusion.

Quentin interrupts his narrative of Sutpen's awakening to reconstruct his biography, underscoring his protagonist's discovery of the importance of such details. He tells Shreve that Sutpen's "innocence" (Grandfather Compson's word) was the result of his having been " 'born in West Virginia, in the mountains where—' " but he is interrupted by his Canadian roommate who corrects the historical details of his story. Faulkner encloses their exchange in parentheses: "('Not in West Virginia,' Shreve said. '—What?' Quentin said. 'Not in West Virginia,' Shreve said. 'Because if he was twenty-five years old in Mississippi in 1833, he was born in 1808. And there wasn't any West Virginia in 1808 because—' 'All right,' Quentin said. '—West Virginia wasn't admitted—' 'All right, all right,' Quentin said. '—into the United States until—' 'All right, all right, all right,' Quentin said)" (179). Their contest, represented through the parentheses as an intrusion on the story, in fact underscores the importance of story telling, particularly the power to write history, which is the power Sutpen covets, the power he fears not to have. Faulkner repeats Quentin's historical error in the genealogy that he appended to the novel, ignoring the fact that, as Sutpen points out, West Virginia did not exist as a state until the Civil War, when the region refused to secede from the Union with the state of Virginia. Sutpen is similarly determined to seize historical power over the future, which in his case means control over the terms of genealogy.

Shreve had already named this motivation, interrupting Quentin's narrative with the realization that Sutpen "just wanted a grandson. . . . That was all he was after." But he will not fully understand the impetus of that desire until the end of the evening—and of Quentin's story. Sutpen's fear of social death is political insofar as it prompts his unquestioning adherence to the law of the father, which, in the early nineteenth-century South, was the law of the slaveholders. And Faulkner makes clear that racialized identity is its cornerstone.

Grandfather Compson insists on Sutpen's "innocence" and on his lack of awareness of that innocence, maintaining that even " 'after it [the innocence] finally told him what to do that night he forgot about it and didn't know he still had it' " (194). He depicts Sutpen's actions as instinctive. "Innocence" is an odd word in this context, suggesting a childlike quality, but also raising the question of culpability. Like Jay Gatsby, and so many other "great men" of literature, Sutpen creates a vision fleshed out from a child's encounter, adheres faithfully to the vision, and never doubts the possibility of its realization. Sutpen and Gatsby stand outside the law—not breaking it (as criminals), but oblivious to it in the innocence of their childlike antinomianism. And they succumb to the fate of so many great men: the destruction of self and others unleashed by their monomaniacal innocence. There is perhaps no more destructive force than innocence.

Social Death and the Drama of the Front Door

During the sleepless night following the affront, Sutpen, like so many poor white men of his generation, heads out to make his fortune in "the West Indies." His knowledge of the West Indies, in fact, had come from a book he had heard a teacher read to the class during his three months of schooling. He returns with a white Martinican architect and a band of black men and two women whom his Jefferson neighbors surmise are Haitian slaves (which, in the 1820s, would be an anachronism) to build Sutpen's Hundred, his plantation on a swamp. The landscape of the swamp is particularly suitable to Sutpen's storytelling as it is to Sutpen's Hundred. Monique Allewaert details the violence with which the swamp is imbued in the literature of the early nation; swamp narratives featured an entangled landscape that was dangerous for white trespassers but served as a refuge for self-liberated slaves and maroon communities. As Allewaert explains, the violence is readily associated in such accounts with African revolution; it is apocalyptic and encroaching, with the vegetation of the swamp itself, and must be contained if it is not to result in the dissolution of the surrounding territory—and culture. Temporality and geography do not conform to expectations. Such is life in what Allewaert calls "the plantation zone," which, like the story Sutpen tells, links the many landscapes in the novel.[10]

With dreamscapes and broken plots, the story Sutpen tells, like the swamp, is inconsistent and deceptive, more myth than history. He recounts details haphazardly and disconnectedly, and Grandfather Compson infers a slave uprising, during which Sutpen fought alongside the master and his daughter until he stepped boldly out to confront the rebels, and they mysteriously dispersed. The master's beautiful daughter is his reward. Sutpen's Haiti is hazy and anomalous. As many critics have pointed out, he would in fact have missed the Haitian Revolution—and Haitian slavery—by more than a decade if he had arrived in the early 1820s.[11] One can imagine Faulkner's responding to such questions with the "all right, all right, all right" with which Quentin responds to Sutpen's correction about West Virginia and with which Shreve responds to Quentin's efforts to correct his repeated references to "Aunt Rosa" (instead of "Miss Rosa"). Faulkner's story had to be about Haiti because it was about racial fear, and the Haitian Revolution, for the antebellum South to which Sutpen returns, was the epitome of the slaveholder's fear. And Sutpen's participation in the Civil War was also necessary to the story, making for an impossible temporality.

Those details mandated a time frame that was more important to Faulkner than historical accuracy. His story, moreover, was more about myth than history, and Sutpen's mythmaking has its own temporal and spatial logic.

Haiti had a mythic function not only in Faulkner's novel, but also in U.S. culture more broadly. The U.S. occupation of Haiti between 1915 and 1934 had propelled the island nation into the American imagination, and it was a landscape that appeared frequently, in a variety of incarnations (especially mythic ones), in U.S. fiction of the period.[12] For the South in Faulkner's novel, however, it summoned the fear of black humanity determined to assert itself. It was where, as Aimé Césaire would write in 1938, "Négritude rose for the first time and stated that it believed in its humanity."[13] Haiti was the crucible in which the ideals of the French Revolution were tested and their limits exposed. Like the swamp, Faulkner's Haiti was the site of violence that hovered between containment and eruption: in Grandfather Compson's words, "a spot of earth which might have been created and set aside by Heaven itself . . . as a theatre for violence and injustice and bloodshed and all the satanic lusts of human greed and cruelty, for the last despairing fury of all the pariah-interdict and all the doomed—a little island set in a smiling and fury-lurked and incredible indigo sea, which was the halfway point between what we call the jungle and what we call civilization, halfway between the dark inscrutable continent from which the black blood, the black bones and flesh and thinking and remembering and hopes and desires, was ravished by violence, and the cold known land to which it was doomed, the civilised land and people which had expelled some of its own blood and thinking and desires that had become too crass to be faced and borne longer, and set it homeless and desperate on the lonely ocean" (202). The liminal space of this former French colony affords Sutpen not only wealth, but the opportunity to become fully white and therefore to begin the construction of his genealogy according to his design.

Sean Latham astutely describes the clash of racisms between the French colonial system and U.S. slavery, reading "*Absalom, Absalom!* . . . as a text in which the ideology of American slavery is contested by the sudden 'abruption' of an imperialist model of racial difference."[14] For him, Sutpen is a figure of discomfort for his neighbors because he challenges the American logic of slavery when he returns, having been socialized into slavery colonial style. But Sutpen does not in fact come home a colonialist. Haiti gave him the wealth to implement the design he had conceived in Tidewater. And to that design he is faithful. He returns speaking the language of American slavery, which is black and white. He is curiously untouched by Haiti, despite almost being killed, being married, having a child, and "putting away" his family while he is there. Racial difference is, for him, necessary to a realization of his design, so the fact that it takes a different form in Haiti is of no consequence.

Sutpen is obsessed by race, since whiteness is key to his design. But he does not share the biases of his neighbors. Latham remarks on the care Sutpen takes to keep the Haitians from harming the captured architect as an example of the inversion of the familiar terms of a slave hunt. Yet, there is no indication that Sutpen would have treated escaped black men differently. He certainly stages fights among them, but he is an eager participant in those events, and they are the sole acts of violence against them in which we see him engage; they are as allowed to bloody him—if they can—as he them in this "sport." And when his neighbors, following the South's defeat in the Civil War, try to enlist him in clanlike activities against the formerly enslaved, Sutpen dismisses them. When they tell him his refusal means war, he responds with the assurance that it would not be the first time. He has seen through racial difference, and it seems to have no meaning to him personally, which accounts for the discomfort he produces in his neighbors. Nonetheless, he enters fully into its terms because of the design. It compels him to accede to the mandates of slavery *despite* his understanding of the arbitrariness of racial distinction. The design is so pernicious, in fact, because of the dehumanization it entails. No one's humanity—not the black men and women, nor the architect—is relevant to Sutpen; everyone is instrumental to him. The astonishing evacuation of humanity to which his fear leads him applies even to the person of Thomas Sutpen. He fights alongside of the master of the plantation with an apparent impersonality, and evident imperviousness to bodily harm, just as he later joins a regiment during the Civil War, because for him Thomas Sutpen had become fully an idea, and part of a design, rather than a man. Social existence supercedes physical survival. His vision is born of political expediency and fear; there is no thought of morality, and he is dangerous in his innocence.

With his dramatization of the fall of the House of Sutpen, Faulkner depicts the racial tragedy of the South as a clash of temporalities and spatialities. The French colonialism of New Orleans allows Sutpen's racially hybrid son, Charles Bon, to grow into gentlemanhood, but the Louisiana Purchase brought New Orleans into the American South, and there Bon embodied the clash that Latham describes. Neither the South nor Sutpen can accommodate the racial identity that Bon inhabits. Terms such as "octoroon" and "mulatto" have too much significance and must be incorporated quickly into a binaristic U.S. system, unleashing a tragic plot that recurs throughout U.S. literature, especially of the South. The fear of the social death that Charles Bon at once threatens and enacts prompts Sutpen to try to make his own mythic vision conform to the temporality of a historical frame. That effort requires him to subordinate everything, including humanity, to the need to know that he exists, which is to say to social knowledge: to the idea without the materiality of "human being." The consequences are inevitably apocalyptic. The House of Sutpen dissolves into the swamp as first Bon and then Wash Jones, the grandfather of the girl Sutpen impregnates and abandons when she fails to produce a son, each ironically reenacts in his own way the drama of the front door. With Sutpen's death, his story is left to a cadre of interpreters, and the lineage to Jim Bond, the "idiot" grandson of Charles Bon.

Shreve pronounces the final irony (in terms Faulkner will reiterate in "On Fear") when he tells Quentin "that in time the Jim Bonds are going to conquer the western hemisphere . . . and so in a few thousand years, I who regard you will also have sprung from the loins of African kings" (302). He appears here to have taken from Sutpen's story the lesson of history: how collective identity and the social existence it confers—hence the genealogy of Shrevlin McCannon—is subject to the stories we tell about the past. The "I," then, is literal; the conquest of the Jim Bonds may well result in the disappearance of whiteness through intermarriage, but more importantly it suggests a retold story in which Shreve, Quentin, and their progenitors—not just their descendants—were already the descendants of Africans.

Fear and Human History in the Genome Age

Shreve's prophecies have come true in the genomic discoveries that have allowed population geneticists to trace a genetic heritage from the DNA of human remains in Africa through the entire living population of the world. With such statements as "we are literally most alike where it matters, under the skin" and "'we are all Africans at the Y chromosome level and we are really all brothers,'" they promise a new narrative of human history that they believe will definitively refute the claims of racism.[15] If we are all descendants of Africans, then what sense do claims of racial distinctions make? Quite a bit, it seems. For, even as they proclaim the senselessness of racism, population geneticists—often in the same articles—pronounce the important distinctions of ancestry that correspond at least roughly to (racial) populations.[16] And race is at the center of a current debate in the medical journals as well as the mainstream media about genomic medicine; the debate concerns whether or not racial categories offer useful medical information and should, therefore, be central to the collection of data for medical research.

Ironically, Faulkner's work might well offer important insight into this resurgence of interest in racial categories in the very areas and at the very moment in which their insignificance is ostensibly heralded. In his analysis, apocalyptic fear is the fear of social death writ large, since it leaves no one to tell the story that bestows social existence and the measure of immortality that memory confers. The histories of racial slavery and colonization offer dramatic examples of social death and insist on its fundamental racialization, not just in Faulkner's South, but in the contemporary United States. As Faulkner's invocation of those histories suggests, "apocalypse" refers not only to the literal annihilation of a population, but also to the disappearance of a culture with which one identifies. It is, then, not surprising that the heralding of a new genealogy of human history would elicit the invocation of the familiar ancestors. The stories of human history that have surfaced in the mainstream media as well as the medical debates manifest an overwhelming tendency to conform to a familiar evolutionary—and racialized—narrative. Despite our evident similarly "under the skin," we are certainly not yet all descended from the loins of African kings.

Faulkner's inheritance, as he understood it, was a postapocalyptic landscape that he believed offered an important lesson for the atomic age. Apocalyptic fear named the threat of literal annihilation from nuclear weapons and social annihilation from an ideology of enslavement. Nothing better represented that enslavement, nor posed a greater challenge to its opposition, than the inequity—and tragedy—of race relations in the South. But the Faulkner of the public addresses could only begin to grasp what white Mississippians, including himself, were afraid of. The remarkable achievement of *Absalom, Absalom!* is its depiction of more than the author knew that he saw: the racialized politics of fear. The continuing relevance of this insight attests to the animating presence and power in our daily lives of the specter of social death.

NOTES

I wish to thank Donald Kartiganer and Cathy Schumann for their helpful feedback on this essay as well as the audience at the 2005 Faulkner and Yoknapatawpha Conference at the University of Mississippi for the excellent questions that made the essay better.

1. William Faulkner, "Address upon Receiving the Nobel Prize for Literature," *Essays, Speeches, and Public Lectures by William Faulkner*, ed. James B. Meriwether (New York: Random House, 1965), 119. Subsequent references in the text are to this collection.

2. William Faulkner, "Address to the Graduating Class University High School," *Essays, Speeches, and Public Lectures by William Faulkner*, 122–23.

3. William Faulkner, "To the Youth of Japan," *Essays, Speeches, and Public Lectures by William Faulkner*, 82.

4. William Faulkner, "On Fear: Deep South in Labor: Mississippi," *Essays, Speeches, and Public Lectures by William Faulkner*, 105.

5. Faulkner took a strong stand against compulsory integration and advocated patience on the part of African American leaders in "Letter to a Northern Editor" (originally

published as "A Letter to the North"), which was published in *Life* in March 1956, and reiterated his position in "A Letter to the Leaders in the Negro Race" (originally published as "If I Were a Negro"), which was published the following September in *Ebony*. See "A Letter to a Northern Editor," *Essays, Speeches, and Public Lectures by William Faulkner*, 86–91, and "A Letter to the Leaders in the Negro Race," *Essays, Speeches, and Public Lectures by William Faulkner*, 107–12.

6. Corey Robin, *Fear: The History of a Political Idea* (Oxford: Oxford University Press, 2004), 19–20. Subsequent references in the text are to this edition.

7. W. E. B. Du Bois, "Of Our Spiritual Strivings," *The Souls of Black Folk, W. E. B. Du Bois: Writings* (New York: Library of America, 1986), 364.

8. William Faulkner, *Absalom, Absalom!* (New York: Vintage Books, 1986), 186. Subsequent references in the text are to this edition.

9. Orlando Patterson, *Slavery and Social Death: A Comparative Study* (Cambridge: Harvard University Press, 1982), 6, 5. Subsequent references in the text are to this edition.

10. Monique Allewaert, "Race Revolution in the Plantation Zone" (PhD dissertation, Duke University).

11. The 1990s witnessed a proliferation of essays on Faulkner's use of Haiti in *Absalom, Absalom!* that included discussion of why the important role of Haiti in this novel had so long been ignored. It would have been impossible for Sutpen to have been in Haiti during a slave revolt, since the Haitian revolution and the abolition of slavery had preceded his arrival there by many years, but there is considerable disagreement among critics about whether the error is Faulkner's or Sutpen's—or, in fact, whether it is an error at all or just an assumption on the part of readers that the revolt was engineered by slaves or by plantation workers who were indistinguishable from slaves. Hortense Spillers initiated discussion of Haiti in the novel with her reference to the anachronism as typical of the U.S. South's repression of its position in the Atlantic slave trade. According to Richard Godden, it was crucial to the plot, illustrating the subduing of black Jacobins by white supremacy; Sutpen, he contends, needs to be understood as a slave owner rather than a capitalist, thinking of Charles Bon as his property in that sense rather than as his son. For Barbara Ladd and John T. Matthews, there is in fact no anachronism, since Faulkner never names the "wild Negroes" as slaves. The mistake could be Sutpen's (certainly his innocence is stressed in the novel) or any of the subsequent narrators who recounts and tries to interpret his story. Maritza Stanchich is more critical of the "marginal, unnamed, assumed, but nonetheless useful presence of the Caribbean; the exploited, cartoonish artchitect; the imagined cache of Spanish coins; and the first-born rejected mulatto son—all [of which] make *Absalom, Absalom!* an American imperialist representation of the Caribbean. . . . The marginalized empire is subordinate to the story, even though the story can't exist without it" (610–11). Sean Latham is more interested in what the use of Haiti in the novel demonstrates regarding slavery and colonialism as repressed histories than in whether or not there is a deliberate or unwitting anachronism. For him, Sutpen's sojourn in Haiti allows the novel to explore the clash between alternative systems of racialization under colonialism and U.S. slavery. Ramon Saldívar reads the Haitian episode as underscoring Sutpen's tragic acquiescence—even investment—in the terms that ultimately destroy him.

See Hortense Spillers, "Who Cuts the Border?: Some Readings on 'America,'" *Comparative American Identities: Race, Sex, and Nationality in the Modern Text*, ed. Hortense Spillers (New York: Routledge, 1991), 1–25; Richard Godden, "*Absalom, Absalom!* and Faulkner's Erroneous Dating of the Haitian Revolution," *Mississippi Quarterly* 47.3 (Summer 1994): 489–95, "*Absalom, Absalom!*, Haiti and Labor History: Reading Unreadable Revolutions," *ELH* 61.3 (Fall 1994): 685–720, and *Fictions of Labor: Faulkner and the South's Long Revolution* (Cambridge: Cambridge University Press, 1997); Barbara Ladd, "'The Direction of Howling': Nationalism and the Color Line in *Absalom, Absalom!*," *American Literature* 66.3 (September 1994): 525–51 and *Nationalism and the Color Line in George W. Cable, Mark Twain, and William Faulkner* (Baton Rouge: Louisiana State University Press, 1996); John T. Matthews, "Recalling the West Indies: From Yoknapatawpha to Haiti and Back," *American Literary History* 16.2 (Summer 2004): 238–62; Maritza Stanchich, "The Hidden Caribbean 'Other' in William Faulkner's *Absalom, Absalom!*: An Ideological

Ancestry of U.S. Imperialism," *Mississippi Quarterly* 49.3 (Summer 1996): 603–17; Ramon Saldívar, "Looking for a Master Plan: Faulkner, Paredes, and the Colonial and Postcolonial Subject," in *The Cambridge Companion to William Faulkner*, ed. Philip M. Weinstein (Cambridge: Cambridge University Press, 1995), 96–120.

For my purposes in this essay, I found Edouard Glissant's formulations about Faulkner's mythmaking in *Absalom, Absalom!* especially generative. See *Faulkner, Mississippi*, trans. Barbara Lewis and Thomas C. Spear (New York: Farrar, Straus, and Giroux, 1999). The original French edition appeared in 1996.

On Haitian history, see especially Robert Debs Heinl Jr. and Nancy Gordon Heinl, *Written in Blood: The Story of the Haitian People, 1492–1971* (Boston: Houghton, 1978) and C. L. R. James, *The Black Jacobins: Toussaint L'Ouverture and the San Domingo Revolution*, 2nd ed. rev. (New York: Vintage Books, 1963).

12. See Mary A. Renda, *Taking Haiti: Military Occupation and the Culture of U.S. Imperialism, 1915–1940* (Chapel Hill: University of North Carolina Press, 2001).

13. Aimé Césaire, *Notebook of a Return to the Native Land: The Collected Poetry*, trans. Clayton Eshleman and Annette Smith (Berkeley: University of California Press, 1983), 47.

14. Sean Latham, "Jim Bond's America: Denaturalizing the Logic of Slavery in *Absalom, Absalom!*," *Mississippi Quarterly* 51:3 (Summer 1998): 462.

15. Alan G. Thorne and Milford H. Wolpoff, "The Multiregional Evolution of Humans," *Scientific American* 226 (April 1992): 76, and Douglas C. Wallace, quoted in Nicholas Wade, "The Human Family Tree: 10 Adams and 10 Eves," *New York Times*, 2 May 2000, F1, F5.

16. For a more extended discussion of this issue, see my "Future Perfect: Genes, Grammar, and Geography," *New Literary History* 4.31 (Autumn 2000): 681–70.

Plaintive Reiterations and Meaningless Strains: Faulkner's Blues Understandings

Adam Gussow

Blues Literature and the Proximity Effect

This occasion marks, as some of you know, my maiden voyage into the brave new world of Faulkner studies. It has been an unnerving journey. As historian Joel Williamson noted when he made his own debut here several years ago, "If one takes [Faulkner's] work as a whole, it is difficult to make any assertion at all that will not justly bring down upon one's head some of that vast band of dedicated, brilliant, and virtually lifelong professional Faulkner scholars."[1] Nevertheless I intend to venture a number of assertions about Faulkner and the blues, doing my best to shed light on a subject that *ought* to have been strip-mined by the vast band years ago but for some reason has managed to escape relatively intact. Scholars such as Thadious Davis, Charles Peek, Carol Gartner, Ken Bennett, and H. R. Stoneback have done excellent critical work on individual texts, sniffing out biographical clues and possible lyric influences, but certain larger patterns connecting the works with each other, with the life, and with the blues literary tradition as a whole have remained obscure.[2] I've entitled my paper "Plaintive Reiterations and Meaningless Strains" because Faulkner attaches those provocative descriptors to blues music in *Sartoris*—one of his few representations of actual blues performance— and because I am indeed provoked to ask about the experiential grounds of Faulkner's blues understandings. What did Faulkner know about the blues, and when did he know it? How did he transform that knowledge into works of literature? Finally, and only slightly tangentially: in what ways have the terms "Faulkner" and "blues," as iconic Southern referents, come to be associated in the American cultural imagination? Do these pure products of Mississippi deserve, in fact, to be peddled from the same little roadside stand?

I'll begin with a brazen claim for the purposes of clearing the air: Faulkner's place in the blues literary tradition is, it seems to me, much closer to the margins than the center. When I speak of that tradition, I'm thinking about novelists, poets, and playwrights such as Langston Hughes, Albert Murray, Zora Neale Hurston, August Wilson, Sterling

Plumpp, Sterling Brown, Arthur Flowers, Alice Walker, and Sherley Anne
Williams, not to mention blues autobiographers such as W. C. Handy,
Big Bill Broonzy, Mezz Mezzrow, David Honeyboy Edwards, Mance
Lipscomb, and B. B. King. These are writers and oral storytellers who
foreground blues performance practices and the journey from appren-
ticeship through mastery that lead to their profitable deployment; writers
who conjure with blues lyricism, particularly the AAB stanzaic form and
black-snake-crawling, peach-tree-shaking sexual double-entendre; epic
poets and raconteurs who sing of train-whistle guitars, Saturday night juke
joints, crossroads devil-pacts, and audiences that come from miles around
to be healed by the voices of Ma Rainey, Shug Avery, Stagolee Dupas, and
the Beale Street Blues Boy. Faulkner can't be wholly excluded from this
tradition, but neither do his collected works self-evidently center him in
it. Blues scholar David Evans shares my opinion; "[f]rankly," he wrote in
a recent e-mail, "the scarcity of blues description in Faulkner is what has
always struck me."[3] Folklorist Alan Lomax makes the same point much
more irritably in his magnum opus on Mississippi blues, *The Land Where
the Blues Began*:

> The longer I listened to the life stories and songs of the black folk of the Delta,
> the more [Faulkner's] work puzzled me. One-half of Mississippi, perhaps the
> more interesting half, had been left out of . . . his account. Faulkner scarcely
> gives the reader a hint at what black life or feelings are like.
>
> As I talked to the black levee-camp workers, farmers, prisoners, mothers,
> and children of the Delta, as I comprehended that the music they had made
> out of their tribulation was becoming the music of the whole world, I wondered
> how Faulkner could have remained so provincial. Did he ever hear such music,
> such songs as are described in these pages? He must have, yet it wasn't clear.[4]

There's a grain of truth in Lomax's charge, but also a kind of territorial-
ity—a desire to speak for "his" Mississippi blues people against the prior
claims of Daddy Faulkner—that leads the folklorist astray. Although
Faulkner did, by virtue of his Mississippi homeplace and regional travels, have a surprisingly variegated exposure to live blues performance
and a passionate investment in one particular blues song, W. C. Handy's
"St. Louis Blues," he grew less interested in representing overt blues performance as his career progressed, even as he grew more interested in
imagining himself into the lives of black subjects overwhelmed with blues
feeling and struggling vainly to articulate that condition. Apart from the
passing mention of a "young, black, lean-hipped" Delta blues guitarist in
The Wild Palms (74), Faulkner's claim on the blues literary tradition arguably rests on four texts: one story, "That Evening Sun"; the "Pantaloon
in Black" chapter of *Go Down, Moses*; and perhaps twenty pages all told
in *Soldiers' Pay* and *Sartoris*.[5] The "Negro cornetist" (*SP* 186), "blind

Negro beggar" (S 108), and "three Negroes and a bull fiddle" (S 127) who briefly but pointedly serenade white audiences for pay in those two novels from the mid-1920s are supplanted, in 1931, by the sound that was "[n]ot singing and not unsinging" (TES 300) made by the death-haunted Nancy Manigoe of "That Evening Sun." Nancy, with her powerful but unprofessionalized expressive gift, is in turn supplanted in 1940 by Rider, the bereaved and inconsolable protagonist of "Pantaloon in Black," who log hauls his blues, drowns his blues in corn liquor, razors his blues into the windpipe of a dice-rolling white timber mill foreman, and finally cries his blues in big, heavy drops, yelling as he does so. But Rider never *sings* his blues, because he lacks a practitioner's competence in that vital and cathartic expressive art. Rider *has* the blues, without question, and he has a name sourced squarely in the blues tradition, but he's neither a blues-man *per se*, nor a member of a blues-consuming audience. In fact, he suffers precisely the suicidal "failure of nerve" that Albert Murray warns against in *Stomping the Blues*—a failure in the face of life's inevitable disasters that blues music was designed to help alleviate in both perform-ers and audience members alike.[6] He's overwhelmed by the blues, rather than sustained by an art form that purges them.

Even as I elaborate my claims about Faulkner's relative marginality to the blues literary tradition, I would be the first to admit that the signifiers "Faulkner" and "blues" have an overdetermined relationship—indeed, a cozy and mutually sustaining relationship—within American culture as a whole and the Mississippi tourism industry in particular. In this post-modern, hypercommodified age, both "Faulkner" and "blues" bespeak a kind of dirty-South authenticity, particularly when that third signifier, "Mississippi," is tacked on. Like single-malt Scotch, Faulkner and the Mississippi blues are icons of the Real: rough-hewn but subtle, not to everybody's taste, hailing from polysyllabic postage stamps of ancestral ground (Yoknapatawpha, Indianola, Glenmorangie), they burn a little going down. That rough-edged alterity is, of course, precisely what makes "Faulkner" and "Mississippi blues" seductive to the mainstream.[7] Both signifiers are amenable to commodification; a taste for Faulkner and the Mississippi blues allows you to attend both the Faulkner and Yoknapatawpha Conference and the Blues Today symposium at Ole Miss, visit Rowan Oak and the Delta Blues Museum, buy the books and CDs and T-shirts and coffee mugs. Oprah's Book Club is in on the action. But the actual stuff lurking behind the signifiers remains at least somewhat resist-ant to the culture industry's signal-smoothing impulse. Rosa Coldfield and R. L. Burnside, the furious old dowager and indomitable old bluesman, bruise us with their harsh, disruptive refusal to be wholly domesticated. They keep the Real alive in a way that Mountain Dew simply can't.[8]

The truth is that "Faulkner" and "Mississippi blues," as terms in a contemporary conversation about culture, find themselves sorted into the same folder in a range of ways that have little to do with Faulkner's literary indebtedness to the blues. We might call these modes of association *proximities*; together they help explain why some people assume that Faulkner must be writing a kind of blues literature, even when the evidence doesn't support that claim. The most obvious of these proximities is *geographic* proximity, invoked in the service of a familiar kind of cultural tourism agenda. "Visitmississippi.org," the state's official Web site, for example, offers a "Music Heritage Tour Itinerary" that bundles Faulkner and the Delta into Day 2. "Continue the journey to Oxford," enthuses the virtual docent, "a quaint college town immortalized in the writings of William Faulkner. . . . Begin the day with a tour of Rowan Oak, Faulkner's home, then visit the Center for the Study of Southern Culture, a research center for Southern music, folklore and literature housed in an antebellum observatory on the campus of the University of Mississippi. Enjoy a tour of the college campus before continuing on to the Mississippi Delta, the 'Birthplace of the Blues.' Visit the Delta Blues Museum in Clarksdale, which houses memorabilia of such music greats as Muddy Waters, Robert Johnson and B. B. King."[9] Faulkner *must* be bluesy, the inner logic of such touristic writing convinces us; why, he lived just around the corner from all those famous blues guys—and I can visit both ancestral stomping grounds in one day! Should a cultural tourist decide to get serious about the study of Southern culture after the hills-to-Delta whirlwind of Day 2 and visit the Web page for the University of Mississippi's Graduate Program in Southern Studies, he or she would quickly gain a sense of what this small postage stamp of academic soil cares about. "Students can study an array of Southern topics and issues," the Center's pitch begins, "from Faulkner to the blues, from the Civil War to the Civil Rights Movement, from folk art to fundamentalism."[10] The inner logic here is also vaguely touristic, but once again Faulkner and the blues are paired and foregrounded: the monumental literary artist and the primal folk music, linked trailheads into the intellectual hinterlands of the One True South.

A second mode of linkage connecting Faulkner with the Mississippi blues might be called *chronological* proximity. Faulkner is bluesy, according to this logic, not just because Rowan Oak and the Delta Blues Museum—and the ancestral territories over which they preside—are geographically adjacent and thus spiritually aligned, but because Faulkner, entering the world in 1897, was born when the blues were born. As Howard Odum noted in a 1953 essay entitled "On Southern Literature and Southern Culture," "[Faulkner] has been contemporaneous with the growth stage of a folk-regional culture."[11] The first generation of full-fledged blues singers, according to Paul Oliver, was born in the half-dozen years that frame Faulkner's birth; his contemporaries include performers such as Blind Lemon Jefferson, Memphis Minnie, Tommy Johnson, Sleepy John Estes, and Whistling Alex Moore.[12] Karen McFarland, past president of the Mississippi Valley Blues Society, invokes both geographical and chronological proximity when she writes, "Like his musical counterparts, Faulkner was born near the turn of the century . . ., about 50 miles east of the Delta. . . . At the same time that Faulkner was honing his craft of writing (including visiting the juke joints of Clarksdale in the early 1920s), Charley Patton, 'King of the Delta Blues,' was refining his music. Faulkner's 'genius' period of writing (late 1920s to mid-1940s) coincides with the 'golden age' of the Delta blues."[13] Now, Faulkner did indeed visit the juke joints of Clarksdale in the early 1920s, a way in which geographical and chronological proximity might seem to contribute directly to his actual—rather than presumptive—blues understandings. What McFarland works tendentiously to evoke, however, is the sense of Faulkner and Patton as twin toilers in the field of blues-toned art making, secret sharers of the Mississippi mojo. This skirts the question of why Faulkner, with his apparently impeccable blues pedigree, never wrote about those Clarksdale juke joints and devoted no more than a couple of sentences during his "genius" period to the bluesmen who worked them.

The third proximity that leads people to impute an unmerited bluesiness to Faulkner's writings is what I'll call *thematic* proximity: the fact that Faulkner and the great Mississippi blues artists create their art out of imaginations shaped by the same set of Jim Crow social relations, albeit from opposite sides of the race/class divide, and share certain thematic interests bred by those social relations: cotton sharecropping, lynch law, hard drinking, recklessness, a culture of honor and vengeance arbitrated by guns and blades, a love-hate relationship with the home place. "Similarities abound between Faulkner and the blues in themes," insists McFarland, and the somewhat more general themes she lists include "love/ loss," "effects of the past and mistreatment," and "movement."[14] Well, those are indeed themes shared by *Light in August, Absalom, Absalom!*, and any number of Charley Patton songs, but they're also the themes of novels such as *Anna Karenina* and *Portrait of a Lady*—works that hardly count as blues literature. Faulkner and Patton are both masterful, powerful Mississippi-born artists who came of age during the Jim Crow era and evoke cotton sharecropping, lynch law, and a range of associated social practices; I'm not sure what we gain by insisting that the author, like the performer, is a blues artist, or why some commentators feel the need to insist on that equivalence—unless it be a backdoor way of reassuring ourselves that Faulkner, as it might have been put fifty years ago, "really *does*

understand the Negro," and really *has* stolen the Promethian fire that
the blues represent as Mississippi's most influential African American cultural legacy. "[W]hatever we now think," writes David Krause in this vein,
invoking the blues literary pantheon, "whatever we now feel about the
legitimacy of [Faulkner's] remakings of Afro-American heritage, experience, and language into something 'not Negro anymore,' we can still
speak about Faulkner's blues, if we've listened to . . . Wright, Ellison and
Baldwin."[15] Thematic proximity has shaded here into something more
like stylistic or spiritual proximity, but the underlying logic is old, familiar,
and retrograde: a white boy—praise the Lord!—can sing the blues just as
convincingly as his darker-skinned brothers across the tracks. Few commentators feel a similar need to reassure us that Muddy Waters, Robert
Johnson, and B. B. King were urbane modernists and self-conscious aesthetic innovators—and Faulkner's peer in that regard—even though that's
exactly what Waters, Johnson, and King were.[16] The proximity effect, in
this case, requires that the black blues-purveyor remain an earthbound
folk-cultural resource, singing his immemorial song—a song that the
white writer simply absorbs along with the weather, the crop cycles, the
occasional lynching, and assorted other aesthetic influences. This strikes
me as a paternalistic double standard.

An accurate appraisal of Faulkner's blues understandings, I'm suggesting, might do well to begin in the spirit of positivist inquiry, avoiding
Lomax's intemperate dismissals on the one hand and the familiar—and
potentially misleading—invocations of Faulkner's Mississippi-born proximity to some primal blues source on the other.[17] Borrowing from the
recursive structure of the classic blues stanza, I will return to my initial
question, with emphasis: What *did* Faulkner actually know about the
blues, and when did he know it?

Pop, Regional, Homespun: Faulkner's Blues Education

We know that Faulkner was as fond of one particular blues-tinged composition, Gershwin's "Rhapsody in Blue," as he was averse to radio and
jukeboxes; he claimed to have worn out three recordings of "Rhapsody"
while writing *Sanctuary* in an effort to "set the rhythm and jazzy tone" of
the novel.[18] Faulkner accumulated most of his knowledge of the blues,
however, from direct exposure to blues performers in a range of geographic locations, including Oxford and the Ole Miss campus, Memphis,
New Orleans, Clarksdale, Harlem, and his rural Lafayette County
homestead, Greenfield Farm. His first significant contact with the blues
came through the mediation of W. C. Handy, whose pop hits "Memphis
Blues" and "St. Louis Blues," in 1912 and 1914, brought blues melodies,

harmonies, and AAB stanzaic form into mass circulation for the first time. While the rest of America absorbed Handy's pop-blues through sheet music, Faulkner was fortunate enough to live within the touring radius of Handy's Memphis-based band and doubly fortunate to circulate, as a teenager, within Oxford social circles where a "fond parent," according to Blotner, "might spend $75 to bring . . . [in the] amiable forty-year-old Negro" and his ensemble to play those upbeat hits on trumpet and piano.[19] Handy and young Faulkner crossed paths at the Oxford home of Myrtle Ramey between 1912 and 1914, where the future author danced with his future wife Estelle, and at the Red and Blue dances in the Gordon Hall ballroom on the Ole Miss campus over the following half decade, where Faulkner, not yet enrolled, was Oxford's version of a gate-crashing townie. Ben Wasson remembered Faulkner barging into his dorm room one night when a band—most likely Handy's—was playing and announcing, "Listen, man, listen to that band. Hear that saxophone. Revelry is underway. Let's join it," before pulling Wasson downstairs so the two young men could watch couples in evening clothes twirling across the dining room.[20] On-campus spectatorship was quickly supplanted by responsive performance. "I shall always remember the time that W. C. Handy played for a dance at Ole Miss," remembered Clifton Bondurant Webb, "and Mr. Faulkner led the grand march. At that time young men wore white shirts with fancy fronts, stovepipe derbies and cutaway coats with tails. Men looked very handsome then. When Mr. Faulkner came on the ballroom floor, he created a picture of the storybook type. A wonderful dancer, he created another splendid scene when the band played a waltz."[21] By the time Faulkner officially enrolled at the University in the fall of 1919, Handy had departed Memphis for New York's Tin Pan Alley, although his band may well have continued to play at university functions.[22] In 1921 Faulkner contributed a sketch of a seven-piece jazz ensemble to the Ole Miss yearbook that seems clearly have been based on his memories of Handy; the piano player—Handy's stand-in—is hidden behind a twirling white couple.

As these vignettes suggest, Faulkner's initial understandings of the blues were shaped by Handy's ability to present blues as commercialized, lighthearted dance music, an appropriate soundtrack for the mating rituals and masculine displays of white Southern youth. It was a tangy and culturally miscegenated music, interspersed with waltzes and other Euro-American dance repertoire yet redolent with deeper folk-blues tonalities that Handy had himself added to his compositional palette relatively recently, after his 1903 relocation from the Midwest (where he'd been on tour with Mahara's Minstrels) to the Mississippi Delta. The forty-one-year-old African American bandleader who composed "St. Louis Blues" in

1914 and the twenty-eight-year-old white Mississippian who fictionalized the bandleader in *Soldiers' Pay* a decade later, although a generation apart, were both ambitious modernists, as eager to escape backward-looking rusticity as they were to ground their art in the South and its distinctive folk inheritance. "St. Louis Blues," in any case, with its opening declamation about how the female singer "hate[s] to see that evening sun go down," long remained one of Faulkner's favorite songs. When Faulkner visited New York in the fall of 1931, as the blues-suffused story "That Evening Sun" was being republished as part of a collection entitled *These* 13, his editor Bennett Cerf convinced a reluctant Carl Van Vechten to shepherd the Mississippi author through Harlem. Van Vechten "piloted a tipsy . . . Faulkner from high-toned clubs to raucous honky-tonks early one morning," according to David Levering Lewis, and was mildly embarrassed by Faulkner's "unvarying slurred request" that the musicians play "St. Louis Blues," a song that had apparently fallen out of fashion uptown.[23]

If W. C. Handy and his commercialized pop-blues were one early source of Faulkner's blues understandings, then the biographical record also makes clear that he, like Handy, came into contact with more localized Mississippi and Memphis blues traditions as well. In particular, his social life as an Oxford teenager and twentysomething exposed him to black musicians such as Lucius Pegues, who played dances at Estelle and Dorothy Oldham's with a small combo featuring guitar, banjo, and drum.[24] It would be a mistake to call Pegues and his trio "bluesmen," although their repertoire would certainly have included blues material; rather, they were representatives of a string-band tradition that had roots in slave-era entertainments but was in the process of modernizing itself into peppier ensembles called "jug bands." A young black Memphian named Will Shade, who was Faulkner's exact contemporary, heard a record by the Dixieland Jug Blowers out of Lexington, Kentucky, in the mid-1920s and began to purvey the newer style. According to William Barlow, "Shade played guitar, harmonica, and 'bullfiddle,' a stand-up bass made from a garbage can, a broom handle, and a string."[25] I suspect, although I can't prove, that Faulkner and Shade crossed paths when Faulkner and Phil Stone were making their weekend automotive getaways to Memphis's red-light district and Clarksdale's parallel "New World" district in the early 1920s, since the plucky, homespun music Shade made, with or without jug-band updatings, was very much in demand by the white patrons of such establishments.[26] In *Father of the Blues*, for example, W. C. Handy describes his 1904 encounter with a black string band in Cleveland, Mississippi, whose repetitive, blues-tinged melodies leave him unimpressed—until a cascade of silver dollars begins to accumulate at their feet, courtesy of the white dancers whom they have driven "wild." "[T]hey were led," wrote Handy, "by a long-legged chocolate boy and their band consisted of just three pieces, a battered guitar, a mandolin, and a worn-out bass. The music they made was pretty well in keeping with their looks. They struck up one of those over-and-over strains that seem to have no very clear beginning and certainly no ending at all."[27] Will Shade and Lucius Pegues, who played this sort of music, are likely models for Faulkner's depiction in *Sartoris* of a black musical trio, compliant young men who sport a bass viol, guitar, and clarinet and are impressed into service one evening by young Bayard Sartoris, home from the Great War, as he serenades a series of eligible young white women in Jefferson. Faulkner's portrait, with its mention of the clarinet, may also have been inspired the Chatmon family, a multigenerational mulatto ensemble that dominated the party-band scene in Mississippi during the pre- and postwar decades. Born four years before Faulkner, Bo Chatmon started out as a child accompanist around 1900, according to Christopher Waterman,

> playing bass viol, banjo, and guitar behind the fiddling of his father Henderson and brother Lonnie. . . . The first blues that Bo's younger brother Sam remembered learning were published songs such as 'St. Louis Blues,' 'Beale Street Blues,' and 'Sugar Blues,' heard on gramophone records and at the minstrel shows that toured [the region], where the Chatmons heard vaudevillian blues singers such as Ma Rainey and Ida Cox. . . .
>
> From around World War I until 1928, the Chatmon family formed a septet, which played at dances in the hill country and the Delta. . . . On the road they often played with local musicians, usually a trumpet player and drummer . . . and Bo apparently sometimes played clarinet.
>
> The Chatmons' circulation between white and colored communities enabled (and required) them to develop a broad repertoire of square dance music, waltzes, fox-trots, and one-steps, country blues, jazz, and current pop songs.[28]

We know from John Faulkner's memories of the 1920s that "Bill was invited to and went to a great many country dances around Oxford in those days. He never danced at them. He simply sat by the tub of whiskey, taking a drink from a tin cup every now and then and watching and listening."[29] What Faulkner was watching and listening to was almost surely the blues-laced mix of popular music retailed by the Chatmons or their equivalents—a very profitable enterprise indeed, guided by men who defy the romantic/primitivist stereotypes of black bluesmen as unsophisticated purveyors of raw emotion. "We played for parties everywhere," Sam Chatmon told folklorist Alan Lomax:

> For colored and white, too. All we wanted was the money. If we would play two hours and a half, we'd get five dollars a man. When we'd get through with

us crops, late on by in June or July, we'd all get together and take a tour all up through Memphis, Chicago, and different places like that. . . .

Bout fourteen or fifteen of us played together. Every Saturday night we would divide up—let four or five go play at this place, and four or five go to the other. . . . That's the way we got around. . . .

We played for white folks more than we did colored. White folks had something to hire you with and colored folks didn't.[30]

What the evidence suggests, contradicting Alan Lomax's earlier charge of ignorance, is that Faulkner repeatedly encountered, and paid attention to, two different kinds of live blues performance in Mississippi between 1912 and the mid-1930s: the commercialized, Delta-fragranced big band pop of W. C. Handy, a music made by sight-reading professionals; and the more locally inflected, folksy, but still profit-minded and hit-conscious string band music made by unschooled journeymen like Will Shade, Lucius Pegues, and the Chatmons.

A third kind of Mississippi blues—homegrown country blues, made for pleasure rather than profit—swims into view at a slightly later moment in Faulkner's life, when he was beginning work on what would become "Pantaloon in Black," with its evocation of a blues-stricken young mill worker named Rider. In February of 1938, after selling screen rights to *The Unvanquished* for $25,000, Faulkner purchased a 320-acre farm seventeen miles from Oxford in a rural area of Lafayette County known as Beat Two—"the Free State of Beat Two," its residents called it. Naming his new country residence Greenfield Farm, Faulkner staffed it with black tenant farmers and made his brother Johncy manager. That Fourth of July, Faulkner did what many landowners in the area did: he threw a picnic. "The picnic season," according to Lomax, "came in July and August, when small farmers, renters, and sharecroppers laid by their crops and the religious attended revivals, the worldly went dancing, and, because the Hill country wasn't so 'strict,' many did both. The picnics, often sponsored by a political candidate or some moneyed town dweller who wanted to show his country relatives a good time, were open to the public and largely financed by sales of homemade barbecue and drinks, with red-eye whiskey out in the dark back of the wagons."[31] In his memoir, *My Brother Bill*, John Faulkner describes a blues performance that blossomed spontaneously among his brother's black tenants toward the end of the festivities, after the barbecue had been eaten and the white relatives and guests had gone home. It's not clear from Johncy's description whether Bill, who retires "late in the evening" after working the barbecue pit all day, is actually present; what we can be certain of is that Faulkner, as resident landowner, would have heard this kind of music being made by his tenants from time to time, with or without the dramatic elaborations that accompany it. "Soon one of them on the front steps brought out a mouth organ and began to play," remembered Johncy:

> The first thing he did after taking the harp from his pocket was to knock it against the heel of his hand to get the crumbs and trash out. Then he slid his lips up and down the keys, sort of warming up. All the Negroes stopped what they were doing and listened. He launched into a song they play about a fox hunt. They play the tune and take the part of the dogs too. You can hear them trailing and finally you can hear them tree the fox.
>
> As soon as this first Negro finished, another one took the organ from his hand and played a train song. You could hear the train starting, running and the whistle blowing. Then a Negro from across Cypress Creek snatched the harp and played an old blues, "Jack o' Diamonds." The Negroes all got stiller than before and one by one they began grinning and patting their feet. Soon they were clapping their hands in time to the tune. . . .
>
> The Negro kept on playing "Jack o' Diamonds" and all at once one of the Negroes who had been listening hopped onto the [tractor] slide [in front of the commissary] and began to dance. Soon he improvised a step and began talking as he danced. He would dance to one end of the slide and then suddenly reach out his hand and shy back quickly. Then he would whirl and dance to the other end of the slide. He'd snort and rear his head back just like a mule when you are trying to put the bridle on him.
>
> . . . He took both parts, trying to put the bridle on the mule and dodging back when the mule threw up its head. The other Negroes began laughing and clapping louder than ever and suddenly another of them jumped up on the stage and pushed the first Negro off. He took the bridle and caught the mule, all this in dance time to improvised steps, as he needed them. Another Negro jumped on the slide and let the mule from his stall and took him to the field and hitched him to a plow. Another took his place and began dirting up corn, turning his feet sideways and sweeping them along the edge of the boards. They made a corn crop right there on that slide, three by four feet. (191–94)

Later, after a drunken white man has propositioned their women and Johncy has forcibly ejected him from the party, the black workers begin drifting away. "They called quiet good nights and thanked Bill and me for the party," Johncy remembered, "and it was over."

Although John Faulkner's racial views were notably less progressive than his brother's, he deserves credit here for the attentiveness with which he renders a blues-based community ritual, music made by and for black Mississippians. There is, remarkably, no equivalent description in William Faulkner's collected works—none, certainly, that shows blues music functioning as an articulate and enlivening conversation among black equals, a music improvised for pleasure rather than crafted for profit. The "old blues" mentioned by Johncy, "Jack o' Diamonds," had been a hit for Sippie Wallace and Blind Lemon Jefferson more than a decade earlier,

but it has been reclaimed as North Mississippi folk music by the men of
Greenfield Farm.[32] "Jack o' Diamonds" was a song, according to black
Mississippian Lewis Jones, that railroad men used to sing when they'd go
broke playing card games like "coon can." "Everything going wrong with
him," Jones remembered, speaking of a busted gambler, "and he'll go to
singing and hollering. *Take that ace, deuce, and queen, / It gonna turn
my money green. / Jack o' diamonds a hard card to play.*"[33] It's a hard-
luck, bad-news blues, in other words. Yet it serves here to abet collective
morale and to inspire collective improvisation. That fact, which sets this
performance apart from the other, more commercialized kinds of blues
music made for white consumption from which Faulkner derived his earlier blues understandings, leads me to ask just what effect his residency at
Greenfield Farm may have had on his literary sensibility. Might his daily
contact with blues-singing tenant farmers, for example, have spurred his
decision to imagine himself into Rider's disintegrating, blues-suffused
consciousness in "Pantaloon in Black"?

Reading Faulkner Representing the Blues

Faulkner's blues understandings, it seems to me, move in an essentially
tragic direction, deepening and darkening through the years. Faulkner's
blues begin, in *Soldiers' Pay* and *Sartoris*, as energetic, repetitive, sexualized, and profitable background music made by black performers to support dramas of white self-articulation; they evolve, with "That Evening
Sun" and "Pantaloon in Black," into the feelings that suffuse dramas of
black self-articulation, dramas in which overwhelmed subjects suffer for
their lack of precisely the sort of supportive blues audience Faulkner's
black tenants create for each other at Greenfield Farm.[34] Faulkner misses
two things about the blues: its tragicomic moment and its healing
potential—the way in which blues feeling and blues music work in tandem
to anneal pain with pleasure and revivify African American communities.

Soldiers' Pay (1926), Faulkner's first attempt to transform his youthful
blues understandings into literature, is distinguished by a lengthy dance
sequence set in the small Georgia town of Charlestown in the spring of
1919 and presided over by a "negro cornetist" and his band—an ensemble
plainly modeled on W. C. Handy's outfit. The novel's narrative attentions
flow primarily towards the white dancers and observers who flirt to, revel
in, and critique the aggressive, sexually charged, "modern" rhythms and
melodies with which the band floods the ballroom. The Lost Generation
is ascendant: slim girlish boys and slim boyish girls dirty dance with each
other in ways that leave the recently returned veterans feeling like out-
dated provincials. "Look at them two," complains Gilligan, a hometown

boy: "look where he's got his hand. This is what they call polite dancing, is it? I never learned it: I would have got throwed out of any place
I ever danced doing that. But I had a unfortunate youth: I never danced
with nice people" (*SP* 192). Faulkner highlights the sexual incitements
of this bluesy new music in a range of ways: not just through Gilligan's
ironic commentary, but through repeated quick shifts in point of view.
A white veteran hears "the rhythmic troubling obscenities of saxophones"
(*SP* 191). The negro cornetist, "having learned in his thirty years a century of the white man's lust," blinks his "dispassionate eye" at a white
woman's "young shapeless leg" and "lead[s] his crew in a fresh assault" on
the ballroom—an assault that seems to bring the war home to the small-
town South as the shock of a modernity that overturns sexual morality
(*SP* 188). The entire scene is propelled, as Thadious Davis notes, by an
"understood racial differentiation . . . an implicit syncopation in which
the two races, black musicians and white dancers, play off each other in
a dialogical scheme in which music, rather than words, forms the basis
for discourse." Yet words, too, play a crucial function in mediating this
sexualized musical dialogue between black and white. Faulkner weaves
a number of racy lyrics into the scene, drawn from three different songs
that were popular at the time: "Uncle Bud," "Shake It and Break It," and
"I Wonder Where My Easy Rider's Gone":

> ". . . Uncle Joe, Sister Kate, all shimmy like jelly on a plate . . . ." . . . ". . .
> Uncle Bud, ninety-two, shook his cane and shimmied too. . . ." (*SP* 188–89)

> ". . . throw it on the wall. Oh, oh, oh, oh . . ." ". . . wont never forget his expres-
> sion when he said, 'Jack, mine's got syph. Had her . . .'" "shake it and break
> it, shake it. . . ." "First night in Paris . . . then the other one. . . ." "don't let it
> fall. . . ." ". . . with a gun . . . twenty dollars in gold pinned to my. . . ." (*SP* 196)

> ". . . oh, oh, I wonder where my easy rider's gone. . . ." (*SP* 194)

Thadious Davis traces the third lyric extract to Handy's "Yellow Dog
Blues" (1914)—a playful, sentimental pop song rather than a true blues,
and one that Faulkner almost surely would have heard Handy's band
perform at Ole Miss.[35] An equally likely source is the song from which
Handy himself appropriated the line: "I Wonder Where My Easy Rider's
Gone," a huge pop hit for the Canadian-born black songwriter Sheldon
Brooks in 1913.[36] Both Brooks's original and Handy's "answer" version
sing wistfully of a Miss Susie (or Susan) Johnson whose "easy riding kid,"
a jockey named Lee, has suddenly vanished. Faulkner deploys the line
to double purpose in *Soldiers' Pay*: it comments both on the pathos of
Donald Mahon, the incapacitated war veteran at the center of the novel
who has been chauffeured to the dance in his near-vegetative state, and

on the sexually suggestive dance that the band's performance incites—the overheated mating ritual of a Lost Generation of stay-at-homes whose best young men disappeared overseas for several crucial years, missing the cultural sea change that now disorients them.

The first two lyric extracts, like the third, are drawn from songs that deserve to be called "bluesy" by virtue of the sexual double entendres they deploy and the performers who brought them to life, even though they don't adhere to the AAB stanzaic form that distinguishes blues songs from other kinds of folk and pop songs. Neither "Uncle Bud" nor "Shake It and Break It," intriguingly, is a song that Handy's band would likely have performed. Both are rougher, lower-class, juke joint ditties that also had currency as somewhat more mainstreamed jazz recordings—precisely the sort of material that Faulkner could have absorbed from Lucius Pegues, Will Shade, the Chatmons, and their equivalents at country dances in the hills and gambling joints and cathouses in Memphis and the Delta, but also material that he might have encountered during his stay in New Orleans in 1925. Bluesman Charley Patton recorded "Shake It and Break It" in 1929, but he'd been performing it throughout the region for at least a decade before that; the song was also recorded by Ladd's Black Aces (1921), Seven Black Dots (1921), Sam Lanin (1921), and others.[37] "Uncle Bud," according to Zora Neale Hurston, was a "social song for amusement . . . well known all over the South," often in far more obscene versions, and "[n]ever . . . sung before respectable ladies."[38] "Uncle Bud" also had a second life in commercial translation: composed (or appropriated) by Bob Miller, it was recorded by the Tampa Blue Jazz Band (1921) and Leona Williams (1922). Williams, a New Orleans native, also recorded a tune entitled "I Wish I Could Shimmy Like My Sister Kate" (1922).[39]

What Faulkner has done with the blues in *Soldiers' Pay*, I would suggest, is dirty up Handy's relatively tame pop-blues repertoire with more salacious material; he's deliberately made that "Negro cornetist" into more of a sexual provacateur than Handy, a conspicuously chaste exemplar of black uplift, himself actually was. Here is the South's Lost Generation, Faulkner seems to declare, white boys and white girls jooking it up with orgasmic abandon—"feeling the beat of the music," he writes, "toying with it, eluding it, seeking it again, drifting like a broken dream" (*SP* 191). Faulkner has crafted the scene out of his personal encounters with blues music, but he's also highlighted the disruptive sexual modernity he senses in the blues and demanded that the music serve as a register of the brokenness of a young white southern generation. Neither of these meanings is intrinsic to the music itself; they're Faulkner's projections *onto* the blues, Faulkner's extensions *of* the blues in the direction of his artistic vision.

In *Sartoris* (1929), written two years after *Soldiers' Pay*, Faulkner again filters his representations of blues music through the disillusionments of the Lost Generation by placing his death-haunted young protagonist, Bayard Sartoris, at the scene of musical production. Bayard's encounters with blues performance are foreshadowed by images of black blues calls that fail to find adequate white responses. As the novel begins, Bayard's grandfather, old Bayard, is literally deaf to the blues singing of his African American housekeeper, Elnora. "From the kitchen, invisible from this window, Elnora's endless minor ebbed and flowed, unheard by [old] Bayard, upon the lazy scene" (*S* 33). When the novel shifts to Miss Jenny's point of view, Faulkner again configures the blues as a kind of Southern pastoral, of a piece with Nature's timeless song. "[A] shrill monotone of crickets rose from the immediate grass, and further away, from among the trees, a fairylike piping of young frogs like endless silver small bubbles rising. . . . [F]rom the rear of the house, up the dark hall, Elnora's voice floated in meaningless minor suspense" (*S* 49). Faulkner's subtle manipulations of point of view make it unclear whether the word "meaningless" is to be read literally, as the novel's own judgment on Elnora's blues song, or ironically, as Miss Jenny's failure to perceive meaning where meaning does indeed inhere. Still, Faulkner's use of the word is significant; the history of representations of African-derived musics in Western discourse is, after all, a history of claims about "barbaric" rhythms, "primitive" vocalizations, and lack of redeeming musical value. Such dismissals invariably fail to engage the range of meanings that performers themselves attach to these performances—as Elnora, for example, surely intends her song to mean *something*, even if it's not a something Miss Jenny, or Faulkner himself, has enough cultural knowledge to decode. Faulkner deploys the discourse of what might be called musical Africanism in a relatively benign way here, but later he invokes the discourse more pointedly in connection with the blues when young Bayard encounters a blind black musician playing for tips in the Jefferson town square. The novel frames their encounter, as Africanism always does, as a contrast between Western emplacement in history—evoked here by Bayard's noting of the exact time on the courthouse clock after he has swooped into town in his fast new car—and black emplacement in a changeless, immemorial, mythic present that is situated reassuringly, if also somewhat abjectly, outside of modernity. "Negroes slow and aimless as figures of a dark, placid dream," the novel notes through Bayard's eyes, "[murmur and laugh] among themselves" (*S* 108), and his gaze soon lights upon the bluesman:

> Against the wall, squatting, a blind Negro beggar, with a guitar and a wire frame holding a mouth-organ to his lips, patterned the background of smells

and sounds with a plaintive reiteration of rich, monotonous chords, rhythmic
as a mathematical formula, but without music. He was a man of at least forty
and his was that patient resignation of many sightless years. . . . His weathered
derby was encircled by an officer's hat-cord, and on the pavement between his
feet sat a tin cup containing a dime and three pennies.

Bayard sought a coin in his pocket, and the beggar sensed his approach and
his tune became a single repeated chord, but without a break in the rhythm,
until the coin rang into the cup, and still without a break in the rhythm and the
meaningless strains of the mouth-organ, his left hand dropped groping a little,
to the cup and read the coin in a single motion; then once more guitar and
mouth-organ resumed their monotonous pattern. (*S* 108–9)

An adequate reading of this scene requires that I make an autobiographical
confession. Between 1987 and 1991 I spent a great deal of my time playing blues harmonica for tips on the streets of Harlem and Times Square
with an African American guitar man from Mount Olive, Mississippi.[40]
Although I'm neither blind nor black, I have shared the stage with several
such men, including Blind Mississippi Morris and Harmonica Fats. I can
confidently assert that *no* mouth-organ player would take at face value
Faulkner's characterization of this blind bluesman's playing as "meaningless strains." We would understand Faulkner's words, instead, as a cultural
outsider's inadvertent confession of cultural illiteracy: a nonblues person's
misunderstanding of the way in which blues performers employ micro-
tonal subtleties to create melodic meaning. We would respond similarly
to the word "monotonous," knowing as we do that the first charge leveled
by nonblues people against the blues is that our music is repetitive—as
W. C. Handy, for example, initially derided the "disturbing monotony"
and the "over and over strain" of the black string-band he encountered in
Cleveland, Mississippi. Such charges, we know, are made by people who
can't hear, or won't allow their bodies to feel, the call-and-response dialogues that African-based rhythms create within themselves through the
use of repetition with variation, and the altered consciousness that results
from greatly extending those dialogues in performance. Finally, we would
laugh at the dismissal of the blind bluesman's performance as somehow
"without music," since music is a form of communication and something
powerful is being communicated in this scene. What are the bluesman's
plaintive reiterations and monotonous strains if not a supremely deliberate and effective rhetorical performance, one that skillfully reaches into
young Bayard's pocket and plucks profit?

It may seem as though I'm accusing Faulkner of distorting the meaning
of the blues here in the act of representing it, but that's not exactly the
case. What Faulkner is evoking, as a subtle modulation of narrative point
of view, is the consciousness of young Bayard; his blues understandings

are conditioned by his troubled need to reassure himself, at the moment his world has been fractured by his brother's death and his own harrowing experience as a military aviator, that "his" black people are still *there*: still anchored in the "dark, placid dream" of his Southern childhood, still child-like, immobilized, available, intimately known and yet ultimately inscruta-ble: "[T]here was in their consonantless murmuring something ready with mirth, in their laughter something grave and sad—country people, men in overalls or corduroy or khaki and without neckties, women in shape-less calico and sunbonnets and snuff-sticks—groups of young girls in still mail-order finery, the young heritage of their bodies' grace dulled already by self-consciousness and labor and unaccustomed high heels, and soon to be obscured forever by childbearing—youths and young men in cheap, tasteless suits and shirts and caps, weather-tanned and clean-limbed as race-horses and a little belligerently blatant" (*S* 108). This passage and the description of the bluesman that follows it, whatever they tell us about Faulkner's own blues understandings, masterfully counterpose Faulkner's broken young protagonist with the dreamlike tableau of his black-and-white boyhood home, a home he's at once alienated from, struggling to reenter, and just beginning to see clearly for the first time. The blind black bluesman is apart from Bayard, and yet a part of him; Bayard *feels* him, even if he doesn't understand the music he's making, and that's pre-cisely Faulkner's point: as they did in *Soldiers' Pay*, black and white are communicating in this scene, however imperfectly, and blues music is the medium of that communication.

Later this same day, after injuring himself badly on a runaway stallion and drinking a great deal of bootleg whiskey, young Bayard, bandaged up and drunk, gets in his car and goes a-courting with two white locals, Hub and Mitch, and a black string band, described as "three Negroes and a bull fiddle in the rear seat" (*S* 127). Faulkner's possible models for this trio were multiple, as I've suggested, and drawn from wide experience: Lucius Pegues, the Chatmons, perhaps Will Shade. W. C. Handy, too, may have provided a model, as Thadious Davis notes, since subunits of Handy's large dance band were often contracted out. "Their most inno-vative performances," she writes, "were instrumental serenades outside the homes of the sweethearts of young white men who hired them."[41] Faulkner initially frames the black trio, as he earlier framed Elnora's blues singing, within the tropes of Southern pastoral. "The moon stood pale and cold overhead, and on all sides insects shrilled in the dusty undergrowth. In the rear seat the Negroes murmured among themselves" (*S* 127). Like shrilling insects, like the whippoorwills who coo as the car passes, the sonorous young black musicians take their place in what Craig Werner has identified as Faulkner's familiar "narrative of endurance."[42] Rather than canny, ambitious, profit-minded agents of culture—which is what Handy, the Chatmons, and many black musicians of the time clearly were—these men, as the novel represents them, are passive and compliant bearers of the ageless Song of the South, placeholders for the premodern from which young Bayard's wartime traumas seems to have alienated him. Yet they are, at the same time, something more than this. Faulkner, searching for his voice early in his novelistic career, discovers in these black musicians a source of native poetry, distinctly Southern and *miscegenated* poetry, that offers him a signpost for what his own Mississippi-born art might be:

> They stopped here, in shadow. The Negroes descended and lifted the bass viol out, and a guitar. The third one held a slender tube frosted over with keys upon which the intermittent moon glinted in pale points, and they stood with their heads together, murmuring among themselves and touching plaintive muted chords from the strings. Then the one with the clarinet raised it to his lips.
>
> The tunes were old tunes. Some of them were sophisticated tunes and formally intricate, but in the rendition this was lost, and all of them were imbued instead with a plaintive similarity, a slurred and rhythmic simplicity; and they drifted in rich, plaintive chords upon the silver air, fading, dying in minor reiterations along the treacherous vistas of the moon. They played again, an old waltz. The college Cerberus came across the dappled lawn to the fence and leaned his arms upon it, a lumped listening shadow among other shadows. Across the street, in the shadows there, other listeners stood. A car approached and slowed to the curb and shut off engine and lights, and in the tiered windows heads leaned, aureoled against the lighted rooms behind, without individuality, feminine, distant, delicately and divinely young.
>
> They played "Home, Sweet Home," and when the rich minor died away, across to them came a soft clapping of slender palms. Then Mitch sang "Good Night, Ladies" in his true, oversweet tenor, and the young hands were more importunate, and as they drove away the slender heads leaned aureoled with bright hair in the lighted windows and the soft clapping drifted after them for a long while, fainter and fainter in the silver silence and the moon's infinitude. (*S* 129)

The repeated word "plaintive" and the phrases "slurred and rhythmic simplicity" and "minor reiterations" are markers for the bluesness of the trio's music; they're Faulkner's way of representing audible blackness. Yet what is striking about Faulkner's description is its articulation of the serenade as a scene of racial intermixture, not racial purity: the black trio seamlessly fuses African-sourced rhythms and tonalities with Euro-American repertoire, including "sophisticated and formally intricate" old tunes, an "old waltz," and "Home, Sweet Home." As Mitch follows the trio with his own rendition of "Good Night, Ladies," miscegenated music is supplanted by a miscegenated performance space; every man's call finds a responsive audience among white Southern womanhood. Soon Bayard, Mitch, and Hub are sharing their jug of whiskey directly with their black coconspirators rather than dispensing doses into an oily metal receptacle they've been periodically prying off of Bayard's car. "[T]hey had lost the breather-cap," writes Faulkner, "and as they moved from house to house, all six of them drank fraternally from the jug, turn and turn about" (S 135–36). The interracial idyll enabled by liquor, blues, and the seductions of the Southern night finally ends when the town marshall shows up. Bayard gives some money to the leader of the trio and the three black men disappear, Faulkner tells us, "quietly down a side street" (S 137).

In the space between noon and midnight, young Bayard Sartoris has exploded back into the collective life of his small Mississippi town; his rebirth as a Lost Generation trickster, a figure of enlivening, poetry-generating disorder, is bracketed by two moments in which he gifts a black male blues performer with money. In symbolic terms, these bracketing vignettes represent Faulkner's offering to his own muse—which is to say, to the *genius loci*, the African American blues spirit, of his Mississippi homeplace, with which he found an unexpected and productive way of aligning himself in *Sartoris*. As Faulkner worked his own way through the scene, it seems to me, he discovered that the modern art he sought to create would need to be sourced in the rich, nuanced, problematic dialogue of black and white, of African and European on southern soil, rather than simply echoing his fin de siècle European influences. In vernacular terms, he'd need to drink deep from the common jug if he wanted to write the really good stuff.

Faulkner's 1931 story "That Evening Sun" is both a fully realized work of miscegenated art—a blues text through and through—and a turn away from the race-bridging potential of blues music. The story takes its title, as many critics have pointed out, from the opening line of W. C. Handy's "St. Louis Blues," although the principal narrative action is arguably set in 1898 or 1899, fifteen years before Handy composed his song.[43] Faulkner has written a blues story that speaks, in historical and psychological terms, from the blues' originary moment. Black blues performance for profit is nowhere to be found, but black blues feelings are evoked with far greater subtlety and intensity than in *Soldiers' Pay* and *Sartoris*. The call-and-response dialogue engendered by blues performance in both novels—the "Negro cornetist" calling to the white dancers in the former, the blind black bluesman and black trio calling to Bayard, Mitch, and the white maidenhood of Jefferson in the latter—has been hollowed out, reduced to a travesty of responsive interchange. Nancy Mannigoe, a Jefferson washerwoman, repeatedly communicates her terror of her estranged

lover, Jesus, to her employer, the Compsons, but fails to elicit an adequate response.[44] She does this through vocalized worrying about the violent end that allegedly awaits her after the evening sun goes down, and
through the eerie moan she makes in an upstairs hallway later that night,
an originary blues cry that "was like singing and . . . wasn't like singing,
like the sounds that Negroes make" (*TES* 296). Her fearful blues calls
are patronized by Mr. Compson and emulated by the children with their
own childish ghost stories. Faulkner uses the flat, affectless reports of his
white narrator, Quentin Compson, to convey Nancy's worried blues far
more intimately than either of the earlier novels conveyed the feelings of
its black blues characters. Her blues, Faulkner makes clear, predate Jesus;
both her blues feelings and the singing that issues from them are sourced
in the sexual exploitation and violence she has suffered at the hands of a
white man named Mr. Stovall, a bank cashier and Baptist deacon whom
she tells off one day as she's being taken to jail. Her diatribe, as Charles
Peek has noted, takes the form of an AAB blues stanza, with additional
repetitions for emphasis:[45]

> "When you going to pay me, white man? When you going to pay me, white
> man? It's been three times now since you paid me a cent—" Mr Stovall knocked
> her down, but she kept on saying, "When you going to pay me, white man? It's
> been three times now since—" until Mr Stovall kicked her in the mouth with
> his heel and the marshall caught Mr Stovall back, and Nancy lying in the street,
> laughing. She turned her head and spat out some blood and teeth and said, "It's
> been three times now since he paid me a cent."
>
> That was how she lost her teeth, and all that day they told about Nancy and
> Mr. Stovall, and all that night the ones that passed the jail could hear Nancy
> singing and yelling. (*TES* 291)

I've argued elsewhere that disciplinary violence—white violence designed
to silence, terrorize, and immobilize black Southerners—is a generative
influence on the blues tradition; this passage helps situate Faulkner's
story in that tradition, particularly when we frame Nancy more narrowly within a cohort of "beaten blueswomen" evoked by singers such as
Billie Holiday and Ma Rainey and writers such as Alice Walker, Bernice
McFadden, Gayl Jones, and Wanda Coleman.[46] White disciplinary violence not infrequently finds itself linked in blues texts with two other
violences—black retributive violence against white violators and black
intimate violence against black lovers and romantic rivals—and both
violences are vividly in evidence in "That Evening Sun." Jesus, as Peek
and Carol Gartner have noted, makes use of blues vernacular tropes and
the repetition with variation of blues stanzaic form to signify on both
the sexual liberties Stovall has taken with Nancy and the razor-borne

retribution he is contemplating against the man whose "vine" is respon-
sible for the "watermelon" under her dress.[47] Faulkner's text is double
voiced: although Nancy and Jesus communicate with devastating clarity
behind their signifying talk, young Caddy fails to understand the deep
blues song of violation and revenge that is being sung:

> Jesus was in the kitchen, sitting behind the stove, with his razor scar on his
> black face like a piece of dirty string. He said it was a watermelon that Nancy
> had under her dress.
> "It never come off your vine, though," Nancy said.
> "Off what vine?" Caddy said.
> "I can cut down the vine it did come off of," Jesus said.
> "What makes you want to talk like that before these chillen?" Nancy
> said. . . .
> "Talking what way?" Caddy said. "What vine?"
> "I can't hang around white man's kitchen," Jesus said. "But white man can
> hang around mine. White man can come in my house, but I can't stop him.
> When white man want to come in my house, I aint got no house. I cant stop
> him, but he cant kick me outen it. He cant do that." (*TES* 292)

Later, when Mr. Compson teases Nancy that Jesus "is probably in St. Louis
now. Probably got another wife and forgot all about you," she responds,
"If he has, I better not find out about it. . . . I'd stand there right over
them, and every time he wropped her, I'd cut that arm off. I'd cut his
head off and I'd slit her belly and I'd shove—" (*TES* 295). Such violently
expressive figurations have an extensive history in the blues lyric and literary tradition, from Bessie Tucker's "Got Cut All to Pieces" and Uncle
Skipper's "Cuttin' My ABCs" to Bea Ella Thornhill's evisceration of her
two-timing lover, Beau Beau Weaver, in Albert Murray's *Train Whistle
Guitar*.

Trying to trace the origin of Faulkner's stories to particular biographical episodes is an imprecise art, but one provocation for "That Evening
Sun" may have been an important and neglected early blues novel entitled *Sweet Man* (1930). The author, Gilmore Millen, sent Faulkner a copy
in June of 1930 inscribed, "[F]or William Faulkner, author of 'The Sound
and the Fury' a profound and true book I sincerely appreciate."[48] Millen's
literary talents were distinctly second-rate, but *Sweet Man* is an ambitious
attempt to do for the Mississippi Delta, Memphis, and Los Angeles what
Claude McKay had done in *Home to Harlem*: depict the struggles and
triumphs of a black male protagonist from humble origins in a loud, sexy,
violent urban milieu, with lots of AAB blues stanzas woven into the narrative as choral commentary. In fact, in his portrait of Beale Street, Millen
had turned to his own sensationalistic purposes a song that Faulkner had

included in *Soldiers' Pay* four years earlier, tossing in W. C. Handy for good measure:

> There, at Second Street where the crowds are thickest of a Saturday night, is where the old Pewee saloon stood, and Handy and Bynum used to wait for white folks to come to hire their bands for dances. . . . Across the street, in front of that barber shop, two white women came screaming from Gayoso Street, a block over, and cut each other, for love of each other, with knives until their flesh fell like potato peelings on the sidewalk. In that alley, in front of the store across the street, by that fire plug, in that stairway negroes died, shot by policemen. A cocaine-crazed negro came yelling naked out of that side street in the old saloon days, chasing all the women out of a bawdy house before him with a meat cleaver, because their electric piano would not play "I Wonder Where My Easy Rider's Gone" when he wanted it to. (*SM* 152)

Millen had poached on Faulkner's home ground, in short, and made sure the Mississippian knew it. Although I can find nothing in the biographical record to substantiate my hunch, I like to think of Faulkner tossing Millen's novel aside in disgust and resolving to write the deepest, truest blues story he could—a story that rejected sensationalism while acknowledging the expressive power of brutal violence, but also a story that acknowledged the failure of white Southerners to take black blues feelings seriously even as it manifested Faulkner's own determination to take them very seriously indeed.

Ten years separate "That Evening Sun" from "Pantaloon in Black," the fourth and final text in Faulkner's blues oeuvre. Where *Soldiers' Pay* and *Sartoris* foreground professionalized black blues musicians in responsive dialogue with white audiences, "That Evening Sun" retains black blues performance as powerful but unprofessionalized singing that evokes inadequate responses from the white Compson family. "Pantaloon in Black" dismisses with blues musicianship altogether to concentrate its evocative power on the blues-laden desolation and self-destructive trajectory of its black male protagonist, a twenty-four-year old sawmill worker named Rider whose beloved wife of six months, Mannie, has inexplicably just died. If Nancy's Jesus in "That Evening Sun" may be read, as Peek argues, as an incarnation of the blues badman, a violent trickster at large, then Rider has been happily domesticated and sanctified by Mannie's love, transformed from a wild young rounder into an honorable mate—until Mannie's death, when the Devil gets the upper hand.[49] Trudier Harris has theorized a mode of blues textuality she terms "no outlet for the blues," which is to say an African American protagonist suffused with blues feeling but incapable of expressing those blues in a way that offers catharsis and communal affirmation; Rider hews to this paradigm.[50] At the end of the story, after he's drunk himself into a stupor and slit the throat of his white bossman at the sawmill, he ends up immobilized in the county jail under a pile of chain-ganged black prisoners who've been sent in to subdue him—"laughing," Faulkner's narrator, a white sheriff's deputy, tells his wife incredulously, "with tears big as glass marbles running across his face and down past his ears and making a kind of popping sound on the floor like somebody dropping bird eggs, laughing and laughing and saying, "Hit look lack Ah just cant quit thinking. Look lack Ah just cant quit" (*PIB* 154). Laughing-while-crying is a variation of laughing-to-keep-from-crying, an enduring mode of blues expressiveness described by Langston Hughes and various blues singers.[51] (Faulkner's original title for a draft version of "That Evening Sun" was "Never Done No Weeping When You Wanted to Laugh.")[52] The laughing/crying dialectic is framed here by Faulkner's clueless, racist narrator as pathos, spiritual isolation, and failure: the helpless breaking of eggs rather than the stoic ethos of "tears hardened with laughter" noted by Hughes. Rider's final words, too, are an admission of failed nerve couched in the AA repetitions of blues lyric utterance. The B line is missing altogether—which is to say, the most soulful and death-haunted black blues call in Faulkner's canon fails utterly to provoke an adequate white response, finding only mockery and disbelief from a townsman who regards Rider as a crazed and unfeeling animal.

I've already suggested that Faulkner may have been spurred to imagine himself into Rider's blues-besieged consciousness as a result of being brought into daily proximity with the blues-singing tenants of his new country residence, Greenfield Farm. Rider's name, in any case, is clearly sourced in the blues tradition, although it's unclear whether Faulkner intended to reference a particular song or songs. H. R. Stoneback cites the refrain included in *Soldiers' Pay*, "oh, oh, I wonder where my easy rider's gone," as evidence for Faulkner's familiarity with "Easy Rider" and several related blues songs, but claims that another blues, "I Know You, Rider," is in fact the "objective correlative" for "Pantaloon in Black," the source of compacted images that Faulkner elaborates into narrative.[53] The version of "I Know You, Rider" cited by Stoneback, which he claims to have notated "from oral tradition as learned in Southern Mississippi in 1962," does indeed align with Faulkner's story—in a stanza, for example, that seems to anticipate Rider's final helpless admission of defeat: "I laid down last night trying to take a rest; / I laid down last night trying to take a rest; / But my mind kept rambling like the wild geese in the West."[54] Thadious Davis, by contrast, invokes two songs by W. C. Handy, "Yellow Dog Blues" and "The Memphis Blues," both of which reference an "easy rider," and both of which Faulkner would surely have known. Neither of Handy's compositions, however, evokes the sort of crushing desolation sounded by "Pantaloon in Black."

Although I'm intrigued by the textual parallels supplied by Stoneback and persuaded by Davis that Handy's music remained a lifelong influence on Faulkner, I'm not convinced that source hunting is the most productive critical approach to this particular story—or, for that matter, to any of the four blues texts I've discussed. Biographical and historical research can give us a good sense of the blues performers Faulkner encountered during his formative years and beyond, but the blues understandings that actually emerge from the texts are nuanced, idiosyncratic, part of a larger and more comprehensive artistic vision. The master trope undergirding all four texts, it seems to me, is call and response as racial dialogue: black blues calls linked dialectically with white responses, or nonresponses, to those calls. As Faulkner probes the emotional sources and signifying registers of black blues expression with increasing subtlety in the course of his career, he also finds more evidence for the inadequacy of white response—which is to say, as his blues-literary art grows blacker, it also grows more pessimistic about the power of the blues to engender interracial understanding. Yet the blues, beginning with W. C. Handy's wistful "St. Louis Blues," managed somehow to draw young Faulkner into their orbit and prompt his own journey towards responsive, if partial, understandings of his African American friends and neighbors—understandings that deepened the whole of his literary achievement, not just the scattered texts I've discussed. Faulkner may stand closer to the margins of the blues literary tradition than some critics have argued, in other words, but blues music, as mode of interracial conversation in a highly racialized society, stands closer to the center of Faulkner's achievement than we may have realized.

NOTES

I'd like to thank Don Kartiganer for first suggesting that I work up a paper on Faulkner and the blues for the 2005 Faulkner and Yoknapatawpha Conference. I'd also like to thank Joe Urgo, Ann Abadie, Greg Johnson, Elliott Hurwitt, Steve Tracy, Travis Montgomery, and Bill Steber for offering research leads and answering my pesky questions with unfailing generosity. Jay Watson read a draft of my presentation and offered numerous helpful comments, several of which crucially shaped my reading of "Pantaloon in Black." David Evans, a scholar's scholar of American music, not only suggested research leads but also read a prepublication version of this paper and saved me from several grievous errors on points of musical fact. Finally, I'd like to thank Noel Polk, Judith Sensibar, Terrell Tebbetts, Jon Smith, and other unnamed but immensely supportive and generous presenters and audience members at Faulkner and Yoknapatawpha 2005, where a shorter version of this paper was first presented.

1. Joel Williamson, *William Faulkner and Southern History* (New York: Oxford University Press, 1993), 355.

2. See Thadious Davis, "From Jazz Syncopation to Blues Elegy: Faulkner's Development of Black Characterization," in *Faulkner and Race: Faulkner and Yoknapatawpha, 1986*, ed. Doreen Fowler and Ann J. Abadie (Jackson: University Press of Mississippi, 1987), 70–92; Thadious Davis, *Faulkner's "Negro": Art and the Southern Context* (Baton Rouge: Louisiana

State University Press, 1983), 32–64; Charles Peek, "'That Evening Sun(g)': Blues Inscribing Black Space in White Stories," *Southern Quarterly* 42.3 (Spring 2004): 130–50; Carol B. Gartner, "Faulkner in Context: 'That Evening Sun' through the Blues," *Southern Quarterly* 34.2 (Winter 1996): 50–58; Ken Bennett, "The Language of the Blues in Faulkner's 'That Evening Sun,'" *Mississippi Quarterly* 38.3 (Summer 1985): 339–42; H. R. Stoneback, "Faulkner's Blues: 'Pantaloon in Black,'" *Modern Fiction Studies* 21.2 (Summer 1975): 241–45.

 3. David Evans, e-mail to Adam Gussow, 3 April 2005.

 4. Alan Lomax, *The Land Where the Blues Began* (New York: Pantheon Books, 1993), 327–28.

 5. Quotations from Faulkner's works, all cited internally, are taken from the following editions: *The Wild Palms* [*TWP*] (New York: Vintage Books, 1966); "That Evening Sun" [*TES*], *Collected Stories of William Faulkner* (New York: Random House, 1950); "Pantaloon in Black" [*PIB*], *Go Down, Moses* (New York: Vintage Books, 1990); *Soldiers' Pay* [*SP*] (New York: Liveright, 1997); *Sartoris* [*S*] (New York: New American Library, 1964).

 When I presented this paper at Faulkner and Yoknapatawpha 2005, two potential additions to my short list of Faulknerian blues texts were suggested: "Peter" (1925), an early uncollected sketch set in New Orleans, and *The Town* (1957). While neither work strikes me as requiring a rethinking of my thesis, each is worth a brief discussion.

 Clearly the work of an apprentice, "Peter" evokes African American life in the New Orleans tenderloin. A light-skinned black youth named Peter sits on a stoop and plays lookout for his prostitute mother, who is entertaining a sequence of male visitors upstairs. He thumps his heels in time with "the raucous syncopation" of an unseen "victrola in which has been prisoned by negroes all the tortured despair of negroes" (489). Faulkner's evocation of a blues recording is notable, coming as it does at an early moment in the medium's history as popular art; so too are the specific terms in which he evokes it, a dialectic of pain ("tortured despair") and pleasure ("raucous syncopation"), totalized in a way that conveys what Houston A. Baker Jr. has described in *Blues, Ideology, and Afro-American Literature* as blues' ability to recapitulate "species-experience." Later in the sketch, the victrola shudders into "tortured syncopation," a phrase that synthesizes two of the dialectic's key terms; Faulkner juxtaposes these two references to a blues recording with what he clearly intends us to understand as the picturesque catastrophe of black life in the tenderloin, evoked through snatches of overheard dialogue mingled with sentimental lyrics that owe little to the blues tradition, as in this example:

A voice—Baby, wrap me round!
A voice—You goddam whore, I'll cut your th'oat.
A voice—And yo' heart within you melt, for the sorrows you have felt. (492)

 Sensationalistic and voyeuristic, simplistic in the blues understandings it purveys, "Peter" is essentially a test run for the blues texts Faulkner was later to create.

 The Town struck several audience members at Faulkner and Yoknapatawpha as germane to my discussion, since it stages a scene in which W. C. Handy ("Professor Handy, from Beale Street in Memphis" [72]) plays a Christmas ball at the Cotillion Club in Jefferson at which the unutterably buxom Eula Varner Snopes dances in such "splendid unshame" (75) with Major de Spain that Gavin Stevens is moved to assault de Spain for having impugned her (nonexistent) chastity and virtue. Handy is merely named, and only once; neither he nor the members of his band nor the music with which they presumably incite Ms. Snopes and the Major to public misbehavior is described in any way. Faulkner's comic tone leaves no doubt that Stevens's blues feelings, such as they are, aren't to be taken seriously. Although Handy's momentary reappearance as a sexual provocateur late in Faulkner's corpus is worth noting, I see no reason to consider *The Town* a blues text.

 Citations from the two texts above are taken from "Peter," *Uncollected Stories of William Faulkner*, ed. Joseph Blotner (New York: Vintage Books, 1981), and *The Town* (New York: Vintage Books, 1961).

 6. Albert Murray, *Stomping the Blues* (1976; New York: Da Capo Press, 1987), 10. In *The Blue Devils of Nada: A Contemporary American Approach to Aesthetic Statement*

(New York: Pantheon Books, 1996), Murray adjudges Hemingway more of a blues artist than Faulkner, at least attitudinally: "It was Ernest Hemingway the Midwesterner-become-cosmopolitan, however, not William Faulkner the race-oriented Mississippian, who wrote fiction that always expresses essentially the same fundamental sense of life as that which underlies the spirit of the blues. . . . Much of what Faulkner wrote not only includes blues idiom, wit, and wisdom; in some instances it also appears to be conscious extensions of Negro folklore. But as richly interwoven with Negro idiom as his highly distinctive rhetoric so frequently is, and as close to the feeling of some Negro spirituals as he comes from time to time, the fundamental sense of life that his fiction represents is always more closely related to the conventional Greco-Roman tradition of tragedy, comedy, farce—of destiny, the fateful curse, doom, of honor, hubris, and outrage than to the blues tradition of pragmatic American existentialism" (179–80).

7. The cultural process I'm invoking here is theorized with far greater subtlety in Douglas B. Holt's *How Brands Become Icons: The Principles of Cultural Branding* (Boston: Harvard Business School Press, 2004), a text that should be required reading for students of contemporary Southern cultures. To the extent that they submit to commodification and enable subcultural affiliations, both "Faulkner" and "Mississippi blues" have, in Holt's terms, paradoxically become *iconic brands*, material embodiments of *identity myths* set in the same Dixie-flavored *populist world*—a place "separated not only from everyday [i.e., 'mainstream'] life but also from the realms of commerce and elite control" in which people "act the way they do because they want to, not because they are being paid to or because they seek status or power" (8–9). I am indebted to Jon Smith for bringing Holt's text and ideas to my attention during his presentation at the 2005 Faulkner and Yoknapatawpha Conference.

8. Holt offers an extended discussion of the way in which Mountain Dew has repeatedly been repositioned through canny advertising—as a hillbilly drink in the 60s, a redneck drink in the '70s, a slacker drink in the '80s—to sustain its brand iconicity within the riptides of American mass culture. My claim is that "Faulkner" and "Mississippi blues," no matter how shrewdly developed into iconic brands, nevertheless (and simultaneously) resist that process in a way that merely material commodities do not: by deliberately violating the Fordist protocols of production-line time, for example. Both Rosa Coldfield and R. L. Burnside *take their time*, in blues-vernacular terms, to tell the story that needs telling.

9. Mississippi Development Authority, Division of Tourism Development, http://www.visitmississippi.org/itineraries/themes_music_heritage_itin.asp.

10. University of Mississippi, http:// www.olemiss.edu/depts/south/Southern_Studies_Program/Graduate_Program.shtml.

11. Qtd. in Lynn Moss Sanders, *Howard W. Odum's Folklore Odyssey: Transformation to Tolerance through African American Folk Studies* (Athens: University of Georgia Press, 2003), 58.

12. Paul Oliver, *Songsters and Saints: Vocal Traditions on Race Records* (New York: Cambridge University Press, 1984), 259–60.

13. Karen McFarland, "Blues: More than Music," in *Up the Mississippi: A Journey of the Blues*, ed. Dr. Eunice Boardman (Davenport, Iowa: Mississippi Valley Blues Society, 2002), 5.

14. Ibid., 6.

15. David Krause, "Faulkner's Blues," *Studies in the Novel* 17 (Spring 1985): 81.

16. I take my cue here from Elijah Wald's salutary reframing of the Delta blues as part of a continuum of American popular music, rather than as autochthonous "pure" folk music of narrowly regional origins. See *Escaping the Delta: Robert Johnson and the Invention of the Blues* (New York: Harper Collins, 2004), 72: "White urbanites, for obvious reasons, are fascinated by a creation myth in which genius blossomed, wild and untamed, from the Delta mud, and are less interested in the unromantic picture of Muddy Waters sitting by the radio and listening to Fats Waller, or a sharecropper singing Broadway show tunes as he followed his mule along the levee."

17. Also potentially contributing to the public's penumbral sense of Faulkner's bluesiness is the fact that two celebrated blues singers, Odetta and Ethel Waters, play key

supporting roles in film versions of *The Hamlet* (*The Long Hot Summer*, 1958) and *The Sound and the Fury* (1959), respectively.

18. Robert W. Hamblin and Charles A. Peek, *A William Faulkner Encyclopedia* (Westport, Conn.: Greenwood Press, 1999), 260. For more on Faulkner's celebrated dislike of jukeboxes, see Amy Evans's interview with Annnette Seay Hines, daughter of the owners of The Mansion restaurant ("Restaurants of Oxford's Past Oral Histories," http://www.southernfoodways.com/oral_history/oxford/OX07_themansion.shtml) and Cheryl Lester, "Make Room for Elvis," http://www.isc.senshu-u.ac.jp/~thb0559/No2/lester.htm: 16–18.

19. Joseph Blotner, *Faulkner: A Biography*, 1-vol. ed. (New York: Random House, 1984), 40–41. See also Thadious Davis, "From Jazz Syncopation to Blues Elegy," in *Faulkner and Race*, 70–71, 74.

20. Ben Wasson, *Count No 'Count: Flashbacks to Faulkner* (Jackson: University Press of Mississippi, 1983), 36–37.

21. Clifton Bondurant Webb, "Swing Low for Sweet Callie," in *William Faulkner of Oxford*, James W. Webb and A. Wigfall Green (Baton Rouge: Louisiana State University Press, 1965), 126.

22. Wasson, *Count No 'Count*, 30.

23. David Levering Lewis, *When Harlem Was in Vogue* (1981; New York: Oxford University Press, 1989), 183. See also Nathan Irvin Huggins, *Harlem Renaissance* (New York: Oxford University Press, 1971), 100.

24. Williamson, *William Faulkner and Southern History*, 173. See also Thadious Davis, "From Jazz Syncopation to Blues Elegy," in *Faulkner and Race*, 70–71.

25. William Barlow, *"Looking Up at Down": The Emergence of Blues Culture* (Philadelphia: Temple University Press, 1989), 202–28.

26. For brief mention of Faulkner's trips to Memphis and Clarksdale, see Susan Snell, *Phil Stone of Oxford: A Vicarious Life* (Athens: University of Georgia Press, 1991), 124, 129. Faulkner may have steered clear of juke joints later in his career. Junior Doughty (Webmaster of "Junior's Juke Joint," a guide to juke-joint life in the Deep South), reports that "William Faulkner once stayed at nearby Melrose Plantation" when visiting Melrose, Louisiana, "and, according to Raymond and Bubba Metoyer, who opened Bubba's back in 1942 and still run it today, Mr. Faulkner kept to the Big House and didn't visit the juke joint" a quarter-mile down the road: http://www.deltablues.net/bubba.html.

27. W. C. Handy, *Father of the Blues* (1941; New York: Da Capo Press, 1991), 76–77.

28. Christopher A. Waterman, "Race Music: Bo Chatmon, 'Corinne Corinnna,' and the Excluded Middle," in *Music and the Racial Imagination*, ed. Ronald Radano and Philip V. Bohlman (Chicago: University of Chicago Press, 2000), 174–75.

29. John Faulkner, *My Brother Bill: An Affectionate Reminiscence* (London: Victor Gollancz Ltd., 1964), 177.

30. Lomax, *The Land Where the Blues Began*, 384.

31. Ibid., 339.

32. I'm grateful to David Evans and Greg Johnson for clarifying this point of blues history. "Jack o' Diamonds" may also have been transmitted to Faulkner's tenants through live performances by regional stars such as Lum Guffin (b. 1902), a Memphis resident who later recorded the song in the 1970s. See Max Haymes, "Back to the Land of California: Robert Johnson and 'Sweet Home Chicago'": www.earlyblues.com/essay_california.htm.

33. Qtd. in Lomax, *The Land Where the Blues Began*, 175.

34. Thadious Davis argues for a related progression in the course of Faulkner's career: a shift in emphasis from "jazz syncopation" ("a configuration of collectivity and syncopation, reverberating with meanings of group cohesiveness (particularly in relation to presumed 'racial' traits), with meanings of race differentiation dependent upon encounter between blacks and whites, and with meanings of amassed motion and rhythm that, though distinctive, discourage individuation and forward comic portraiture") to "blues elegy" ("an impulse towards blues as a mode of development . . . marked by what I term a structure of emotion, a structure grounded in the folk existence of blacks. It magnifies an internal life that is substantially unaffected by the immediacy of the white world, yet simultaneously reflective of that world's past enslavement and present oppression of blacks. And it is primarily elegiac

in tone"). See Davis, "From Jazz Syncopation to Blues Elegy," in *Faulkner and Race*, 81, 84–85.

35. Ibid., 74. For the lyrics to "Yellow Dog Blues," see W. C. Handy, ed., *Blues: An Anthology* (1926; New York: Da Capo Press, 1990), 86–89.

36. For biographical information on Shelton Brooks, see http://www.jass.com/sheltonbrooks/brooks.html. For lyrics of "I Wonder Where My Easy Rider's Gone," see http://ucblibraries.colorado.edu/cgi-bin/sheetmusic.pl?RagIWonder&Rag&1.

37. See, for example, http://redhotjazz.com/tampabluJB.html. I'm indebted to David Evans for clarifying crucial points of fact in this discussion of "Uncle Bud" and "Shake It and Break It." Any errors that remain are mine alone.

38. Cited in Pamela Bordelon, ed., *Go Gator and Muddy the Water: Writings by Zora Neale Hurston from the Federal Writers' Project* (New York: W. W. Norton Co., 1999), 167–68.

39. See http://redhotjazz.com/leonawilliams.html.

40. See Adam Gussow, *Mister Satan's Apprentice: A Blues Memoir* (New York: Pantheon Books, 1998).

41. Thadious Davis, *Faulkner's "Negro,"* 75.

42. Craig Hansen Werner, *Playing the Changes: From Afro-Modernism to the Jazz Impulse* (Urbana: University of Illinois Press, 1994), 30–32.

43. Working backward from the date of Quentin Compson's suicide in *The Sound and the Fury*, Hamblin and Peek suggest this two-year window in *A William Faulkner Encyclopedia*, 396. I say "arguably" because I received a great deal of argument from the audience at Faulkner and Yoknapatawpha 2005—albeit not from Hamblin and Peek—when I invoked the 1898–1899 dates. My point stands, regardless of such quibbles: Faulkner clearly intends the action of the story, including Nancy's blues singing, to stand in a premodern moment *vis a vis* the (framing) narrative present in which the older Quentin relates it—a narrative present fifteen years and a world apart from that remembered childhood dream of singing black washerwomen and their incomprehensible fears. Nancy's tuneless originary blues song is to the hand-delivered wash of the story's narrative past, I would argue, as a pop-blues such as Handy's "St. Louis Blues" is to the motorcar-delivered wash of the story's more impersonal and rationalized (but somehow less numinous) "modern" narrative present.

44. See Peek for a superb articulation of this point. "That Evening Sun(g)," 143.

45. Ibid., 134–35.

46. See Adam Gussow, *Seems Like Murder Here: Southern Violence and the Blues Tradition* (Chicago: University of Chicago Press, 2002).

47. Peek, "'That Evening Sun(g),'" 135; Gartner, "Faulkner in Context," 55.

48. See Gilmore Millen, *Sweet Man* (New York: Viking Press, 1930). A copy inscribed to Faulkner is housed in Special Collections at the Library of the University of Mississippi.

49. Peek, "That Evening Sun(g),'" 137–38.

50. See Trudier Harris, "No Outlet for the Blues: Silla Boyce's Plight in *Brown Girl, Brownstones*," *Callaloo* 18, vol. 6, no. 2 (Spring-Summer 1983): 57–67. Judith L. Sensibar argues compellingly that Faulkner used Rider in "Pantaloon in Black" as an outlet for his own deep grief at the recent death of Callie Barr—a grief, mixed with shame and a kind of tortured ambivalence, that he had no legitimate way of expressing apart from the racial masking Rider's fictive persona made possible. See "Who Wears the Mask? Memory, Desire, and Race in *Go Down, Moses*," *New Essays on "Go Down, Moses*," ed. Linda Wagner-Martin (New York: Cambridge University Press, 1996), 101–27.

51. "[S]ad as Blues may be, there's almost always something humorous about them—even if it's the kind of humor that laughs to keep from crying." Langston Hughes, "Songs Called the Blues," *Phylon* 2.2 (1941): 144. "I know very little to tell you about the Blues. They always impressed me as being very sad, sadder even than the spirituals because their sadness is not softened with tears but hardened with laughter, the absurd, incongruous laughter of a sadness without even a god to appeal to." Langston Hughes, letter to Carl Van Vechten, qtd. in Arnold Rampersad, *The Life of Langston Hughes: Volume 1: 1902–1941: I, Too, Sing America* (1986; New York: Oxford University Press, 2002), 111. Examples of blues lyrics in this vein include the following: "Said I work for you baby, I treat you like a

baby child / While you laughing at me now mama, you'll be crying after a while" (Walter Davis, "Why Shouldn't I Be Blue" [Chicago, 12 July 1940]); "It's getting so I can't sleep for dreaming, and I can't laugh for crying" (Ethel Waters, "Ethel Sings 'Em" [New York, June 1923]); "Baby, you don't know my mind / When you see me laughing, I'm laughing just to keep from crying" (Rosetta Crawford, "My Man Jumped Salty on Me" [New York, 1 February 1939]). All lyrics are at http://www.dylan61.se/taft.htm.

52. Gartner, "Faulkner in Context," 52.

53. Stoneback, "Faulkner's Blues," 241–42.

54. Ibid., 244–45.

Faulkner, Metropolitan Fashion, and "The South"

JON SMITH

While it is no doubt true that the South has long existed as the nation's whipping boy or "abjected regional Other," as Houston Baker and Dana Nelson put it in their introduction to a special issue of *American Literature* a few years ago,[1] the upside to this national and arguably global act of projection is that for several decades the region has also existed as what marketing theorist Douglas B. Holt calls a "populist world." In his 2004 book *How Brands Become Icons*, Holt asks readers to see brands as "historical entities whose meaning and value depends [sic] on how the brand's myth addresses a particular tension in society." These objective tensions, which Holt, for reasons he does not explain, sees as taking place only at the level of the nation, produce subjective anxieties, which the nation's citizens buy particular brands in order to alleviate. Those brands that rise to this level of iconicity do so because for a price they offer a set of particularly compelling palliative myths of authenticity. This perceived authenticity derives in turn from the product's association with "populist worlds," which Holt locates "on the frontier, in bohemia communities, in rural backwaters, in immigrant and African American neighborhoods, [and] in youth subcultures." Such worlds hold appeal, according to Holt, because

1. Populist worlds are perceived as "folk cultures"—their ethos is the collective and voluntary product of their participants. The ethos has not been imposed on them.
2. The activities within the populist world are perceived as intrinsically valuable to the participants. They are not motivated by commercial or political interests.
3. Reinforcing these perceptions, populist worlds are often set in places far removed from centers of commerce and politics. For worlds that have been commercialized (sports and music are key examples), these populist perceptions are much harder to maintain because the participants must fight off the commercial attributions.[2]

Specifically Southern kinds of perceived authenticity have had their ups and downs in the marketplace—recall the soft drink Mountain Dew's repositioning itself from the "rural backwater" populist world of Appalachia to the "youth subcultural" one of skateboarding—but for just this reason I think the model explains rather well the periodic appeal of "the South" as a populist world, whether as, for example, the source of blues music in the folk music revival of the '50s and '60s, in the "Southern rock" of the 1970s so well analyzed by Ted Ownby,[3] or in the turn-of-the-century alt-country repackaging of Johnny Cash and Loretta Lynn by überhipsters Rick Rubin and Jack White, respectively.

It is from marketing theory's understanding of the fundamental *similarities* between "the South" and bohemia, at least in popular consumerist fantasy, that I wish to approach what I consider one of the trickier novels in the Faulkner canon, *The Mansion*, and in particular chapter 7 of that novel, sometimes referred to as the "Greenwich Village" chapter. Consumerism is central to *The Mansion* as a whole: even the unnamed Booker T. Washington-quoting principal of the Negro school Linda Snopes Kohl visits tells Gavin Stevens that the only remaining ties between whites and blacks in the South are consumerist: "There is no place for us now in your culture or economy either. We both buy the same installment-plan automobiles to burn up the same gasoline in, and the same radios to listen to the same music and the same iceboxes to keep the same beer in, but that's all."[4]

In examining a few elegant examples of this consumerism I hope to address some fundamental issues within Southern Studies. For at least the sixty-eight years between *I'll Take My Stand* and Michael Kreyling's *Inventing Southern Literature*, mainstream Southern literary studies overwhelmingly and explicitly presented the region as precisely Holt's sort of populist world, and for nearly as long the field of Faulkner studies—with some notable exceptions—has been about as guilty as any other, however paradoxically, of marketing the South, and the works of Faulkner in particular, as an antidote to the anxieties of Yankee capitalism. Perhaps the high-water mark of this sort of sales pitch was Cleanth Brooks's essay on Faulkner for *The History of Southern Literature*, in which Brooks explicitly contrasted Northern *gesellschaft* with the Southern *gemeinschaft* to be found in Faulkner.[5] Those terms from the German sociologist Ferdinand Tönnies are usually translated respectively as society and community, with all the implications I've been sketching above.[6] By the end of the 20th century, the situation had gotten so bad that critics like Michael Kreyling and Patricia Yaeger were apparently conflating Faulkner with his Southernist critics, positioning not Faulkner studies but Faulkner himself as the "Dixie Limited" that was getting in the way of a fresh and more honest approach to Southern literature; both contemplated "dynamiting the rails" of said Limited.[7]

Yet Faulkner is a good deal hipper than his critics have been. When I began thinking about this paper, I meant that term somewhat ironically. *Hip* was originally an African American term deriving from Wolof

and meaning, roughly, the state of having one's eyes open; it was popular among jazz musicians but was widely picked up by white Beats in
the 1950s. Today, though, *hip* has largely been appropriated by a racially
heterogeneous, but chiefly white, semisubculture living in places like
Williamsburg, Brooklyn; Silver Lake, Los Angeles; and Prenzlauer
Berg, Berlin. In this world, hipness is largely mediated by commodities,
defined, in Sarah Thornton's icy term, as a kind of "subcultural capital." In
her Bourdieuian reading, hipness is little more than a new way in which
one group of people purport to distinguish themselves from an imagined
square "mainstream": in this case, by knowing how to dress—usually
ironically—and what bands and kinds of drinks are cool.[8]

Yet on the shuttle from the Memphis airport to the conference, Don
Kartiganer told me a story Albert Murray had once told him, and it got me
thinking. Apparently Murray was working at Random House in the 1950s
when Ralph Ellison stopped by. Faulkner happened to be in the building,
and Murray arranged a meeting. When Ellison returned, Murray asked
him how it went. Ellison's comment was about dress. He said he'd always
heard Faulkner dressed like a raggedy farmer. Instead, Ellison marveled,
"he dresses like we do!" Given that *Invisible Man*, from its title on down,
is obsessively about the visual presentation of the black Southern male
body, this is both a striking compliment and a telling observation. I do
not think Faulkner "dresses black" in any simple way, and I don't think
that's what Ellison meant. But the need to negotiate between authentic
Southern yam-eating roots and a shifting cosmopolitan identity is something Faulkner absolutely shared with Ellison and, I would argue, with
the whole ethos of bebop, even if his personal musical tastes were more
archaic.

Thus if chapter 7 of *The Mansion* continues to resist interpretation by
the Southernist interpretive community—or society—one reason it has
been unreadable may be that for a long time it has been unbearable. A
long quotation from a contemporary review of *The Mansion* (by one Louis
D. Rubin) should illustrate the point:

> *The Mansion* is a failure as a novel, an unbelievably awkward failure.
>
> All of which goes to prove something about Mr. Faulkner. So long as this
> great Mississippi novelist deals with rural Southern life, so long as his milieu is
> primitive and pre-modern, he is matchless. From the earliest Yoknapatawpha
> tales right down through Mink Snopes in the present novel, Mr. Faulkner is the
> greatest novelist of his generation.
>
> But when he attempts to deal with a sophisticated, modern milieu, with
> characters living in the present and requiring the subtle, intellectual charac-
> terizations of moderns, his technique fails, his rhetorical gifts emphasize the
> failure, and our greatest American writer falls flat on his face. It is not his world;

as a writer, his universe is bounded by Nineteenth and early Twentieth Century Yoknapatawpha county. Within those boundaries he has no peers. But let him attempt to step outside the time or the place and he is lost.[9]

Lost to whom?

Faulkner seems to play for the wrong team here, to present the South as embodying a kind of lack that can only be filled in the populist world of Greenwich Village. If for Agrarians and neo-Agrarians the problem with urban life is alienation and anomie, for Faulkner (as for others) the problem with the traditional South is—in *The Mansion*, at least—boredom. If at first glance this seems a comedown from the grander themes of works like *Absalom, Absalom!*, it is not, in fact, a trivial matter either theoretically or empirically. In *Boredom: The Literary History of a State of Mind*, Patricia Meyer Spacks notes that "boredom in its verbal renditions usually masks another condition," often aggression, and links the very acts of reading and writing to boredom's avoidance: "as action and as product, writing resists boredom, constituting itself by that resistance. In this sense all writing—at least since 1800 or so—is 'about' boredom, as all physical construction is 'about' entropy."[10] (Her observation seems particularly applicable to Modernist writing, especially Faulkner's.) In *The Feminine Mystique*, Betty Friedan characterized 1950s American women as suffering a kind of epidemic of boredom. And of course, in *The Mansion*, Eula Varner Snopes is agreed to have committed suicide out of boredom and even Flem Snopes is hypothesized to have done so.

Unsurprisingly for a book published in 1959, these issues of Modernity and the Good Life, if I might fairly call them that, get worked out in Faulkner's treatment of material culture, of more or less everyday objects: in particular, an abstract sculpture, a piece of wood, two ties, and a pistol. "The fifties," Joanne Jacobson reminds us, perhaps a bit too nostalgically, in a review of Alison Clarke's important book on Tupperware, "may have been the last great moment when Americans entrusted their dreams of transformation to the material world. In the postwar years rationed hunger was let loose on a whole new world of goods, visible manifestations of the possibilities of upward mobility that were renewed in the boom economy. More even than symbol, the material world became a theater of transformation. On the glowing, capacious stage of *things*—cars, hula hoops, rockets—our destiny of motion was revealed. And our destiny of metamorphosis: as malleable as Silly Putty, Play-Doh and Jell-O."[11] In this context, Faulkner's lifelong and obvious love of well-designed objects—both in the trilogy and in his own fastidious taste in clothes—should remind us that, for Faulkner at least, there are different kinds of bourgeois consumption and "identity construction." The author's profound distaste for conformist small-town Southern peasant-cum-bourgeois consumerism is matched by his admiration for more individualist small-town-cum-big-city bourgeois consumerism. In other words, his disdain for the pursuit of respectability is matched by his admiration of the pursuit of beauty, particularly when that pursuit, that "excessive" consumerism, puts food on the tables of artists and designers. The Snopes trilogy begins with what I would call Flem's protopunk critique of small-town bourgeois masculine identity—a turn to what art critic Hal Foster once labeled the antiaesthetic. Richard Godden has already noted that Flem's tiny two-inch black bow ties, with what Faulkner calls their "quality of outrageous overstatement of physical displacement," sitting against Flem's white shirts, link him, in the eyes of men of small means, to his rebellious peasant barn-burning father.[12] It is but a small step to characterizing these ties as protopunk, in their ironic, combative minimalist commentary on the whole notion of bourgeois male business dress, on the whole notion of vanity.[13] (Flem is said to buy these ties by the gross, and in Hell the Prince of Darkness can't buy him with the vanities because he has brought a gross of them along with him, a clear reference to those ties.[14]) But in *The Mansion*, the trilogy closes with a kind of dialectical return to the aesthetic. By the end, then, Faulkner's aesthetic focus on objects *as* objects—as neither symbols nor signs—will also disrupt a cultural studies that would associate fashion, or even art, with the punkish deconstruction of tradition. To both the tweedy neoagrarian and the black-spectacled Communist antecedents of contemporary Southern studies and cultural studies, Faulkner says, a plague on both your outfits.

In *The Mansion* Faulkner follows the retold story of Eula Snopes's suicide with what might seem a bit of comic relief: Ratliff and Gavin Stevens making an almost carnivalesque trip to Greenwich Village to attend her daughter Linda's wedding to Jewish Communist sculptor Barton Kohl. I'd like to defer the obvious Cold War implications of this for a moment to look at what I take to be a related phenomenon: not only does Linda choose to marry a maker of beautiful things, but the chapter also appears structured by the contrast between two design objects. Flem, who has taken over Major de Spain's bank, has the entire De Spain house done over to look like Mount Vernon because, in Ratliff's words, "the house [Flem's depositors] would see him walk into ever evening until time to unlock the money tomorrow morning, would have to be the physical symbol of all them generations of respectability and aristocracy that not only would a been too proud to mishandle other folks' money, but couldn't possible ever needed to" (153). Yet Ratliff makes an interesting distinction: "it was jest the house that was altered and transmogrified and symbolized: not him. The house [may have changed], but the feller the owners of that custodianed money seen going and coming out of it was the same one they had done got accustomed to for twenty years now: the same little snap-on bow tie he had got outen the Frenchman's Bend mule wagon in and only the hat was new and different. . . . It wasn't that he rebelled at changing Flem Snopes: he done it by deliberate calculation" (154–55). Faulkner here appears to deploy—unconsciously, I think—two very different, even contradictory, figures for the self. On the one hand, the self seems to be—in good cultural studies fashion—conflated with clothes and hence with performance: as an appositive, for example, "the same little snap-on bow tie" *renames* "the same feller," a function the phrase "only the hat" repeats through its parallel grammatical, or more properly ungrammatical, relation to the phrase about the tie. On the other hand, in *The Mansion*, domestic *interiors*—modeling an old public/private split— repeatedly appear to suggest a more traditional model of a stable, "authentic," and even rather precious private, noumenal self hidden from public gaze.[15] In these private recesses, Flem has done something unusual: on one of the fireplaces "with colonial molding and colyums and cornices," he has had his carpenter cousin nail up what Ratliff calls "not a defiance, not a simple reminder of where he had come from but rather as the feller says a reaffirmation of his-self and maybe a warning to his-self too: a little wood ledge, not even painted, nailed to the front of that hand-carved hand-painted Mount Vernon mantelpiece at the exact height for Flem to prop his feet on it" (156). Here Faulkner appears to reinscribe the notion of the South as an antifashion—more on this term in a moment—populist world, for it is hard to miss what is surely an intended contrast between this secret, humble bit of wood, this "reaffirmation" of Flem's authentic self, and the very different object Ratliff buys in New York a few pages later in the same chapter. Ratliff (or Faulkner) appears to set this contrast up as a joke at Ratliff's expense. When Gavin Stevens drives Ratliff to the Jefferson train station, we are told he "stopped and opened the door and looked at me and then done what the moving pictures call a double take and says, 'Oh hell.' 'It's mine,' I says. 'I bought it'" (165). The object referred to is a necktie, which—unlike his shirts—Ratliff pointedly has bought, not made. In curiously class-based terms, we soon learn that the problem is not just that he is wearing a tie, changing his signature "look"—which is a powerful reinforcer, like Flem's, of his professional and personal petit-bourgeois "brand identity"—in a way that, contrasted with Flem's "calculation," seems surprisingly reckless. The problem is also that the tie is ugly: "It was all right as long as just railroad conductors looked at it but you cant face a preacher in it," insists Stevens. In fact, not only is the tie ugly in itself, but for reasons known only to Ratliff, he has also chosen to wear with his trademark blue shirt a tie that is "pink and green" (167).

Having thus declared this necktie unacceptable on a mix of class and aesthetic grounds, Stevens, adopting a kind of mentor role, takes Ratliff to a particular sort of New York boutique: "a store," as Ratliff describes it, "with a show window, a entire show window with not nothing in it but one necktie" (166). There is nothing inside the store either, "except some gold chairs and two ladies in black dresses and a man dressed like a congressman or at least a preacher, that knowed Lawyer by active name" (167). In a complicated exchange to which I will return, Ratliff ends up paying Myra Allanovna, the designer and boutique owner, one hundred and fifty 1936 dollars—over two thousand 2005 dollars[16]—and obtains two ties. Dressed in one of them at a Greenwich Village party that evening, and in the new white shirt Stevens has had the tie people send out for, Ratliff is presumed to be either an Oklahoma oilman or a Texas cattleman, and two different people recognize his tie admiringly as "an Allanovna" (170, 172).

At first glance, then, Faulkner seems to be taking a stab, perhaps even a cheap shot, at the absurdities of New York commodity culture. "Seventy-five dollars for a necktie?" exclaims Ratliff to Stevens at one point. "I cant! I wont!" (169). Indeed, later in the novel Faulkner will make Mink Snopes's trip to Memphis to purchase his own design object—a rusty, snub-nosed pistol[17] of questionable functionality that "looks like a cooter" (291)— echo this trip to the city that never sleeps: "Now [Mink] was in what he knew was the city. For a moment it merely stood glittering and serried and taller than stars. Then it engulfed him: it stooped soaring down, bearing down upon him like breathing and the vast concrete mass and weight until he himself was breathless, having to pant for air. Then he knew what it was. It's un-sleeping, he thought. It ain't slept in so long now it's done forgot how to sleep" (285). "The city had never slept," Faulkner repeats of Memphis four pages later, just as Stevens had earlier teased Ratliff in Manhattan that at 7 a.m. "They haven't even gone to bed yet. This is New York, not Yoknapatawpha County" (166).[18] Yet the trip to purchase the pistol puts Mink in mind of an earlier trip to Memphis to visit the brothel "which he had entered with his mentor that night forty-seven years ago" (290). And just as Mink is led to meditate on the pistol in terms of its appearance and "function" (when Flem is shot, Stevens reports grimly of the pistol that "it functioned"), so too does he think of the prostitutes as design objects, literally and quite oddly defined by shape and color and function: "women not only shaped like Helen and Eve and Lilith, not only functional like Helen and Eve and Lilith, but colored white like them too" (395, 290).[19] In a particularly grim bit of irony, Faulkner carefully notes— from the point of view of a necessarily omniscient narrator—that while the New York trip successfully reunites Linda with Hoake McCarron, her biological father, and she recognizes him, Mink's last Memphis trip takes him past the same brothel he'd visited in 1899, where "he didn't know it of course and probably wouldn't have recognized her either, but his younger daughter was now the madam of it" (290). In this context, coupled with Allanovna's insistence during their bargaining that Ratliff kiss her, New York designer boutiques and commodity culture come to look like little more than the rich man's bawdy house.

Yet Faulkner, I would like to believe, is rarely given to cheap shots, and what looks like stark contrast (or parodic comparison) may well be something more complex. Fashion theory can offer us a provisional way in here. While Mink's pistol is crucial to my argument, Faulkner appears to juxtapose most closely—in the same chapter—Ratliff's ties and Flem's footrest as embodying the two poles of what almost thirty years ago Ted Polhemus and Lynn Procter identified as fashion and antifashion.[20] (Despite some notable problems, their article remains powerful in fashion circles, still serving, for example, as the theoretical starting point of the 2002 second edition of *Fashion as Communication*, Malcolm Barnard's popular introductory textbook.) Writing in the heyday of Birmingham School cultural studies, Polhemus and Procter observed that "anti-fashion is composed of numerous and unrelated body and clothing symbols. Fashion, on the other hand, is a unified system of arbitrary body and clothing signs" (18). In their now-famous example, a prostitute dressed like a prostitute is saying "I am sexually available"; an art student dressed like a prostitute "does not in her style mean 'I am sexually available.' Her message is simply 'I am fashionable.' Three months ago she may have looked like Chairman Mao, and in six months' time she may look like an innocent adolescent schoolgirl" (19). This difference between symbols and signs is, in their argument, profoundly political in all the ways we associate with Birmingham School cultural studies, which arose as the youth of post-imperial England, like those of the post–civil rights South, struggled to slough off a hierarchical culture overdetermined by the importance of knowing one's place: "Traditional societies are by definition conservative: they seek to preserve their culture despite the threat of change and instability. Anti-fashion, especially when the body is permanently customized, is perhaps the most powerful weapon with which a society can protect itself. Anti-fashion is a time capsule which one generation leaves for the next, a machine designed to symbolically defy and destroy change" (22). Fashion, on the other hand, is "the natural, appropriate language of the socially mobile, those between rather than within social groups. While symbolizing social mobility and change, fashion also symbolizes the social rootlessness, anomie, alienation, and atomization which are the requisite and the result of this social change. Fashion's function is to represent and identify the social and cultural limbo of modern urban society" (20).

Ratliff's Allanovna ties seem to be the epitome of fashion in just these terms: not unlike the Invisible Man's zoot suit and dark glasses in Ralph Ellison's novel of eight years earlier (in which, of course, another Southerner comes north to New York City) they lead to a comic case of mistaken identity, of unexpected social mobility in a destabilizing urban setting. This social mobility is heightened by contrast, and doubly complicated, because Ratliff's initial tie purchase results from his quest to reclaim his own social roots. One purpose of this trip for Ratliff is a "sentimental pilgrimage": a visit to Saratoga, where Ratliff's first American ancestor, "that-ere first immigrant Vladimir Kyrilitch," served with the Hessians in the English General Burgoyne's defeated army (175, 164). In preparation for that trip, back in Jefferson he buys his first tie "to let all them V. K. Ratliff beginnings look at me for the first time. Maybe it's them I'm trying to suit. Or leastways not to shame" (165).[21]

Conversely, Flem's unpainted footrest seems to be the epitome of anti-fashion: seemingly tucked away from public gaze "like a secret chapel or a shrine" in a house to which "he hadn't never invited nobody in," nailed on a fancy mantelpiece not only in disregard of but as an assault on the fake colonial décor, and described in terms of pure function, as complete absence of ornament, it seems to operate not as a sign but as one true symbol among the faux-colonial many (159, 155). More than anything else except perhaps his patiently waiting for Mink to pull the trigger a second time, it is this little wooden ledge, this organic residuum of authentic Flem-self hinting at crucifixion, that has generated a fair amount of critical sympathy for Flem at the end of the trilogy.

Yet given the salted-mine trick by which Flem in *The Hamlet* has conned Ratliff and Henry Armstid into buying a worthless old mansion by digging in the garden as if for buried treasure and as if no one were watching him, and given Ratliff's suggestion Flem himself had more recently chalked the anti-Semitic graffiti outside his own house to generate sympathy in the community, the authenticity of the ledge-gesture is hard to, well, authenticate. Ratliff himself notes Flem has put it up "like one of them framed mottoes you keep hanging on the wall where you work or think, saying *Remember Death* or *Keep Smiling* or *-Working* or *God is Love* to remind not jest you but the strangers that see it too, that you got at least a speaking acquaintance with the fact that it might be barely possible it taken a little something more than jest you to get you where you're at." Ratliff's simile suggests the footrest is only partly about humility and partly about advertising that humility to "the strangers that see it too." Moreover, while "Remember Death" and "God is Love" might point to humility, "Keep Smiling" and "Keep Working" make the overall list less redolent of private reflection than of technologies of disciplining employees, forms of

Taylorist manipulation. Ratliff metaphorically figures the "little wooden additional ledge" as *both* private residuum of Flem's peasant roots and public bourgeois supplement to his success. As Ratliff also shrewdly notes, that ledge exists not in simple contradiction to the hand-carved, hand-painted mantelpiece (here denoting less craft than consumption) but in "unpainted paradox" to it, implying that any contradiction is only apparent (157).

If Faulkner carefully subverts our admiration for Flem's ledge, so too does he undercut our rather petit-bourgeois—or is it peasant?—disdain for those excessive ties. Initially, Ratliff is conveyed as understanding the importance of antifashion to his status in the conservative Southern business community every bit as much as Flem does: "I jest cant," he explains to Myra Allanovna. "I sells sewing machines in Missippi. I cant have it knowed back there that I paid seventy-five dollars apiece for neckties. But," he continues, "if I'm in the Missippi sewing-machine business and cant wear seventy-five dollar neckties, so are you in the New York necktie business and cant afford to have folks wear or order neckties and not pay for them. So here" (176).

But the situation is a good deal more complicated than this. At an early age Faulkner himself forcibly rejected the conservative, provincial white Southern businessman as a masculine role model. This is not at all to say he was opposed to more urbane sorts of consumption. While Faulkner was no Elvis, throughout his life the novelist was neither blind nor immune to spectacular dress. His letters are peppered with references to clothes; he would sometimes draw them for his reader. In 1925, traveling in England, he gushed about finding "the best-looking sport jacket you ever saw"; in 1960, upon his admission to the Farmington Hunt Club outside Charlottesville, he wrote Albert Erskine, "I have been awarded a pink coat, a splendor worthy of being photographed in," an observation Joseph Blotner felt important enough to include in his highly selective chronology of Faulkner's life for the Library of America volumes.[22] And, in fact, Faulkner *did* have himself famously photographed in that very coat, though we should also note that, as a uniform Faulkner had for once actually earned, the coat chiefly operated at least among the Albemarle County cognoscenti as antifashion: as symbol, not sign.[23] Yet in this letter, Faulkner seems at least as enthusiastic about the more purely aesthetic "splendor" of the coat,[24] and photographs and letters attest that throughout his life Faulkner was, at least when he chose to be, impeccably dressed. In his younger years, the attire was often a kind of costume: the RAF uniform he had no right to wear; his bearded Parisian artiste getup of the early '20s. As he grew older, costume generally matured into style (with certain exceptions for posing theatrically as decayed gentry or mustachioed horseman). But even early on, he was remembered as a "fashion plate" at Ole Miss dances, perhaps, Joel Williamson suggests, because even back then he bought his clothes in Memphis.[25]

Most importantly, I don't think I have ever seen a photograph of Faulkner wearing an ugly necktie. In *William Faulkner and Southern History*, Williamson captions the 1942 J. R. Cofield photograph of Faulkner "A Worried Man, 1942." With no small degree of melodramatic projection, he intones, "Summer, 1942, age forty-four. The years of genius have passed. He will never again write a great novel. He is broke, and he had difficulty staying sober for an interview. . . . In a sense, he is dying, an uncounted casualty in the Hollywood War."[26] Me, I'm admiring Faulkner's tie, its knot held in place under the starched collar by a perfectly placed tie pin. The tie, so far as I can see, is of an elegantly minimalist yet varied design: a pattern of small dots and small horizontal and vertical line segments, a clean mix of order and variety. Nobody who dresses like that is likely to write about designer ties merely as satire.

Certainly Faulkner's language points us in other directions. Through Ratliff, he sets up the shop-window scene in language that is, at best, straining for effect: "at least some weather was jest made for New York. In which case, this was sholy some of it: one of them soft blue drowsy days in the early fall when the sky itself seems like it was resting on the earth like a soft blue mist, with the tall buildings rushing up into it and then stopping, the sharp edges fading like the sunshine wasn't just shining on them but kind of humming, like wires singing" (166). This neither sounds much like Ratliff ("the sky itself seems like it was resting on the earth"?) nor even very good writing (the too-close repetition of the phrase "soft blue"). But unlike the prose of so many writers bent on describing urbanity's alienation from nature, here sky and earth are in harmony with each other and with the skyline, whose "sharp edges" fade like Ratliff's shirts into a "soft blue," and where sun and buildings combine to make "singing," quite unapologetically the peculiarly high tech variety made by power lines. And it is at this moment of exquisite urban harmony between nature and culture that Ratliff sees his first Allanovna tie.

A page later, in the shop, Ratliff fantasizes to Allanovna: "I was jest thinking that if you could jest imagine a necktie and then pick it right up and put it on, I would imagine one made outen red with a bunch or maybe jest one single sunflower in the middle of it" (167). Stevens has already described Greenwich Village as "a little place without physical boundaries . . . where young people of all ages below ninety go in search of dreams" (151), so the idea of the place as a magical one where fantasies materialize has already been established. In his fantasy, Ratliff prefers primary colors—he wishes his pink and green tie were yellow and red, and he favors blue shirts—but

Allanovna first brings out one much subtler than that: "it looked like the outside of a peach, that you know that in a minute . . . you will see the first beginning of when it starts to turn peach. Except that it dont do that. It's still jest dusted over with gold, like the back of a sunburned gal." "This one for now," explains the designer, "Tomorrow, the other one, red with sonnenblume" (167, 168).

It seems clear the man writing this rather *likes* the *gesellschaft* of the modern metropolis, which appears here as a magical playground, not—as for the Nashville Agrarians or for Cleanth Brooks (or T. S. Eliot, or, for that matter, Theodore Dreiser[27]or the Birmingham School)—a hotbed of alienation and spiritual emptiness. Indeed, immediately after Ratliff pays Allanovna and refuses to take the ties, she brandishes another design object whose form belies its use—as Ratliff describes it, "a thing on the desk that looked like a cream pitcher until she snapped it open and it was a cigarette lighter" (176)—and threatens to burn the money, which is what he himself has in effect already done by refusing to accept what he has paid for, by writing the money off as a loss. Ratliff balks, of course, and instead of getting outcapitalized by Flem, gets outsacrificed by Allanovna. After soliloquizing that "only the gauche, the illiterate, the frightened and the pastless destroy money," she continues, "You will keep it then," but she means not the money but the one tie he pays for: "You will take it back to . . . Missippi. Where is one who, not needs: who cares about so base as needs? Who wants something that costs one hundred fifty dollar—a hat, a picture, a book, a jewel for the ear; something never never never anyhow just to eat—but believes he—she—will never have it, has even long ago given up, not the dream but the hope— This time do you know what I mean?" And Ratliff replies, "I know exactly what you mean because you jest said it" (177). (Notably, "Missippi" is figured here precisely as a drab place where dreams *don't* materialize unless you bring them back from New York.) In their compromise, then, Ratliff buys one tie for $150 and Allanovna gives him the second. This second tie, he explains to Chick Mallison years later, "is a private matter"; Mallison has never seen it and, says Ratliff, "I doubt if you will" (232). If Flem's ostensibly private wooden ledge seems to operate as symbol, however questionably, Faulkner makes it difficult to assign a single meaning to "the tie" at all, because we have two ties vibrating unstably, Heisenberg fashion, between purchase and gift.

What Allanovna conveys in her homage to expensive beauty is a desire that Faulkner does not describe as representative of a scandalously excessive capitalism, a horrific *gesellschaft*, but rather a desire that in itself *gemeinschaft*—here, the *gemeinschaft* of the Southern peasantry and petit bourgeoisie—can never fulfill. If it is Ratliff's bourgeois standing that prevents his accepting the ties, Faulkner has Allanovna show us, his ultimately doing so represents a dawning understanding of life beyond the petit-bourgeoisie who amass surplus items solely as symbols of their status, their antifashion respectability.

But if the ties are not antifashion, it also seems clear that neither Myra Allanovna nor Faulkner sees them entirely as fashion in the Birmingham School sense either, for despite Ratliff's experiences at the party, they do not see fashion primarily as communication. Instead, their artistic vision appears closer to what Herbert Blau describes in his iconoclastic 1999 book *Nothing in Itself: Complexions of Fashion*. After discussing a black Koran-embroidered evening dress by Karl Lagerfeld as modeled by Claudia Schiffer in 1994, Blau concludes:

> While it can make a dissident statement, or work for identity politics, at the level of its deepest motives there is no justice in fashion. Which augments the perpetual blush.
>
> We may, as we look in the mirror, be mortified for the moment, but dressing up or dressing down, there's a certain expectancy in clothes, as if woven into the fabric, even technofabrics, with something of the sensuousity of sewing or weaving itself. . . . If there's no last word in fashion, despite all the exquisite, ravishing, undeniably elegant things, that's because even what we think of as timeless is suffused with anticipation. Even before the garment is worn there's something erotic in the prospect of wearing, unsubdued by evanescence, the thing half understood, what makes fashion fashion, if sinister, threatening, even aroused by that.[28]

Blau's central project is to redirect our gaze toward the fashion object as aesthetic, even of course erotic, object; he wants to acknowledge the designer's exquisite craft even in the most "political" seeming garb. An Allanovna tie is, perhaps above all else, an "exquisite, ravishing, undeniably elegant thing," and her list of items—"a hat, a picture, a book, a jewel for the ear"—deliberately blurs the boundary between design and art.[29] This is an important step for Faulkner, whose characters up to this point have generally, in their progress from peasantry to respectability, amassed design objects solely as markers of their status: what Shreve McCannon in *Absalom, Absalom!* mercilessly calls Thomas Sutpen's "crystal tapestries and . . . Wedgwood chairs."[30] To put it perhaps a bit too cynically, after his New York visit, Ratliff seems to graduate from reading *Southern Living* to reading *Wallpaper*.[31]

Faulkner's mocking characterization of Sutpen's status-bestowing Design Objects as made of ludicrously fragile china and crystal is more than echoed, though with an overtly erotic twist, two decades later in *The Mansion* in Ratliff's strangely fearful approach to the second tie: "I hadn't even teched [it] yet because I was afraid to. It was red jest a little under what you see in a black-gum leaf in the fall, with not no single sunflower nor even a bunch of them but little yellow sunflowers all over it in a kind of diamond pattern, each one with a little blue center almost the exact blue my shirts get to after a while. I didn't dare touch it" (176). What are we to make of Ratliff's fear in the face of Allanovna's Object, "red jest a little under" and packed with *jouissance*? Why the strange disjunction between seeing and touching? We seem to be back in the rich man's bawdy house, Ratliff's fear like that of Clyde Griffiths's when visiting his first prostitute in *An American Tragedy*: "She might charge him more than he could afford. He was afraid of her—himself—everything, really—quite nervous and almost dumb with his several fears and qualms."[32] Yet ultimately, it will be this tie that Ratliff chooses to display in his home "on a rack under a glass bell" next to one of Barton Kohl's sculptures (231); the peach-colored tie, even more sensual as it recalls the back of a sunburned girl, that he keeps genuinely private. Perhaps from time to time he even touches it. All Mink has to play with, on the other hand, is a pistol. Firearms are phallic enough without embellishment, but Faulkner embellishes: "snub-nosed, short-barrelled, swollen of cylinder and rusted over, with its curved butt and flat reptilian hammer it did resemble the fossil relic of some small antediluvian terrapin." "Hit's dirty inside," complains Mink (291, 292).

Yet even though these objects appear to stand in for eroticized body parts, I am still not convinced this is fetishism, exactly, at least not on Faulkner's part. For one thing, as Victoria de Grazia reminds us on the opening page of the essay collection *The Sex of Things*, "In Western societies, acts of exchange and consumption have long been obsessively gendered, usually as female," and some recent work by Bill Brown suggests that psychoanalysis has made objects inexorably symbolize body parts—breasts, genitals, etc.—only because it has underestimated the appeal for humans of things in themselves.[33]

For another thing, the association of big city objects with forbidden human sexuality extends in the novel even to Barton Kohl's sculpture. Admittedly, here the sexuality is chiefly a matter of Chick Mallison's insinuation to Ratliff: "It's that sculpture you liked: the Italian boy doing whatever it was you liked that Gavin himself who has not only seen Italian boys before but maybe even one doing whatever this one is doing, didn't even know where first base was. But it's all right. You don't have a female wife nor any innocent female daughters either. So you can probably keep it right there in the house" (203–4). Mallison later confesses to the reader that "if Gavin was still looking for first base, I had already struck out because I didn't even know what it was, let alone what it was doing" (232). Chick insinuates a double sexuality: that the boy is doing something with his genitals, and, via the baseball analogy, that understanding abstract sculpture is somehow like sex. (If this line of thinking seems adolescent, well, that's Chick Mallison, who keeps joking about how *"once you get the clothes off those tall up-and-down women you find out they aint all that up-and-down at all"* [205]. Hubba hubba.) Here Ratliff succeeds where the two Harvard graduates fail. To view his sculptures, Kohl leads him away from the party to the private section of the house—"a room not jest where folks used but where somebody come off by his-self and worked" (172). (Functionally if not aesthetically, this is of course just the sort of space where Flem will keep his ledge and Ratliff his peach tie.) In the loft, Ratliff gazes "at some I did recognise and some I almost could recognise and maybe if I had time enough I would, and some I knowed I wouldn't never quite recognise, until all of a sudden I knowed that wouldn't matter neither, not jest to him but to me too. Because anybody can see and hear and smell and feel and taste what he expected to hear and see and feel and smell and taste, and wont nothing much notice your presence nor miss your lack. So maybe when you can see and feel and smell and hear and taste what you never expected to and hadn't never even imagined until that moment, maybe that's why Old Moster picked you out to be the one of the ones to be alive." Ratliff's artistic education is proceeding apace. If Mallison and Stevens, Harvard aesthetes though they may imagine themselves to be, still imagine art to be fundamentally representational, Ratliff—in only his first experience of abstract sculpture—almost immediately, "all of a sudden," comes to realize the essence of art is, instead, formal innovation: experiencing "what you never expected to and hadn't never even imagined until that moment" (173).This Modernist emphasis on experiential newness is virtually indistinguishable from Faulkner's description, in his Nobel Prize speech, of his own attempts "not for glory and least of all for profit . . . to create out of the materials of the human spirit something which did not exist before."[34] None of this is how Kohl expects Ratliff to react. "Shocked? Mad?" he asks after giving Ratliff "time and room both to look." "Do I have to be shocked and mad at something just because I never seen it before?" asks Ratliff. Kohl's answer is curious: "At your age, yes. . . . Only children can stand surprise for the pleasure of surprise. Grown people cant bear surprise unless they are promised in advance they will want to own it" (173).

In its celebration of childhood and its rejection of getting and spending, it's an oddly Romantic attitude for a Modernist sculptor, certainly a more "innocent" vision than Chick Mallison's. Kohl's attitude nevertheless recalls Stevens's description of Greenwich Village as a place "where young people of all ages below ninety go in search of dreams" (151). And youth in this chapter is pitted, to make matters still more complicated, against totalitarianism: "Young people today don't have any [time] left because only fools under twenty-five can believe, let alone hope, that there's any left at all," declares Stevens, going on to declaim against totalitarians in Italy and Germany and Spain and at home, whom he describes partly in terms still appropriate today as "the fine names confederated in unison in the name of God against the impure in morals and politics" (160, 161). Of the domestic totalitarians listed, none is associated with Greenwich Village, but the South has plenty: "Long in Louisiana and our own Bilbo in Mississippi, not to mention our very own Senator Clarence Egglestone Snopes," plus its fair share of the Klansmen and Silver Shirts Stevens also mentions. Ratliff adds Russia to the list, of course, but Stevens goes on again: "when you are young enough and brave enough at the same time, you can hate intolerance and believe in hope, and, if you are sho enough brave, act on it." And Ratliff adds, with a hint of corrective parody suggesting he's a bit skeptical about dividing the world up so easily into hopeful youth and intolerant elders, "I wish I was either one of them. To believe in intolerance and hope and act on it" (161).

Thus chapter 7, seemingly a light jaunt to Greenwich Village, comes on the heels of a beautiful woman's suicide from boredom and ends with apocalypse: "and now we watched the lights go out in Spain and Ethiopia, the darkness that was going to creep eastward across all Europe and Asia too, until the shadow of it would fall across the Pacific islands until it reached even America." Kohl dies, and Linda, they predict, will return to Yoknapatawpha because "it's doom" (177–78). Yet the enemy here is not capitalism, patriarchal or otherwise, but rather what Faulkner labels "intolerance," a remarkably mild word for National Socialism, fascism, Stalinism, and so on, but one aptly suited to the reception of startling, difficult art in the South. It's that intolerance that leads to boredom by expelling the surprising, the creative.

I don't want to suggest that Faulkner plays down the murderousness of totalitarianism. But if Priscilla Wald's essay in this volume has reminded us all of the complex relations between big fears and small fears, I think *The Mansion* reminds us of the complex relations between big acts of resistance and dignity and small ones. For various kinds of oppressed men—gay men and African American men in particular, but in much fashion theory working-class white Britons as well—snappy dressing has derived from an insistence on dignity, an assertion of a kind of sophistication readable only to others in the know, sometimes even "a black thing you wouldn't understand." Ellison's Invisible Man uses fashion as a kind of flashy invisibility: he becomes flashy to those who get it, invisible to those who don't. In such a context, a $1,000 necktie is not some decadent bourgeois excess. It is a celebration of beauty, an assertion of personal dignity, and most of all, an affirmation of selfhood.[35] Faulkner was not, of course, oppressed in

the ways gay and black men have been. But for much of his life he was
miserable for other reasons, reasons that often did have to do with mainstream America's "intolerance," its hatred of surprise, its drive, especially
in the Fifties, toward a world that any artist would find boring.

A few days ago one of my early-morning runs took me by Faulkner's
grave. Left there was the usual assortment of whiskey bottles. Myself
the child of an alcoholic, I find such "tribute" tremendously depressing.
In my own ideal world, in St. Peter's Cemetery people would not leave
empty flasks of alcohol. Faulkner's grave would be festooned with beautiful neckties.

NOTES

The author wishes to thank Richard Godden and Jack Matthews for their patient and helpful readings of an early draft of this essay, and Judith Sensibar for directing my attention to
references to fashion in Faulkner's letters.

1. Houston A. Baker Jr. and Dana D. Nelson, "Preface: Violence, the Body, and 'The
South,'" *American Literature* 73:2 (June 2001): 236.

2. Douglas B. Holt, *How Brands Become Icons: The Principles of Cultural Branding*
(Boston: Harvard Business School Press, 2004), 12, 59, 58–59.

3. Ted Ownby, "Freedom, Manhood, and White Male Tradition in 1970s Southern
Rock Music," in *Haunted Bodies: Gender and Southern Texts*, ed. Anne Goodwyn Jones and
Susan Donaldson (Charlottesville: University Press of Virginia, 1997), 369–88.

4. William Faulkner, *The Mansion* (New York: Random House, 1959), 224. Subsequent
citations are made parenthetically.

5. Cleanth Brooks, "William Faulkner," in *The History of Southern Literature*, ed.
Louis D. Rubin Jr. et al. (Baton Rouge: Louisiana State University Press, 1985), 333–42.

6. Holt himself, for example, discusses crises in "society" and sees solutions in
smaller units such as the "bohemia community." In *Against the Romance of Community*
(Minneapolis: University of Minnesota Press, 2002)—which is not really about the South,
though the cover photo was taken in Tupelo—Miranda Joseph quite thoroughly decon-
structs the false opposition between community and capitalism, arguing in part that "local
heterogeneity does not necessarily imply resistance to globalization either in the form of
authentic original otherness or excess" (150). The most masterful treatment of this concept
in Southern literary studies, of course, is Scott Romine, *The Narrative Forms of Southern
Community* (Baton Rouge: Louisiana State University Press, 1999).

7. Michael Kreyling, *Inventing Southern Literature* (Jackson: University Press of
Mississippi, 1998); Patricia Yaeger, *Dirt and Desire: Reconstructing Southern Women's
Writing, 1930–1990* (Chicago: University of Chicago Press, 2001). Kreyling's and Yaeger's
metaphor of the literary critic as Luddite guerrilla obviously pertains to my argument
about modernity in this essay. In the fifty years since Flannery O'Connor's original depiction of Faulkner as a relatively high-tech Modernist express train, Faulkner's modernity has
become, metaphorically, the problem itself. Yaeger's embrace of the metaphor is meant
chiefly as a way of distancing herself from Kreyling's ultimate unwillingness to follow through
on the implications of his own project. Kreyling's use is more complex. For the record, I *like*
express trains, and wish the contemporary South had some.

8. Sarah Thornton, *Club Cultures: Music, Media, and Subcultural Capital* (Hanover:
University Press of New England, 1996).

9. Louis D. Rubin, "The Trilogy of the Snopes Family Complete," Baltimore *Evening
Sun*, 27 November 1959, rpt. in *William Faulkner: The Contemporary Reviews*, ed.
M. Thomas Inge (New York: Cambridge University Press, 1994), 499.

10. Patricia Meyer Spacks, *Boredom: The Literary History of a State of Mind* (Chicago: University of Chicago Press, 1995), x, 1.

11. Joanne Jacobson, "Exploding Plastic Inevitable," review of *Tupperware: The Promise of Plastic in 1950s America*, by Alison Clarke, *The Nation*, 27 December 1999.

12. Richard Godden, "Earthing *The Hamlet*, an Anti-Ratliffian Reading," *Faulkner Journal* 14:2 (Spring 1999): 77–79.

13. The classic treatment is, of course, Dick Hebdige's *Subculture: The Meaning of Style* (New York: Methuen, 1979), and most other works on punk style have followed Hebdige's lead, even as they increasingly dissent from Hebdige's idea of punk as subversively heroic.

14. William Faulkner, *The Hamlet*, 3rd ed. (New York: Random House, 1940), 58, 151.

15. See discussions of Ratliff's tie and Kohl's sculpture below.

16. According to a conversion table provided on the Web site of Oregon State University political science professor Robert Sahr: http://oregonstate.edu/Dept/pol_sci/fac/sahr/cv2004.pdf.

17. Costing $11, or $88 today.

18. As if to reinforce an already obvious contrast, Faulkner almost anxiously repeats the line "This is New York" five times in six pages.

19. The pistol itself is also associated with Ratliff's ties. Both are bargained for; in a grim bit of class parody, the pistol comes out of the blue-jowled pawnshop owner's "private stock," and just as Ratliff and Allanovna attempt to soften the commerciality of their transaction, so too, through semantics, must Mink "reclaim" rather than "buy" the pistol (291). And when at the end of the novel Ratliff hesitates to walk right in on Mink's hiding place, he might not explicitly recall his own two-for-one tie purchase, but we do: "You never seen that pistol," he says to Stevens. "I did. It didn't look like no one-for-ten-dollars pistol. It looked like one of a two-for-nine-and-a-half pistols. Maybe he's still got the other one with him" (432).

20. Ted Polhemus and Lynn Procter, *Fashion and Antifashion: An Anthropology of Clothing and Adornment* (London: Thames and Hudson, 1978). Subsequent citations are made parenthetically.

21. For a full recent treatment of the importance of Ratliff's sentimental pilgrimage, see Randy Boyagoda, "Imagining Nation and Imaginary Americans: Race, Immigration, and American Identity in the Fiction of Salman Rushdie, Ralph Ellison, and William Faulkner" (PhD diss., Boston University, 2005).

22. William Faulkner, *Selected Letters of William Faulkner*, ed. Joseph Blotner (New York: Random House, 1977), 30, 450; William Faulkner, *Novels 1936–1940*, ed. Joseph Blotner and Noel Polk (New York: Library of America, 1990), 1104.

23. The Farmington Hunt Club Web page notes that "In order to wear the colors, members must prove their ability in the hunting field, and must be awarded their colors by the master" (http://farmingtonhunt.org/history.html). However, given the social dynamics of Albemarle County—where I grew up—it's safe to say the coat symbolizes more than hunting ability.

24. Good design is rarely *purely* aesthetic. For example, like line or shape, color draws some of its meaning from context: some colors look fresher for not having been used in design for a while—or, conversely, because they are currently "in." (Avocado and gold, for example, looked a lot better in 1970 than in 1980.) In 1960, pink had been "in" for a while, especially paired with black, and Faulkner may have been drawn to two or more incongruous combinations: first, an "in" mid-century modern tone paired with the coat's classic, conservative tailoring and expensive traditional materials—a coat that functions simultaneously as sign and symbol—and, second, the allegedly feminine pink's standing for his hunting prowess.

25. Joel Williamson, *William Faulkner and Southern History* (New York: Oxford University Press, 1993), 173.

26. Ibid., n.p.

27. There is a world of difference between the most famous shop-window scene in American literature, Dreiser's account of Hortense Briggs ogling a fur coat in *An American Tragedy*, and Faulkner's version. Yet Walter Benn Michaels's now rather hoary observation about Dreiser, that he "didn't so much approve or disapprove of capitalism; he desired

pretty women in little tan jackets with mother-of-pearl buttons, and he feared becoming a bum on the streets of New York" (19), has not been taken sufficiently to heart by writers of the rather large body of critical work treating the Snopes trilogy as Faulkner's critique of *gesellschaft* or capitalism, patriarchal or otherwise. Walter Benn Michaels, *The Gold Standard and the Logic of Naturalism* (Berkeley: University of California Press, 1987).

28. Herbert Blau, *Nothing in Itself: Complexions of Fashion* (Bloomington: Indiana University Press, 1999), 252.

29. As Serge Guilbaut argues in *How New York Stole the Idea of Modern Art* (Chicago: University of Chicago Press, 1983), New York in the 1950s supplanted Paris as the center of the art world.

30. William Faulkner, *Absalom, Absalom!,* in *Novels 1936–1940*, ed. Joseph Blotner and Noel Polk, 148.

31. I exaggerate. According to Chick Mallison, Ratliff's parlor three or four years later holds, in addition to the tie and Kohl's sculpture, a "fireplace filled with fluted green paper in the summer but with a phony gas log in the winter" (231), a *Southern Living* tableau if ever there was one, especially along with the spotlessly waxed melodeon in the corner and the waxed chairs.

32. Theodore Dreiser, *An American Tragedy* (New York: Signet, 2000), 67.

33. Victoria de Grazia, ed., *The Sex of Things: Gender and Consumption in Historical Perspective* (Berkeley: University of California Press, 1996), 1; Bill Brown, "Object Relations in an Expanded Field," talk delivered at Dortmund University, June 2005.

34. William Faulkner, "Banquet Speech," http://nobelprize.org/literature/laureates/1949/faulkner-speech.html.

35. Though such an affirmation can degenerate into the desperate ghetto pursuit of Air Jordans and other logoed products, the ghetto version suggests a different aesthetic, since it emphasizes conformity, not the individuality of dress espoused by Ellison, Faulkner, and others.

Light in August, Faulkner's Angels of History, and the Culture of Jim Crow

SUSAN V. DONALDSON

When *Light in August* first appeared in late 1932, it was widely—and perhaps surprisingly—hailed in a good many newspaper reviews as a socially conscious novel that fiercely condemned the most notorious and conspicuous failings of the U.S. South—lynching, racial oppression, injustice, religious fundamentalism, extreme poverty. One review in particular—in the *Chicago Daily News*—was accompanied by a highly revealing caricature of the young novelist surrounded by the debris that historian George B. Tindall would catalogue decades later as the many telltale signs of "the Benighted South" so obsessively mused upon during the heyday of H. L. Mencken—bottles of moonshine, hooded figures, hysterical women, a shabby cabin, and a hangman's noose (Figure 1).[1] It is a caricature that hints at the novel's—and the writer's—obsessive engagement with the cultural heritage of the region, its witches' brew of violence, race, sex, bigotry, and crumbling mementoes of the past. It is also an image that evokes something of the entrapment in history that marks so many of the novel's characters, "volitionless servants of an irrevocable past," as the *Times Literary Supplement* reviewer so aptly pronounced them.[2] Perhaps more to the point, the *Chicago Daily News* caricature captures both the form and the reading experience of *Light in August*—a fragmentary narrative stubbornly resistant to unity and nearly bursting with hidden histories brought suddenly to light and with highly visual passages so cinematic in their impact that they threaten to unreel off the page.

There is in that caricature a haunting and uncanny anticipation of an epigrammatic meditation on history and its attendant disasters, inspired by Paul Klee's 1920 watercolor *Angelus Novus* (Figure 2), that a German refugee and scholar named Walter Benjamin wrote in 1940, a few months before he tried and failed to escape wartorn France and subsequently committed suicide. Benjamin had bought the painting in 1921, kept it in his Berlin residence for years, and then fled with it into exile in France when Hitler came to power. Over the years the painting served as "a picture for meditation," in the words of one of Benjamin's closest friends, and Benjamin's musings upon its elusive meanings eventually resulted in

Figure 1: Roy C. Nelson, "As caricaturist Roy C. Nelson sees Novelist William Faulkner, surrounded by the deep, dark, bloody South." *Chicago Daily News*, 5 October 1932:16. William Faulkner Collections (#6074), Special Collections, University of Virginia Library.

the ninth fragment of his "Theses on the Philosophy of History," which is worth quoting here in full:[3]

> A Klee painting named "Angelus Novus" shows an angel looking as though he is about to move away from something he is fixedly contemplating. His eyes are staring, his mouth is open, his wings are spread. This is how one pictures the angel of history. His face is turned toward the past. Where we perceive a chain of events, he sees one single catastrophe which keeps piling wreckage upon wreckage and hurls it in front of his feet. The angel would like to stay, awaken the dead, and make whole what has been smashed. But a storm is blowing from Paradise: it has got caught in his wings with such violence that the angel can no longer close them. This storm irresistibly propels him into the future to which his back is turned, while the pile of debris before him grows skyward. This storm is what we call progress.[4]

Writing just after his release from a French internment camp and in anticipation of German invasion, Benjamin drew on his fascination with Jewish mysticism and his affiliation with Marxist history to evoke his angel of history as an antagonist of the history of the powerful, of its continuity and progress, and as a champion of the oppressed, the silenced, and the discarded.[5] The historian, he famously declared, must "brush history against the grain" and hence resist the lure of continuity and progress proffered by conventional, "official" histories for the fragmentation and discontinuity he saw defining "the tradition of the oppressed."[6] Anticipating a postmodern suspicion of narrative and its embrace of the visual, Benjamin wrote elsewhere that "history decays into images, not into stories."[7] He saw his charge as a materialist historian, accordingly, as investigating, deciphering, and reassembling the fragmented debris of the past, in the words of one of his most sensitive commentators, Graeme Gilloch, into

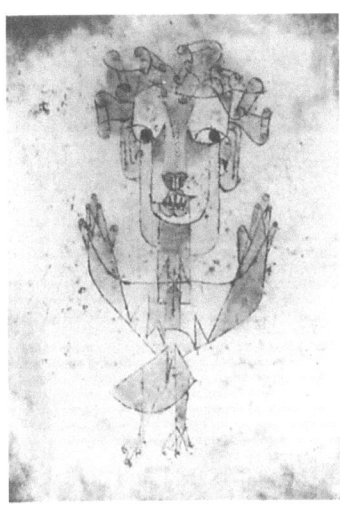

Figure 2: Paul Klee, *Angelus Novus*, 1920.
2005 Artists Rights Society (ARS), New
York/VG Bild-Kunst, Bonn, Germany.

"a powerful, illuminating mosaic or montage" capturing the dialectical tension between past and present.[8]

Separated by geography, history, and biography, Benjamin and Faulkner nonetheless intersect in the contested terrain of excavating and decipher-ing history and in a manner of speaking their own inheritances, especially in their willingness to interrogate "official" histories, in their attraction to the modernist aesthetics of montage and fragmentation, and above all to the politics of vision and visibility undergirding what histories are told and what histories are not. In a novel that hesitates between the present and long stretches of narrative looping back into the past, Faulkner resorts to something like his own angels of history in the shape of figures who live in the margins of his imagined landscape and who in many respects embody and survey an increasingly fractured color line—the disgraced Presbyterian minister Gail Hightower, the wandering mother-to-be Lena Grove, and the shadowy Joe Christmas, whose slippage back and forth between the color line culminates in a horrifying lynching, the ultimate weapon, as we're reminded, from early twentieth-century lynching photo-graphs, of white control over African Americans under Jim Crow.[9] Drawn together initially by the fire that consumes the house of yet another out-cast, Joanna Burden, Faulkner's own angels of history survey the wreckage of a society all too confident in its categories of whiteness and blackness and in its powers of surveillance and control, and the steadiness of their gaze upon that wreckage interrogates and destabilizes the surveillance they fall under themselves as misfits, outcasts, and debris of a rigidly seg-regated society. Contesting the gaze of Jim Crow defining their marginal

positions in society, they end up dislodging and disrupting what Robyn
Wiegman would call its "economies of visibility"—its control of what can
be seen and what cannot, its reliance upon visual signs for designating
the length and breadth of the color line, and its authorization of what
visual representations of the past can be circulated and what cannot.[10] In
a word, Faulkner's own angels of history end up disrupting codes of recognition designating the boundaries between black and white, man and
woman, self and other, upon which the white South depended to define
its racial and social order and its very sense of whiteness.[11] In doing so,
Light in August anticipates many of the battles over visual representation
in the media fought in the streets of Southern cities and in magazine photographs and television screens a generation later.[12]

That *Light in August* does in many respects foreground battles over
visibility and invisibility in its examination of segregation, race, and
identity politics is not so surprising when we consider Faulkner's own
preoccupation with vision and acts of looking, a preoccupation that has
drawn much commentary from many of the speakers at past conferences
of Faulkner and Yoknapatawpha, including Noel Polk, André Bleikasten,
Candace Waid, Doreen Fowler, Leslie Fiedler, Joseph Urgo, Michel
Gresset, Panthea Reid, Judith Sensibar, Lothar Hönnighausen, Jay Watson,
and Carolyn Porter, to name just a few. Faulkner himself in *The Sound and
the Fury* provided something of his own commentary on gazing in the disconcerting eye in the electric sign that taunts Jason Compson, in fruitless
chase after his runaway niece, to "keep your eye on Mottson."[13] Faulkner's
earliest work was in many respects shaped by the motif of "nympholepsy,"
the eternal chase of an elusive female before the onslaught of a quest-
ing male gaze that Faulkner had undoubtedly inherited from a host of
Romantic poets and in particular from Conrad Aiken, as Judith Sensibar
tells us.[14] A good deal of *The Sound and the Fury* was structured by that
yearning glimpse to catch sight of the ever-absent Caddie Compson.[15]
But one of the things most haunting about that novel is the way the narrative gazes of the three Compson brothers suddenly open and expand
as we read the first pages of the fourth section and see the long-suffering
Compson cook Dilsey Gibson for the first time, apart from Benjy's grief
and yearning, Quentin's obsessive ponderings on African Americans as
signifiers of white identity, and Jason's frankly racist, Bilboesque fulmina-
tions. We see her as something like wreckage left in the wake of the white
Compsons' decline, consumed by the years, the third-person omniscient
narrator suggests, "until only the indomitable skeleton was left rising like
a ruin or a landmark."[16] Focusing directly on Dilsey herself, no longer
veiled by the Compson brothers' obsessions, the narrative gaze makes a
significant shift from the claustrophobic concerns of the Compsons—and

Figure 3: Eudora Welty, *A woman of the 'thirties*, Hinds County, 1935. Copyright Eudora Welty, LLC; Eudora Welty Collection, Mississippi Department of Archives and History. Used by permission of Russell & Volkening as agents for the author's estate.

Faulkner's own aesthetic of vision, gender, and artistic authority—to a far wider and more socially aware vision, one that awards Dilsey her own privilege of vision—of having seen the first and the last of the white Compsons. Some twenty years ago Thadious Davis made a persuasive argument for the way Dilsey herself seems to represent the only true "clear vision" in the novel,[17] and from this perspective Dilsey's singularly clear gaze aptly parallels one of Eudora Welty's astonishingly direct and empathetic photographs of the 1930s, in which the photograph's black subject looks unflinchingly at the camera and the white photographer in a world that militated against the very idea of African Americans looking back (Figure 3).

Richard Gray has suggested that a similar widening of vision characterizes the narrative representations of looking and being looked at in *Light in August*, Faulkner's seventh novel, which lacks, he says, "the sometimes claustrophobic personal focus" of both *The Sound and the Fury* and *Sanctuary*.[18] But then, by 1931, Faulkner, like so many other writers of his generation, had begun to look up from his own aesthetic preoccupations and become attuned to the social and economic misery engulfing his own community and that of the country at large. In *Light in August* he was ready, his most recent biographer, Jay Parini, tells us, to face directly the workings of racism in the segregated South.[19]

Indeed, within the manuscripts of the novel that began as "Dark House," his own narrative gaze—and that of the characters who began to emerge—underwent a kind of shift and expansion.[20] Months before he began the manuscript, he had apparently sent a letter defending the practice of lynching—on the time-worn basis of protecting white womanhood—to the Memphis *Commercial Appeal*, the discovery of which we have Noel Polk and Neil McMillen to thank.[21] The manuscript itself began with the obsessive yearnings over tales of Confederate military glory by a middle-aged white man named Gail Hightower, whose own gaze is focused narrowly on the burgeoning Cult of the Lost Cause enshrining the Confederacy in white memory. As the writing unfolded in late 1931 and early 1932, the figure of Lena began to emerge—although in later years Faulkner himself would claim that he began the novel with no more idea of its central concerns than that of a young woman, he said, "pregnant, walking down a strange country road."[22] Finally, though, the figure of Joe Christmas and his tortured trajectory through the politics of race and identification took on increasing importance as Faulkner apparently drew upon the now-famous Nelse Patton lynching in 1908 and possibly the 1919 shooting of an escapee on his way to the local courthouse for the details of Joe's own lynching at the hands of white avenger Percy Grimm. In the final published version Christmas's history and death are framed—and contained—by Lena Grove herself, who opens and concludes the narrative.[23] To a startling degree, that narrative framing, Lena's story confining and containing Joe Christmas's story, suggests not just the transformation the manuscript had undergone since its early preoccupation with Gail Hightower's visions of past glory but also its indebtedness to, certainly strong echoes of, Jean Toomer's 1922 poem "Portrait in Georgia":

Hair—braided chesnut,
    Coiled like a lyncher's rope,
Eyes—fagots,
Lips—old scars, or the first red blisters,
Breath—the last sweet scene of cane,
And her slim body, white as the ash
    Of black flesh after flame.[24]

That *Light in August* does resonate with earlier texts of lynching, like Toomer's poem, says a good deal about how Faulkner's own notions of the politics of looking and being looked at, of visibility and invisibility, had grown and deepened with an expanding sense of history and an increasing

Figure 4: "The Vampire that Hovers over North Carolina" ("Negro Rule"), Raleigh *News and Observer*, 27 September 1898. Courtesy of the North Carolina Collection, University of North Carolina at Chapel Hill, http://www.lib.unc.edu/ncc/1898/.

sensitivity to the dynamics of black and white at a time when the system of Jim Crow did indeed seem to be at the height of its control over the region and thoroughly impervious to change. Historian Leon Litwack tells us that in a mere twenty-five years, beginning around 1890, white Southerners nervous about the rise of a new generation of African Americans born in freedom and moving into the anonymous space of rising cities of the New South began to pass legislation, already anticipated in the realm of public education, that restricted black access to the franchise, to public accommodations, and to transportation. Frightened by the prospect of "New Negroes" increasingly disinclined to "stay in their place," literally and figuratively, white Southern state legislators took greater and greater pains to ensure the social, political, and economic subordination of African Americans in every facet of daily life—public transportation, the workplace, hospitals, orphanages, homes for the aged and the infirm, even churches and cemeteries.[25] Streetcars and railroads early on became sites of contention, beginning in the 1880s, because it was in the spaces of public transportation, as Litwack and Edward Ayers both argue, that African Americans and whites—but most particularly African American men and white women—were most likely to see each other on something very like equal standing.[26] And it was that possibility that both frightened and enraged white Southerners, who often argued that the protection of white womanhood was one of the prime rationales for segregation as a system (Figure 4). To "the ignorant and brutal young Negro," white novelist Thomas Nelson Page maintained, social equality meant quite simply "the opportunity to enjoy equally with white men, the privilege of cohabiting with white women."[27]

Monitoring the system that became known as Jim Crow, drawing its name from the tradition of blackface minstrelsy in nineteenth-century America, was an extraordinarily complicated and detailed form of surveillance in signs, laws, monitors, and material culture that resembled, finally, as Robyn Wiegman has pointed out, nothing so much as Michel Foucault's notion of the panopticon, strictly designating the boundaries

Figure 5: Bull Durham tobacco poster (early twentieth century). Courtesy of Joanne M. Braxton, Williamsburg, Virginia.

between those who are surveyed and those who have the power to under-take surveillance.[28] Drawing on Jeremy Bentham's diagram of the ideal penitentiary system, Foucault sees the panopticon as a schema of power placing those under surveillance in a series of cells that serve as "small theatres, in which each actor is alone, perfectly individualized and con-stantly visible."[29] Certainly the signs designating "white" and "colored" that proliferated everywhere evoked something of that ever-present sense of white surveillance and compartmentalization of space. So, for that mat-ter, did the explosion of black stereotypes in every conceivable form and on every possible product, from lawn jockeys to Aunt Jemima beginning in the 1890s (Figure 5). In the words of historian Robert Norrell, "coon imagery suffused American advertising and mass communications. Cigar packages offered 'coon' trading cards, and advertisements used coon images to sell a wide variety of products. . . . Newspaper comics serialized coon characters. One could not receive the most commonplace forms of communication in the 1890s without getting constant repetition of blacks stereotyped as lazy, stupid, and animal."[30]

The signs alone provided a constant reminder that African Americans were always under scrutiny (Figure 6). Civil rights activist Pauli Murray

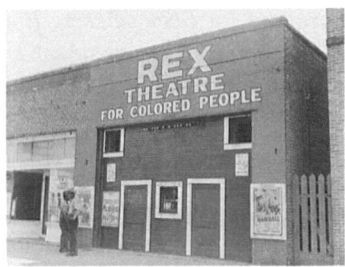

Figure 6. Marion Post Walcott, photo-
graph of segregated theater, Leland,
Mississippi, 1939. Library of Congress,
Prints and Photographs Division, FSA/
OWI Collection (reproduction number LC-
USF34-052508-D).

in her autobiography *Proud Shoes* vividly remembered feeling besieged
by them from every side:

> the signs ... screamed at me from every side—on streetcars, over drink-
> ing fountains, on doorways, FOR WHITE ONLY, FOR COLORED ONLY,
> WHITE LADIES, COLORED WOMEN, WHITE, COLORED. If I missed
> the signs I had only to follow my nose to the dirtiest, smelliest, most neglected
> accommodations or they were pointed out to me by a heavily armed, invariably
> mountainous red-faced policeman who to me seemed more a signal of calam-
> ity than of protection. I saw the names of telephone subscribers conspicuously
> starred '©' in the telephone directory and the equally conspicuous space given
> to crimes of negroes by the newspapers, the inconspicuous space given to
> public recognition and always with the ignominious and insulting "negro" or
> "negress."[31]

Lillian Smith for her part saw the signs as unceasing instruction in the
lessons of Jim Crow: "Few words are needed for there are signs everywhere. *White ... colored ... white ...* over doors of railroad and bus
stations, over doors of public toilets, over doors of theaters, over drinking fountains." There were also the invisible but unmistakable boundaries
between white and black to consider, she noted. "Invisible, but electri-
cally charged with taboo. Places you go. Places you don't go. White town,
colored town, white streets, colored streets; front door, back door. Places
you sit. Places you cannot sit."[32]

Public space, accordingly, was charged with danger for African
Americans, constantly aware that they were under scrutiny by the whites
who made the laws, posted the signs, and inspected their every gesture
and casual glance in public for breaches in racial etiquette.[33] Growing up
largely in isolation from the white world, Richard Wright felt compelled
to laboriously learn the complicated web of racial etiquette protecting
him from white violence. "I had to feel and think out each tiny item of
racial experience in the light of the whole race problem," he wrote in
Black Boy, "and to each item I brought the whole of my life. While standing before a white man I had to figure out how to perform each act and

how to say each word."[34] One of the informants for *Remembering Jim Crow* was even more direct and succinct: "Shit, you couldn't even look at a white woman hard back then when I come up. You would get hung. . . . Blacks couldn't look at no white. But whites could look at blacks all they wanted. Ain't going to be nothing did about it."[35]

It is this sort of danger, in fact, that Joe Christmas seems to flirt with from the beginning since he is remembered arriving for his first day of employment at the Jefferson saw mill in good but soiled clothes, and city clothes at that, which attract the suspicious glances of the white men working there. But what really takes them aback is a look on his face that seems "darkly and contemptuously still."[36] Unable to read and categorize his appearance, they are particularly put off by a look on his face that they cannot identify and that in many respects they have not seen before. "'Except that's a pretty risky look for a man to wear on his face in public,' one said. 'He might forget and use it somewhere where somebody wont like it'" (32). That look keeps worrying the white men at the mill, who find it difficult to read its significance, and what they fail to detect in particular is its quality of interrogation, defiance, and even repudiation, a look that seemingly has no place in a world defined, as the narrative tells us near the end, by "a hidden and unsleeping and omnipotent eye watching the doings of men" (456).

Light in August, in fact, is a novel that fairly bursts with references to mad eyes, cold eyes, judgmental eyes, murderous eyes—eyes that anticipate Foucault's panopticon all too vividly so that Joe Christmas does indeed feel that "all space was still a cage" (160). There are the eyes that survey Lena Grove, heavily pregnant, out in public pursuing her seducer Lucas Burch against all reason and considerations of social propriety, and the eyes that contemplate with disgust and dismissal the disgraced white minister Gail Hightower, unable to police his own wife decades ago and living on the edge of the black section of town. Above all, there are the eyes that watch the "parchmentcolored" Joe Christmas throughout his life—in the orphanage, where he is minutely surveyed by everyone from the children to the mad old janitor, all of whom automatically assume that he is black; on the farm of his foster parents, who monitor his every action for signs of sin and damnation; in the planing mill in present-day Mississippi, where his city clothes contradict "the screen of his negro's job at the mill"; in the manhunt for him as the supposed murderer of Joanna Burden; and in the final moments of his death at the hands of Percy Grimm (120, 36). These are eyes that dismiss all three of these figures—Christmas, Hightower, and Lena Grove—as outcasts and outsiders, those who have failed to meet the criteria for inclusion in the white community by Jim Crow: Lena because she has forfeited the ideal of white women's purity, Hightower because he has failed to police his own wife or his own obsessive sense of historical memory, and Joe Christmas because he is finally designated as black in the cultural script imposed upon Joanna Burden's death. From the perspective of the gaze that surveys them, they suggest something like the white community's refuse, all that is dismissed and negated in the making of a white communal identity and its "official" history under Jim Crow—an impure white woman, a disgraced white minister, and a man designated as a black rapist/murderer, mirror images of the color line as it had emerged in the U.S. South, supposedly protective of white womanhood, enshrined by white religion, barricaded against black encroachment.

Precisely because they are pronounced outcasts of sorts, they evoke something like the "reverse side of history," as Graeme Gilloch calls Walter Benjamin's affiliation with the tradition of the oppressed.[37] This is a history in Faulkner's world that is populated not with the Sartorises and Compsons who agonize on their declining status and diminishing sense of white aristocratic privilege but with those who live on the margins of society—a man who can move back and forth across the color line, a disgraced white minister whose obsession with the past outrages his white neighbors, and a white unwed mother whose very presence seems to contradict the ideal of pure white Southern womanhood. They seem, in fact, to suggest something of the wreckage of the past surveyed by Benjamin's angel of history, the refuse, anomalies, and contradictions expelled in the making of white community and history. Among other things, they all three evoke the potential failure/collapse of the three pillars of Jim Crow—the impermeability of the color line, the white Protestant justification/rationale for slavery, segregation, and white supremacy, and the protection/idealization of white Southern women as, in the words of historian Jacquelyn Dowd Hall, "the repository of white racial legitimacy."[38] It is the specter of that potential failure, represented most vividly by Joe Christmas's easy movement back and forth through the color line that so infuriates those white pursuers intent on capturing what they think is a black rapist/murderer. "He never acted like either a nigger or a white man," observed one of the anonymous members of the milling white crowd in Mottstown, where Joe is captured. "That was it. That was what made the folks so mad. For him to be a murderer and all dressed up and walking the town like he dared them to touch him, when he ought to have been skulking and hiding in the woods, muddy and dirty and running. It was like he never even knew he was a murderer, let alone a nigger too" (350).

In a word, that anonymous white townsman is infuriated that Joe Christmas can be so easily misread in a world where the realm of the visible is subject to such rigid racial regulation and segmentation. As one of the novel's angels of history surveying the wreckage and potential debris of Jim Crow, Joe bears potent testimony to the increasingly indecipherable nature of a system defined by rigid hierarchies of the visible and the invisible and above all by racial codes of recognition designating the boundaries between whiteness and blackness and individual identity itself. But then again, as James Snead observed so acutely in *Figures of Division, Light in August* is nothing if not a novel all about misrecognition, where signs are failing to signify, where people look and see and fail to understand, and where its characters white and black appear to arrive at mistaken perceptions and conclusions about one another with unnerving regularity.[39]

In a world where puzzling figures like Joe, Lena Grove, Gail Hightower, and Byron Bunch periodically come under the public glare of scrutiny as scandals and anomalies, Faulkner's characters one after another seem to be stymied by incidents of mistaken identity and misrecognition. No one could be more glaringly visible than Lena Grove at the novel's opening, on the road for Alabama in pursuit of the man who seduced and abandoned her, but as more than one person she meets along the way discovers, she has no inkling that the story of a woman seduced and abandoned determines who and what she is. Hearing her story, Byron Bunch "gets the picture of a young woman betrayed and deserted and not even aware that she has been deserted, and whose name is not yet Burch" (52). Bunch for his part is initially mistaken for her fugitive lover Lucas Burch, whose name, after all, seems to echo Bunch's. Now going under the name of Joe Brown—and described as "dark complected" (51), Burch in turn is linked and even mistaken at times for Joe Christmas, the two of them serving as doubles of sorts, seemingly anonymous "Joes" who live precariously in the margins of the color line, designated as white, a bit uneasily to be sure by the white men around them but sharing a black cabin on the Burden place and relegated to jobs at the saw mill usually associated with blacks. The narrator even makes a point of referring to how little the whites around Joe Christmas know about him, "what he was actually doing behind the veil, the screen of his negro's job at the mill" (36).

The wording of that last phrase is significant because it echoes the language W. E. B. Du Bois uses in *The Souls of Black Folk*—that of the "Veil" of the color line configuring and obscuring the perception of both whites and blacks, which is to say, what it means for a black person in white America to be recognized and misrecognized, to be on the "reverse side" of Jim Crow, to be, in short, the object of the white gaze and surveillance of segregation.[40] It is, I think, very likely that Faulkner was familiar with *The Souls of Black Folk* because his portrait of Joe Christmas resonates with Du Bois's agonized consideration of "double consciousness," the legacy, Du Bois maintains, facing each African American living in a world "which yields him no true self-consciousness, but only lets him see himself through the revelation of the other world." In words that would echo down the length and breadth of twentieth-century America, Du Bois describes "double consciousness" as "this sense of always looking at one's self through the eyes of others, of measuring one's soul by the tape of a world that looks on in amused contempt and pity. One ever feels his twoness—an American, a Negro; two souls, two thoughts, two unreconciled strivings; two warring ideals in one dark body, whose dogged strength alone keeps it from being torn asunder." The history of African Americans, he maintained, could be encapsulated quite simply by "the history of this strife—this longing to attain self-conscious manhood and to merge his double selves into a better and truer self."[41] What could more succinctly describe Joe Christmas's plight than that "sense of always looking at one's self through the eyes of others," of seeing himself only through the eyes of a Jim Crow world that defines blackness as the negative of whiteness? "*Set out for the nigger*," he thinks as he looks at the food left for him in Joanna Burden's kitchen, the sole space where African Americans traditionally could eat in a white household (238). Or those other times when he seeks out darkness only to brave what is to him a sense of suffocation reminding him of all those barriers militating against his very sense of self.

Perhaps more to the point, Joe's "discovery" of his designated identity as black in the room of the orphanage's white female dietitian resonates with that "stock scene of racial discovery" that Michael Cooke sees as a defining moment for so much African American literature and that Priscilla Wald and Shawn Michelle Smith have explored to such an illuminating degree in *Constituting Americans* and *Photography on the Color Line*, respectively.[42] Du Bois talks quite frankly about that discovery at the beginning of *The Souls of Black Folk* when he looks back to his childhood days and recalls the moment when a new tall young girl in his schoolhouse refuses to exchange visiting cards with him. She "refused my card," he remembers, "—refused it peremptorily with a glance." That was when, he says, he realized that he was indeed "different from the others," "shut out from their world by a vast veil." Wondering why God had made him "an outcast and a stranger in mine own house," the young Du Bois contemplates "the shades of the prison-house [that] closed round us all: walls strait and stubborn to the whitest, but relentlessly narrow, tall, and unscalable to sons of night who must plod darkly on in resignation."[43]

Years later James Weldon Johnson, as both Wald and Smith point out, would expand upon the dynamics of that dismissal "with a glance," a dismissal denying recognition of the black male's subjectivity by withholding an idealized image of wholeness and posing instead a reflection of disintegration and fluidity. In *Autobiography of an Ex-Coloured Man*, Johnson describes the impact of his white fiancée's gaze upon him once he reveals to her his previously concealed African heritage: "I felt her hand grow cold, and when I looked up, she was gazing at me with a wild, fixed stare as though I was some object she had never seen. Under the strange light in her eyes I felt that I was growing black and thick-featured and crimped haired."[44] Through the impact of his white fiancée's gaze, Johnson's protagonist feels his sense of self fissuring, much as Frantz Fanon would describe decades later in *Black Skin, White Masks* the effect of the call "'Dirty nigger!' Or simply, 'Look, a Negro!'" that would create both his sense of blackness and his sense of disintegrating selfhood.[45]

Significantly, both Du Bois's and Johnson's discoveries and/or rediscoveries of race are made through the glance of a white woman, as Shawn Michelle Smith argues in her wonderfully illuminating study of W. E. B. Du Bois and the visual culture of Jim Crow in *Photography on the Color Line*. Smith suggests that double consciousness, that "sense of always *looking at one's self through the eyes of others*," emerges through the intersection and combat of two gazes and visions, white and black, self and other, that compete and collaborate to define "the experiences of *racialization* and *racial identification*."[46] Du Bois, Smith persuasively argues, drew from William James's scenario of the self as "duplex," "'partly known and partly knower, partly object and partly subject,' both '*Me*' and '*I*.'" The "Me" in turn is made up of several different parts, including the material, the spiritual, but most notably "the social me," which James defines as "the recognition which [one] gets from his mates." "Properly speaking," James declares, "a man has as many social selves as there are individuals who recognize him and *carry an image of him in their mind*."[47]

Du Bois's discussion of double consciousness, though, as well as his scene of racial discovery, also anticipates, Smith persuasively suggests, Jacques Lacan's description of ego formation as one grounded in the process of misrecognition—in that moment called the mirror stage when an infant suddenly encounters an idealized image of wholeness that is markedly at odds with the bodily infantile experience of fragmentation and blurred boundaries between self and world. It is through that mirror stage that the ego splits, as Lacan describes it, divided between the bodily experience of fragmentation and that image of wholeness, and thereafter the individual will be impelled by the "perpetual psychological effort," as Smith terms it, "of *suturing* self-identification to image." Smith tries to revise, as it were, Lacan's scenario of the mirror stage, through emphasizing the mother's role; she suggests that the mother—who reassures the infant that the image in the mirror is indeed the infant's self—"provides important social reinforcement for the child's misrecognition through her own approving gaze." But in that "stock scene" of racial discovery that Smith examines so perceptively, the moment of reinforcement is withheld in confrontation with the color line. What Du Bois discovers in that moment of social misrecognition by the tall young girl who refuses his card is something like an "anti-self," a "negation" of the social recognition that James sees as part of the Me that defines oneself. Instead, he discovers a sense of splitting, between the idealized image of wholeness displayed alluringly in the mirror and reinforced by the mother's loving glance and encouragement and the "negation" of that image summed up by the tall young girl's dismissive glance.[48]

It is, I think, something very like this scenario that describes Joe Christmas's own scene of racial discovery and identification at the age of five in the orphanage—and it is a scene that he tries to replay again and again in an outraged effort to alter and reclaim it. We are told that he has been steadily monitored by the mad old janitor who appeared at the orphanage at roughly the same time that Joe did and that the children there taunt him with the label of nigger. But still, it is in the room of the white female dietitian, whose sexual encounter with the young intern is interrupted by the revelation of Joe's presence, that Joe discovers his own sense of difference. Dragged from behind a curtain while he vomits up the toothpaste he has been sampling illicitly, Joe is shaken within an inch of his life by the now-hysterical dietitian, who screams at him, "you little rat! Spying on me! You little nigger bastard!" (122). At that moment Joe experiences, I think, a sense of disintegration and dissolution that is remarkably akin to the sense of alienation and self-division experienced by W. E. B. Du Bois in his New England school house and by James Weldon Johnson shrinking from the horrified gaze of his white fiancée.

From there on in, Joe seems to see himself in terms that Du Bois himself would recognize as the divisive effects of double consciousness, as a figure disintegrating under the outraged white gaze proclaiming him black. That is how we as readers see him when we first penetrate his world "behind the veil" in chapter 5, as he crouches beneath the dark window of Joanna Burden's house and contemplates his body in the darkness, "seeming to watch it turning slow and lascivious in a whispering of gutter filth like a drowned corpse in a thick still black pool of more than water" (107). It is a sensation that intensifies on the manhunt after the death of Joanna Burden and the burning of her house when Joe flees through the countryside eluding his pursuers, forever trapped on that circling paved street that has defined his wandering life and in many respects the white gaze that has proclaimed him black, a gaze he detects on "that mark on his ankles the gauge definite and ineradicable of the black tide creeping up his legs, moving from his feet upwards as death moves" (339).

In many respects, it is as though Joe also keeps seeking out that white gaze as much as he keeps eluding it in his running because over and over again he seemingly stages one confrontation after another with it, as though compulsively reenacting that early discovery of racial identity under the angry gaze of the orphanage dietitian. In chapter 5, where we enter his consciousness for the first time, we see him moving naked in the darkness, after he has slipped his garments off, into the glare of a car's headlights: "He watched his body grow white out of the darkness like a kodak print emerging from the liquid. He looked straight into the head-lights as it shot past. From it a woman's shrill voice flew back, shrieking. 'White bastards!' he shouted. 'That's not the first of your bitches that ever saw. . . . . . .'" (108).

That moment of confronting the white gaze seems to be replayed over and over again in Joe's history—in his sexual encounters with Bobbie the waitress and with Joanna Burden, a descendant of New England aboli-tionists, both of whom in their turn reinforce his objectification as and fragmentation into blackness, and also with the nameless women he meets along that endless anonymous street that turns out to be far more a cage than a metaphor of freedom. It is a moment of confrontation that marks as well that strange and frightening encounter with the young black girl whom Joe unexpectedly—but perhaps not so unexpectedly at that—assaults perhaps because she offers not an opportunity to confront the white gaze but merely the possibility of falling into what seems to him a formless pool of darkness. Bobbie and Joanna at least provide him with a confirmation of sorts of his sense of being, albeit within their own fears and phobias of blackness, but in the eyes of the frightened and abject young black girl he seems to see nothing at all but his own formlessness and invisibility.

Confronting the white gaze again and again, he seeks to make visible what the world of Jim Crow has rendered invisible—the wholly arbitrary nature of the color line, the fantasy of separate whiteness and blackness, the violence required in repressing and repudiating the intersubjective nature of identity, which as Stuart Hall once observed, is founded on "[t]he dialogue of power and resistance, of refusal and recognition."[49] In a strange sort of way, Joe's confrontations with the white gaze, compul-sively reenacting and resisting that discovery of racial identity, also sug-gest something of the kind of oppositional or counter gaze pondered by bell hooks and Homi Bhabha, a counter gaze, Bhabha says, that "turns the discriminating look . . . back on itself," interrogating its very opera-tions and contesting its control over black images.[50] This is the look that W. E. B. Du Bois himself tried to encourage and foster, as Shawn Smith argues, in the 1900 American Negro Exhibition, which countered Jim

Figure 7: Portrait of an African American man, from W. E. B. Du Bois's albums of photographs of African Americans in Georgia exhibited at the Paris Exposition Universelle in 1900. Library of Congress, Prints and Photographs Division (reproduction number LC-USZ62-124665).

Crow stereotypes of African Americans, slyly interrogated American binary definitions of race into whiteness and blackness, and looked back in a way that questioned the very concept of whiteness founded on the subordination and dehumanization of blackness (Figure 7).[51] In a manner of speaking Ida B. Wells was undertaking much the same project in her fierce campaign against lynching, when she directly challenged the official white rationales used to defend lynching as a practice that was becoming peculiarly white and Southern in the late nineteenth and early twentieth century. She looked back at the white gaze that labeled all black men as potential rapists and murderers of white women by excavating the real stories behind incidents of racial violence and lynching—the economic competition between whites and blacks that often prompted violence against individual African Americans and the very real possibility that charges of rape camouflaged consensual relationships between black men and white women.[52] Looking back at white viewers, both Ida B. Wells and W. E. B. Du Bois, in their writings and in Du Bois's 1900 exhibition, ultimately challenge the very notion of white wholeness and solidarity, for what those direct and oppositional gazes pose among other things is a resistance to objectification under the white gaze, to relegation into subordination, to the kind of fragmentation into double consciousness that Du Bois sees as all too representative of those scenes of racial discovery under the heavy pressure of Jim Crow.

This is the kind of challenge that Joe Christmas's very presence in *Light in August* poses to the narrative—to the assumptions and stories that are told about him once it is "revealed" by his erstwhile partner Joe Brown/Lucas Burch that he can be designated as black, information that turns out to be as tenuous and as unreliable as all those scenes of misrecognition that punctuate the narrative. Once Joe Brown makes his information known to the legal authorities, the whites of Jefferson can finally place and categorize the all but unreadable Christmas, who has proven adept indeed at marshaling conflicting signs and signals of whiteness and blackness. And once they categorize him as a black rapist and murderer, Joe Christmas's final end—as well as the history that is told of that end—is all but foreordained—pursuit, capture, escape, lynching, mutilation, death. But what those events and that death ultimately mean remains to be seen precisely because Faulkner's own angels of history excavate the fragments, pieces, questions, and absences that the white townspeople do their best to ignore and shuttle aside.

In the narrative, our last close, direct glimpse of Christmas is toward the end of the chase, as he contemplates the tide of blackness engulfing him under the impact of the white gaze. Thereafter the narrative center shifts to the townspeople in Mottston, where he is captured, seemingly seeking out his pursuers to make them see him at last, to Byron Bunch, still haplessly trying to provide comfort and shelter for Lena Grove, to the townspeople of Jefferson, who exchange details about Christmas's seemingly inevitable death, and finally to Gavin Stevens, the District Attorney, whose Harvard degree, Phi Beta Kappa key, and family antecedents in Jefferson make him nothing if not a highly appropriate narrator of the lynching's "official history." What Stevens tries to do is explain to a visiting friend why it is that Joe Christmas, bursting free from his captors in Jefferson, makes his way to the house of the disgraced minister Gail Hightower, where he is finally shot and mutilated by the enthusiastic young white vigilante Percy Grimm. From his position of authority, Stevens is able to draw the bits and pieces of the elusive, fragmentary story together—the visit to Christmas in jail by Mrs. Hines, the ranting and raving of Doc Hines for a lynching, the break for freedom, the chase, and the final moment of death. An "official" version of murder and death emerges that Stevens weaves together with his theory of Christmas's white/black blood as the motivating force in all his seemingly contradictory actions. Steven's history breaks off with the final shooting of Joe Christmas, but the narrative thread he drops is continued in a manner of speaking once the narrative shifts to a third-person account of the white vigilante who eventually kills Joe Christmas. In a seamless passage of extraordinary visual force, with something very like the immediacy of cinema, Percy gives chase once Joe breaks free, measures his ability as hunter against that of Joe's as the hunted, and tracks him down and kills him in the name of maintaining and preserving white supremacy—although those he seeks to protect seem to be less than attentive to their own designated roles in that endeavor. When Gail Hightower futilely tries to ward off Percy and his fellow vigilantes with an alibi for Joe Christmas's whereabouts, Percy is self-righteously indignant. "'Jesus Christ!'" Grimm cried, his young voice clear and outraged like that of a young priest. 'Has every preacher and old maid in Jefferson taken their pants down to the yellowbellied son of a bitch?'" (464).

Presenting himself as Joe Christmas's ally and possible sexual partner, Gail Hightower ultimately casts into that seamless narrative of white revenge against blackness a stumbling block, a question, an anomalous fragment. So too does Lena Grove, having just given birth to her baby, momentarily wonder whether or not the hotly pursued Joe Christmas is in fact the real father—just as Mrs. Hines is momentarily persuaded in her frenzied fear that Lena's baby is Joe Christmas born again, the child of her long-dead daughter Millie, requiring her grandmotherly protection once again. Ultimately, Hightower, Lena, and Mrs. Hines help disrupt and dislodge that seamless narrative of murder/rape, revenge, and lynching that the white townspeople and Gavin Stevens have woven to make sense of the anomalous figure of Joe Christmas once and for all as a black rapist/murderer who must be ritualistically killed to reinforce and restore the smooth facade of whiteness. They suggest all the anomalies, contradictions, and questions that must be expelled in telling the story of the Burden place fire, Joanna Burden's death, Joe Christmas's flight, final capture, and death. Among other things, they widen that disturbing gap/absence marking the narrative place of Joanna Burden's death. For in all the violent encounters making up Joe Christmas's short and volatile life, encounters that fail, ultimately, in telling him who and what he is, the one that is missing is the final confrontation between Joe Christmas and Joanna Burden. We are led right up to the brink of it, as Joe Christmas watches on the wall the shadow of the Civil War pistol held by Joanna Burden, but we break away as soon as the "cocked shadow of the hammer flicked away" (283). What passes between them eludes our sight, and all we see finally is the ancient pistol that Joe Christmas holds in his hand after he has used it to flag down an approaching car—and here we are reminded as readers of Faulkner how much absences in earlier narratives, Caddy Compson's absence in *The Sound and the Fury* and the absence of the rape scene in *Sanctuary*, disrupt and unsettle Faulknerian narratives.

After that last glimpse of Joe looking in surprise at the pistol he holds in his hand, he begins to sink out of the narrative's sight and out of ours as

Figure 8. *The Lynching of Lige
Daniels, August 3, 1920, Center,
Texas* (postcard, front). From
James Allen et al., *Without
Sanctuary* (Santa Fe, N.M.: Twin
Palms Publishers, 2005),
plate 54.

well as he slips slowly into the narrative of pursuit woven by the whites he
encounters and eventually into the narrative of blood and explanation by
Gavin Stevens. But in the relentless chase by Percy Grimm and his fellow
white vigilantes, he briefly reappears, and as he does, it is as something
very like Faulkner's primary angel of history, his back to the future, gazing
at the wreckage before him, in a way that resembles nothing so much as
yet another visual artifact from the age of Jim Crow, a lynching photograph, one of those horrifying souvenirs that circulated in the heyday of
lynching and segregation and that both reinforced and exposed the making and working of whiteness. Historians Grace Elizabeth Hale and Leon
Litwack have offered cogent and probing analyses of the uses of those
photographs—and the spectacle of lynching, for that matter, under the
visual regime of Jim Crow; for what the photographs and the spectacle
undertook was literally and figuratively putting African Americans back in
their place through ritualistic tortures and murders that sometimes drew
thousands of white spectators in the early twentieth-century South.[53] By
so doing, the rituals and the photographs also endeavored to situate the
viewers as solidly and impregnably white, a visual rendering of the color
line (Figure 8).[54] That project is all too evident in the collection of lynching photographs gathered in the volume *Without Sanctuary* just a few
years ago, and arguably the most disturbing of the images collected in
that book is the double portrait of Frank Embree, photographed from the

back to display the marks of torture upon him and from the front as well. It is in that latter image that Frank Embree squarely faces his tormentors and looks at them head on—at the photographer, at the crowd, and at anyone who looks at the photograph. What the photograph reveals, though, is not a black man hunted down and tortured in a ritual of scapegoating and murder, but the broken, fissured whiteness of his tormentors—and the viewers of the photograph—under his defiant, confrontational gaze, a gaze that resists with astonishing power the objectification required by whiteness and that shows his viewers what it is indeed to see through the eyes of others. It shows the violence required to render him the object of the gaze of Jim Crow—and the ultimate failure of that violence.[55]

Just so does Joe Christmas's own gaze back at his tormentors dislodge, unsettle, and ultimately fragment their whiteness. The narrative tells us Percy Grimm, caught up in the sadistic ecstasy of his successful chase, ritualistically castrates Joe Christmas after he has already been shot five times, hiding behind the table in Gail Hightower's kitchen, and it tells us as well that one of the white men shoulder to shoulder with Grimm vomits when he sees what has been done. Above all, though, that narrative passage tells us that in the last moments of his life Joe Christmas looks back at his murderers, as Frank Embree looked back at his, and confronts them with their own shattered whiteness—the divisions of self and the violence required in the making of whiteness: "For a long moment he looked up at them with peaceful and unfathomable and unbearable eyes. Then his face, body, all, seemed to collapse, to fall in upon itself, and from out the slashed garments about his hips and loins the pent black blood seemed to rush like a released breath. It seemed to rush out of his pale body like the rush of sparks from a rising rocket; upon that black blast the man seemed to rise soaring into their memories forever and ever" (464–65).

Under the impact of that gaze the narrative itself cracks and fissures, like the fissures in the cracked urns that Joe so long ago conjured up in his pondering of female sexuality. For the story then shifts abruptly to Gail Hightower's own vision of Joe's death, forever linked with that of his murderer Percy Grimm, and to Lena Grove, still on the road, now accompanied by her baby and her determined but ineffectual knight and protector Byron Bunch. But what remains in the end are mere fragments, the shards and pieces of the history that the white townspeople and Gavin Stevens do not tell and do not see. With Joe, Gail Hightower, and Lena Grove, we see the wreckage of Jim Crow to come, the violence required to hold what Robyn Wiegman has called its "tenuous geometry of public gazes" and the eventual extinguishing of the white gaze—and of whiteness, for that matter.[56] It is a novel, ultimately, that signaled Faulkner's venture into an ever-widening critique of the cultural inheritance of Jim Crow and slavery, culminating in what critics have increasingly come to see as those postmodern moments of interrogating history itself in *Absalom, Absalom!* and *Go Down, Moses.*[57] For in the end, what Faulkner's angels of history reveal in *Light in August* is that the story of Yoknapatawpha's inheritance is really the story of those who are disinherited.

NOTES

1. Sterling North, "Magnolias, Madness and Mississippi Mud," *Chicago Daily News*, 5 October 1932, 16 (with caricature by Roy C. Nelson), newspaper clipping, William Faulkner Collections (#6074), Special Collections, University of Virginia Library; George B. Tindall, "The Benighted South: Origins of a Modern Image," *The Ethnic Southerners* (Baton Rouge: Louisiana State University Press, 1976), 43–58. Permission by the Albert and Shirley Small Special Collections Library to reproduce the caricature by Roy C. Nelson and to quote from Sterling North's review is gratefully acknowledged.

2. Review of *Light in August*, *Times Literary Supplement*, 16 February 1933, n.p., newspaper clipping in William Faulkner Collections (#6074), Special Collections, University of Virginia Library. Permission by the Albert and Shirley Small Special Collections Library to quote from the review is gratefully acknowledged.

3. Gershom Scholem, "Walter Benjamin and His Angel," in *On Walter Benjamin: Critical Essays and Recollections*, ed. Gary Smith (Boston: MIT Press, 1988), 59–62, 84; Beatrice Hanssen, "Portrait of Melancholy (Benjamin, Warburg, Panofsky)," in *Benjamin's Ghosts: Interventions in Contemporary Literary and Cultural Theory*, ed. Gerhard Richter (Stanford, Calif.: Stanford University Press, 2002), 173, 174; quoted in Hanssen, 173.

4. Walter Benjamin, "Theses on the Philosophy of History," *Illuminations*, ed. and intro. Hannan Arendt, trans. Harry Zohn (New York: Schocken Books, 1955), 257–58.

5. Scholem 84; Graeme Gilloch, *Walter Benjamin: Critical Constellations* (Malden, Mass.: Blackwell Publishers/Polity Press, 2002), 227–28.

6. Gilloch, 182, 227–28; Benjamin, "Theses on the Philosophy of History," 257.

7. Walter Benjamin, N11, 4 [On the Theory of Knowledge,Theory of Progress], *The Arcades Project*, trans. Howard Eiland and Kevin McLaughlin, prepared on the basis of the German volume ed. Rolf Tiedemann (Cambridge: Belknap Press/Harvard University Press, 1999), 476.

8. Gilloch, 182.

9. See in general James Allen *et al.*, *Without Sanctuary: Lynching Photography in America* (Santa Fe, N.M.: Twin Palms Publishers, 2005).

10. See Wiegman's section on "Economies of Visibility" in *American Anatomies: Theorizing Race and Gender* (Durham: Duke University Press, 1995), 21–78. See also Deborah Poole's discussion of "Principles of Visual Economy" in *Vision, Race, and Modernity: A Visual Economy of the Andean Image World* (Princeton: Princeton University Press, 1997), 9–13.

11. Tzvetan Todorov has a very useful overview to offer of the "need for the gaze of the other" emerging in eighteenth-century western philosophical discourse in *Life in Common: An Essay in General Anthropology*, trans. Katherine Golsan and Lucy Golsan (Lincoln: University of Nebraska Press, 2001), 14; see his first chapter, 1–45. See as well Charles Taylor's "The Politics of Recognition," in *Multiculturalism: Examining the Politics of Recognition*, ed. and intro. Amy Gutmann (Princeton: Princeton University Press, 1994), 25–73. Norman Bryson refers to "codes of recognition" as "learning to see socially" ("The Gaze in the Expanded Field," *Vision and Visuality*, ed. Hal Foster, Dia Art Foundation Discussions in Culture No. 2 [Seattle, Wash.: Bay Press, 1988], 92).

12. See two highly useful texts on the political and persuasive uses of photography during the civil rights movement: Steven Kasher, *The Civil Rights Movement: A Photographic*

History, 1954–68 (New York; Abbeville Press, 1996) and Danny Lyon, *Memories of the Southern Civil Rights Movement*, Lyndhurst Series on the South (Chapel Hill: Published for the Center for Documentary Studies, Duke University, by University of North Carolina Press, 1992).

13. William Faulkner, *The Sound and the Fury,* The Corrected Text (1929; New York: Vintage International, 1984), 311.

14. Judith L. Sensibar, *The Origins of Faulkner's Art* (Austin: University of Texas Press, 1984), 118, and Cleanth Brooks, *William Faulkner: Toward Yoknapatawpha and Beyond* (New Haven: Yale University Press, 1978), 40–45. See also my "Cracked Urns: Faulkner, Gender, and Art in the South," in *Faulkner and the Artist: Faulkner and Yoknapatawpha, 1993,* ed. Donald M. Kartiganer and Ann J. Abadie (Jackson: University Press of Mississippi, 1996), 51–81; and Candace Waid, "The Signifying Eye: Faulkner's Artists and the Engendering of Art," in *Faulkner and the Artist*, 208–49.

15. See my "Reading Faulkner Reading Cowley Reading Faulkner: Authority and Gender in the Compson Appendix," *Faulkner and Cultural Studies*, Special Double Issue of *Faulkner Journal* 7: 1&2 (Fall 1991/Spring 1992): 27–42.

16. Faulkner, *The Sound and the Fury*, 266.

17. Thadious Davis, *Faulkner's "Negro": Art and the Southern Context* (Baton Rouge: Louisiana State University Press, 1983), 105.

18. Richard Gray, *The Life of William Faulkner: A Critical Biography* (Oxford: Blackwell, 1994), 178.

19. Jay Parini, *One Matchless Time: A Life of William Faulkner* (New York: Harper/Perennial, 2004), 179.

20. For a summary of the changes the manuscript underwent, see Joseph Blotner, *Faulkner: A Biography*, rev. 1-vol. ed. (New York: Random House, 1984), 281–82. For a fuller account, see Regina K. Fadiman, *Faulkner's "Light in August": A Description and Interpretation of the Revisions* (Charlottesville: University Press of Virginia, 1975).

21. Neil R. McMillen and Noel Polk, "Faulkner on Lynching," *Faulkner Journal* 8.1 (1992): 3–14.

22. William Faulkner, "An Introduction for *The Sound and the Fury*," ed. James B. Meriwether, *Southern Review* NS 8 (1972): 709.

23. Blotner, 281–82, 31–33, 301.

24. Jean Toomer, "Portrait in Georgia," in *Cane*, intro. Darwin T. Turner (New York: Liveright, 1975), 27. Permission by Liveright to quote the poem in its entirety is gratefully acknowledged.

25. Grace Elizabeth Hale, *Making Whiteness: The Culture of Segregation in the South, 1890–1940* (New York: Pantheon, 1998), 135–36; Leon Litwack, *Trouble in Mind: Black Southerners in the Age of Jim Crow* (New York: Random-Vintage, 1998), 218–33.

26. Litwack, 230–31; see also Edward L. Ayers, *The Promise of the New South: Life after Reconstruction* (New York: Oxford University Press, 1992), 136–46.

27. Quoted in Litwack, 221.

28. Litwack, iv–v; Robyn Wiegman, *American Anatomies: Theorizing Race and Gender* (Durham: Duke University Press, 1995), 13.

29. Litwack, xiv; Robyn Wiegman, 37–38; Michel Foucault, *Discipline and Punish*, trans. Alan Sheridan (New York: Random House, 1977), 200; Michel Foucault, "The Eye of Power," *Power/Knowledge: Selected Interviews and Other Writings, 1972–1977*, ed. Colin Gordon, trans. Colin Gordon et al. (New York: Pantheon Books, 1980), 146–48.

30. Robert J. Norrell, *The House I Live In: Race in the American Century* (New York: Oxford University Press, 2005), 31.

31. Pauli Murray, *Proud Shoes: The Story of an American Family* (1956; New York: Harper & Row/Perennial Library, 1978), 268.

32. Lillian Smith, *Killers of the Dream* (New York: W. W. Norton, 1949), 89–90.

33. Robin D. G. Kelley, *Race Rebels: Culture, Politics, and the Black Working Class* (New York: Free Press, 1996), 56.

34. Richard Wright, *Black Boy (American Hunger): A Record of Childhood and Youth*, intro. Jerry W. Ward (1945; New York: HarperPerennial, 1993), 231.

35. Willie Harrell, quoted in *Remembering Jim Crow: African Americans Tell about Life in the Segregated South*, ed. William H. Chafe et al. (New York: New Press, in association with Lynhurst Books of the Center for Documentary Studies of Duke University; distributed by W. W. Norton and Company, 2001), 40.

36. William Faulkner, *Light in August*, The Corrected Text (1932; New York: Vintage International, 1985), 32. Subsequent references to this edition are cited parenthetically within the essay.

37. Gilloch, 226.

38. Jacquelyn Dowd Hall, *Revolt against Chivalry: Jessie Daniel Ames and the Women's Campaign against Lynching*, rev. ed. (New York: Columbia University Press, 1993), 155.

39. James Snead, *Figures of Division: William Faulkner's Major Novels* (New York: Methuen, 1986), 86, 88.

40. Shawn Michelle Smith in her book *Photography on the Color Line* notes that Arnold Rampersad sees the Veil as signifying "the dim perception by the races of each other." She herself argues that the Veil "is that which *dims* perception. See her *Photography on the Color Line: W. E. B. Du Bois, Race, and Visual Culture* (Durham: Duke University Press, 2004), 40.

41. W. E. B. Du Bois, *The Souls of Black Folk*, intro. Donald B. Gibson (1903; New York: Penguin Books, 1989), 5.

42. See in general Michael Cooke, *Afro-American Literature in the Twentieth Century: The Achievement of Intimacy* (New Haven: Yale University Press, 1984). See also Priscilla Wald, *Constituting Americans: Cultural Anxiety and Narrative Form* (Durham: Duke University Press, 1995), 186; and especially Shawn Michelle Smith's discussion, 31–40.

43. Du Bois, 4, 5.

44. James Weldon Johnson, *The Autobiography of an Ex-Coloured Man*, intro. Henry Louis Gates Jr. (1912; New York: Random House/Vintage, 1989), 204.

45. Frantz Fanon, *Black Skin, White Masks*, trans. Charles Lam Markmann (1952; New York: Grove Press, 1967), 109. I am indebted here to Smith's highly perceptive examination of double consciousness as that sense of splitting and dissolution emerging from initial confrontations with the color line militating against any kind of idealized sense of self-wholeness associated, from Lacan's perceptive, with misrecognition in the mirror stage (26–42).

46. Smith, 25.

47. Qtd. in Smith, 29, 30; Smith's emphasis.

48. Smith, 30, 31, 32. See also Jacques Lacan, "The Mirror Stage as Formative of the Function of the I," in *Ecrits: A Selection*, trans. Alan Sheridan (New York: Norton, 1977), 1–7.

49. Stuart Hall, "Cultural Identity and Diaspora," in Williams and Chrisman, 400.

50. Qtd. in Smith, 144. See also bell hooks, "The Oppositional Gaze: Black Female Spectators," *The Feminism and Visual Culture Reader*, ed. Amelia Jones (New York: Routledge, 2003), 94–105; Homi Bhabha, *The Location of Culture* (New York: Routledge, 1994), 47.

51. Smith, 144, 76–77. See in general David Levering Lewis and Deborah Willis, *A Small Nation of People: W. E. B. Du Bois and African American Portraits of Progress* (New York: Amistad/HarperCollins, 2003).

52. See in general Sandra Gunning's discussion of Ida B. Wells and other African American writers and activists participating in the anti-lynching crusade: *Race, Rape, and Lynching: The Red Record of American Literature, 1890–1912* (New York: Oxford University Press, 1996), 77–107.

53. See Hale's chapter in *Making Whiteness*, "Deadly Amusements: Spectacle Lynchings and the Contradictions of Segregation as Culture," 199–239; Litwack, 283–95; and the essays by James Allen, Hilton Als, Congressman John Lewis, and Litwack in *Without Sanctuary: Lynching Photography in America* (Santa Fe, N. M.: Twin Palms Publishers, 2005). See also Smith's examination of lynching photographs and white audiences (113–45).

54. Smith's reading of the whiteness constructed by lynching spectacles is particularly persuasive, and so, for that matter, is her speculative coda on the unsettling and dismantling of whiteness resulting from encounters between white American viewers and the

wide-ranging (and often white-appearing) African American subjects in Du Bois's exhibit of photographs at the 1900 Paris Exposition (113–45).

55. James Allen discusses the three cabinet cards of Frank Embree in *Without Sanctuary*.

56. Wiegman, 41.

57. See in particular Patrick O'Donnell, "Faulkner and Postmodernism," *The Cambridge Companion to William Faulkner*, ed. Philip M. Weinstein (New York: Cambridge University Press, 1995), 31–50. See as well Richard C. Moreland, "Faulkner and Modernism," *The Cambridge Companion to William Faulkner*, 17–30; and John N. Duvall and Ann J. Abadie, eds., *Faulkner and Postmodernism: Faulkner and Yoknapatawpha, 1999* (Jackson: University Press of Mississippi, 2002).

Faulkner's Dark House:
The Uncanny Inheritance of Race

MARTIN KREISWIRTH

"A difference in which everything and nothing differs is uncanny."
—*Stanley Cavell*

"The insanity of racism"

—*Toni Morrison*

From its inception, Sigmund Freud's notion of the "uncanny" has been associated with literary representation. Indeed, in the opening of the 1919 essay on this subject Freud somewhat defensively notes that only rarely does the psychoanalyst, the self-conscious man of science, feel "impelled to investigate the subject of aesthetics."[1] Yet, as the essay goes on to demonstrate, when reviewing "the things, persons, impressions, events and situations which are able to arouse in us a feeling of the uncanny" (226), Freud places the literary in a commanding position. He not only presents the major part of his argument by analyzing the psychological and emotional effects produced by texts by E. T. A. Hoffman, Friedrich Schiller, and other creative writers, but also provides extensive aesthetic (and anti-aesthetic) speculations on the reasons why "imaginative productions" are "a more fertile province" for the uncanny than "real life" (249). Given the prominence placed on it by Freud, it is not surprising that the literary uncanny has received a great deal of attention, particularly in terms of making distinctions in genre (horror, the fantastic, the gothic), and in theories of literary form and reception.

More significantly for my present concerns, however, are those views of Freud's essay and concept, initiated by Martin Heidegger, Hélène Cixous, Ludwig Wittgenstein, Samuel Weber, Stanley Cavell, Jacques Derrida, and, most recently, Nicholas Royle, who have turned the uncanny back upon itself, finding the term and the logic by which it is advanced to be itself uncanny. A practical consequence of such critical interrogations has been to remap the performative realm of the uncanny, deepening and extending its explanatory "province" to include areas of experience and affect that go beyond "what arouses dread and horror," the "frightening," or even "what excites fear in general" (Freud, 219). The uncanny has come to be seen, in fact, as a more basic epistemic and phenomenological operation, a certain almost indefinable complex of disturbing sensations (not only trepidation or terror) caused by, at bottom, a hesitation in the production of knowledge.

While the uncanny eventually "leads back to what is known of old and long familiar" (220), there is a productive gap in the circuit: what is finally recognized and understood goes at first unrecognized. The uncanny is the flash of uncertainty that vacillates within this gap. According to Friedrich Schelling, in a formulation Freud adopted, the "'*Unheimlich' is the name for everything that ought to have remained . . . secret and hidden but has come to light*" (224). And, as Freud insists, repression is the psychic engine for "everything that ought to have remained secret." The uncanny, Freud continues, "is in reality nothing new or alien, but something which is familiar and old-established in the mind and which has become alienated from it only through the process of repression" (241). The "*unheimlich* is what was once *heimisch*, familiar; the prefix '*un-*'," Freud notes, "is the token of repression" (245).

The process by which the uncanny gets produced requires the opening of the space between the known and the repressed. It resides, according to David Spurr, in the "disturbing oscillation, sometimes called anamorphosis, between familiarity and strangeness, in particular the tendency of that which is most familiar and most real to turn on us, to become suddenly defamiliarised and derealised—as one's own face will begin to appear that of a stranger if gazed at too long in the mirror."[2] The uncanny is most powerfully felt, as Gordon Bearn argues, in those situations where there is "the *presence of what ought to be absent,*"[3] particularly in cases when basic and long-held assumptions are mistrusted, such as those that uphold the most elemental understanding of our world, our "heim." The *Unheimlich*, then, is that which moves us away from our ground of being, from what is firm and decidable, from our home. It is not merely doubt about ontological basics, about, say whether some person or event exists or doesn't exist, or whether the identity of our own reflection is real or imaginary. It concerns, rather, the essential undecidability of the distinction between the two possibilities themselves. "Constitutive for the uncanny," according to Samuel Weber, "is not the alternative: reality—imaginary, for this alternative presupposes the identity and meaning of whatever it thus questions, and seeks only to fix its ontological status. Uncanny is a certain indecidability that affects and infects representations, motifs, themes and situations, which . . . always mean something other than what they are and in a manner which draws their own being and substance into the vortex of signification."[4]

When viewed in terms such as these, it would not at all be difficult to argue that *Absalom, Absalom!* and *Light in August* are fundamentally uncanny texts, and that the peculiar combination of frustration and uneasiness that frequently accompanies the reading experience is the result of an elaborate discursive machinery designed to generate epistemic gaps, and gaps within gaps, that put representative undecidability on exhibit, and postpone, for as long as possible, the return of the repressed. What ultimately returns in both these novels is what I want to call the *racial uncanny*. In *Absalom, Absalom!* it is buried deep within the monomania of Rosa's narration, obliquely hinted at through the gentlemanly niceties of Mr. Compson's discourse and, only haltingly, but finally, exhibited through Quentin and Shreve's impossible imaginative recreation; in *Light in August*, it underlies the inscrutability of Christmas's social representation and animates his tortured inner quest for self-identity.

Charles Bon is at the center of the racial uncanny in *Absalom, Absalom!* Yet, like other figures in Faulkner's texts, Bon remains an empty center—projected as much by what he is not as by what he is. Or, more accurately, Bon hovers between the two: awaiting the moment where the secret of what has been both seen and unseen is revealed. In short, Bon's character could be said to be written under the sign of the uncanny. Almost all descriptions of him remain poised between the palpable and impalpable, the visible and the invisible, the present and the absent, particularly in those situations in which he is associated with scenes of female desire or family membership—affiliation or filiation. Rosa, for example, in her depiction of how she became *"polymath love's androgynous advocate,"* says of Bon: *"I never saw him. I never even saw him dead. . . . I had never even heard his voice. . . . [E]ven before I saw the photograph I could have recognized, nay, described, the very face. But I never saw it. I do not even know of my own knowledge that Ellen ever saw it, that Judith ever loved it, that Henry slew it: so who will dispute me when I say, Why did I not invent, create it?"*[5] Mr. Compson's baffled description of the courtship between Bon and Judith that finally leads to the initially incomprehensible murder is presented in similar terms: "You can not even imagine [Bon] and Judith alone together. Try to do it and the nearest you can come is a projection of them while the two actual people were doubtless separate and elsewhere—two shades pacing, serene and untroubled by flesh, in a summer garden—the same two serene phantoms who seem to watch, hover, impartial attentive and quiet, above and behind the inexplicable thunderhead of interdictions and defiances and repudiations" (77). Bon, according to Mr. Compson, is, at bottom, an "impenetrable and shadowy character . . . a myth, a phantom . . . some effluvium of Sutpen blood and character, as though as a man he did not exist at all" (82).

Whatever Mr. Compson's and Rosa's descriptions do, they do not, as Mr. Compson is fond of saying, "explain . . . something is missing" (80). With Bon, one's perceptual apparatuses are seemingly confounded, and this particular semantic disfunction becomes representative of a larger and more general cognitive dissonance: *There are some things which happen to us,*" Rosa notes, *"which the intelligence and the senses refuse just as the stomach sometimes refuses what the palate has accepted but which digestion cannot compass—occurrences which stop us dead as though by some impalpable intervention, like a sheet of glass through which we watch all subsequent events transpire as though in a soundless vacuum, and fade, vanish; are gone*" (122). Attempting to understand Bon, and the "horrible and bloody mischanching of human affairs" (80) that transpires from his relationships with the (other) Sutpens effectively, as Rosa puts it, *stops us dead.*" What we learn through and along with her and Mr. Compson does not provide substance, actuality, or presence, but rather appearance, distance, and mediation, specifically setting into action those mechanisms for the hesitation in knowledge that underwrite the uncanny. Bon is both known and unknown, cognitively tasted but unconsumed, seemingly palatable yet unable to be digested into the body of knowledge. The unperceived, imagined face of Bon, although desired, according to Rosa, is a *"pictured face"* without *"a skull behind it"* (118). There is something in Bon that powerfully attracts, yet the substantive basis of that attraction remains unsettled, disturbing, and perhaps even pathological.

Once Shreve and Quentin take over the narration, however, the other pole of the *heimisch/unheimlich* pendulum swings to the fore and, initially, the shadowy Bon begins to become slightly more distinct, somewhat more known, opening up more possibilities for the familiar and unfamiliar to interact. In an uncanny narrative manoeuver, the tellers, Quentin and Shreve, directly assume the parts of the characters in the tale, and they, and the reader, are reminded again and again that the subject positions of the speakers are doubled and redoubled with those of the figures presented. Here is a typical scene:

> Shreve stood beside the table, facing Quentin again . . . while both their breathing vaporized faintly in the cold room where there was now not two of them but four, the two who breathed not individuals now yet something both more and less than twins. . . . Not two of them in a New England college sitting-room but one in a Mississippi library sixty years ago . . . as free now of flesh as the father who decreed and forbade, the son who denied and repudiated, the lover who acquiesced, the beloved who was not bereaved . . . not two of them there and then either but four of them riding the two horses. (235–37)

It is not only this disconcerting doubling of the characters, where the identities of the living and dead, real and imaginary, inexplicably merge, that adds to the uncanny effects here—incidentally, one of the primary phenomenon eliciting the uncanny, according to Freud, is the doppel-ganger, or double. It is also the consequences of Bon's outlines being filled in by Quentin and Shreve's interactive narrative reconstructions. Through their discussions, hypotheses, reportings, and speculations, we learn, first, that Bon is Judith and Henry's elder brother: there has been a previously unperceived and, more importantly, unperceivable familial linkage—an invisible blood connection: he is the son of Sutpen and a previous wife. Consequently, Bon's heretofore accepted and acceptable relationships with Sutpen's second family—Judith and Henry (and indeed Sutpen, Clytie, and the rest)—must undergo reevaluation. What must be con-fronted, of course, is that Bon has come home (*heim*)—both figuratively and literally. The relationship that had been thought to be permissibly Other turns out to be not so Other as was previously thought. The newly discovered filiation that has increased the level of Bon's intimacy with the Sutpens has also made that intimacy socially impermissible, taboo. The familiar has become far too familiar, raising the age-old specter of incest—the most familiar of family injunctions, the Biblical injunction: "Do not have sexual relations with your sister, either your father's daugh-ter or your mother's daughter, whether she was born in the same home or elsewhere" (Leviticus 18:9). With the knowledge of Bon's hereditary link, the repressed has uncannily returned home, and what was "*heimisch*," as Freud states, has become, at one and the same time, "*unheimlich*."

Yet, this information, of course, marks only one stage in the complex process of narrative disclosure that comprises *Absalom, Absalom!* More about Bon is to be revealed. Quentin and Shreve's reconstructive con-versational activity reaches a climax when the dual telling of the Sutpen's familial trauma becomes a singular, dramatic showing and the crucial rev-elatory scene from the past uncannily obtrudes upon the present, dem-onstrating, as Freud would put it, that what is "most intimately known" can contain within it something "alien and threatening." Here is how this episode is introduced: Now "neither of them was there. They were both in Carolina and the time was forty-six years ago, and it was not even four now but compounded still further, since now both of them were Henry Sutpen and both of them were Bon, compounded each of both yet either neither, smelling the very smoke which had blown and faded away forty-six years ago" (280). As this present-tense, italicized scene unfolds and we learn about Bon's purported genealogical "flaw," formerly hidden racial energies become exposed, affecting both the tellers and the tale.

Even though it has been insisted that both Quentin and Shreve stand in for and, in fact, *become* both Henry and Bon for the purposes of textual regeneration, the imaginatively reconstituted scene is actually centered on

Henry; indeed, unlike the other participating characters, Henry appears throughout the whole italicized present-tense episode, first in conversation with his father, then with Bon, and, with the exception of two sentences where the reader views Henry from Bon's perspective, the entire six-page scene is focalized through Henry: we get his perceptions, thoughts, memories, and language. This is, in many ways, the novel's climactic scene: here Henry (as well as Quentin and Shreve, and, indeed the reader) learns that Bon is not only prohibited from becoming a mate for Judith because he is revealed to be too close for comfort (hers and Henry's half-brother), but rather because he is, as it were, beyond the pale, taboo, truly an "other," a racial other, son of a purportedly part African-descended mother.[6] In short, by the convoluted logic of racial blood fantasies, he is, in terms of the larger culture's mores, not too similar, but, much too different, removed from the sphere of accepted social relations. As Bon himself puts it to Henry, he may be his brother, but he is also, and for Henry, obviously, more importantly, "the nigger that's going to sleep with your sister" (286). In short, Bon has been "passing," and his newly discovered racial makeup trumps both the injunction of incest and the attachment of brotherhood.

Now the former privileges of Bon's gender and class are coupled with and hopelessly confounded by race. As his previously indeterminate racial identification becomes (provisionally) stabilized by Sutpen's revelation, Bon comes to emblemize the fantasized horrors of miscegenation; indeed, he is an overdetermined and highly charged example, both its unwitting product and potential replicator. Given his ultimately uncertain heritage, Bon may be empirically a non- or transracial figure, with no authoritative evidence available to truly decide. Yet to assume subjectivity and social identity in the South of the mid-nineteenth (and early twentieth) century he must of necessity be racially marked. There is no possibility of him remaining between races; he must be "fixed" as either black or white. It is Faulkner's strategy in *Absalom, Absalom!* to have Bon's racial interpellation be the responsibility of two early twentieth-century young white men, Quentin and Shreve, who construct the social imaginary that must inevitably "color" him.

Up until Sutpen's accusatory revelation, Quentin and Shreve (another Other, certainly, from a Southern point of view) have had little difficulty identifying with and narratively working through both "sons'" generalized incest fantasy; if anything, they have spent more narrative time and space imaginatively recreating and identifying with Bon and his past than Henry and his. But things change drastically when the repressed heredity link has come home—has become *heimisch*. Thomas Sutpen's climactic utterance performs what almost amounts to an ontological transformation, but certainly, for the world of Yoknapatawpha, an epistemological and social one: "*His mother's father told me that her mother had been a Spanish woman. I believed him; it was not until after he was born that I found out that his mother was part negro*" (283). This revelation, remember, occurs in the present-tense italicized section of chapter 8, where Shreve and Quentin's psyche are doubled and redoubled with those of Bon and Henry and Sutpen, where the past of the Civil War obtrudes upon the present of the twentieth-century dormitory room in Harvard, and where the historical and demonstrable coalesce with fiction and desire. In short, we have in textual terms an entirely uncorroborated allegation, communicated through a hypothetical conversation, mediated by means of a conjectural multiple narration. Regardless of plausibility or textual authority, once Bon is *said to be* racially part African American, his social categorization for Quentin and Shreve entirely changes; as such, although nothing visible or outward has changed, he is now both the same as he was before, but also wholly different. In terms of the historical South's understanding of sex, blood, and family, Bon has become completely transformed, and, according to the white world of the Sutpens (and of Quentin and Shreve), irrevocably Other. And, as such, he simply disappears from Quentin and Shreve's domestic romantic drama, no longer able to fulfill the familial role of son or brother (or, indeed, lover). Not the lover, son, or brother, he is starkly and blatantly *not*, absent, one who cannot even act, but rather only passively reacts, leaving Sutpen and Henry (and/or Quentin and Shreve) to oversee (in every sense) his life (and death).

Before Sutpen's statement about Bon's mother's purported ancestry racially recategorized him, as it were, he was central to Quentin and Shreve's narration; he was their protagonist and the figure with whom they most closely identified. However, even though nothing about Bon has changed—there are no observable changes in Bon's pigmentation, features, or any other purported racial markers—the moment he becomes verbally identified by his now racialized past, the moment he is labeled as phenotypically dark and a visible "Other," he (paradoxically) becomes socially and narratively imperceptible, both textually and socially, *invisible* (in the sense that Ralph Ellison uses the term). Re-presented as a black man, as it were, he loses autonomy and materiality and functions, as Quentin puts it in *The Sound and the Fury*, "as a form of behavior; a sort of obverse reflection of the white people he lives among."[7] While always portrayed through the voices of others, those voices now specifically, and even stereotypically, depict Bon through the "double-consciousness" of racial difference, whereby, as W. E. Du Bois notes, black identity is never self-generated but always reflected from a dominant Other.[8]

According to the way Quentin and Shreve reimagine him, Bon's former sexual, filial, romantic, and patrimonial identity entirely disappear, and he is left only to perform the role of subaltern and scapegoat, to sacrifice himself *to* and *for* the white Sutpens. This sacrifice is performed literarily—through Henry's agency in fratricide—and figuratively—through the replacement of Judith's picture with that of the "octoroon mistress" in his locket. This exchange of portraits, as Quentin and Shreve speculate, is designed to dramatize Bon's true worthlessness to Judith: "'*I was no good; do not grieve for me*'" (287). His formerly professed love, according to Quentin and Shreve, was either a sham or an unrealizable goal, because of racial division, a division seemingly supported by Bon himself. Once imagined black, as it were, Bon becomes for Quentin and Shreve imaginable only to perform what for Southern whites (and indeed northern Canadians) is a sanctioned, ideologically acceptable sacrificial role, one against which they, as Toni Morrison would put it in *Playing in the Dark*, can posit possibilities for their own identities.[9] In Judith Butler's terms, Quentin and Shreve reinscribe Bon's subjectivity as "citing" the social authority of the dominant culture's racial supremacist norms.[10] The traditional, and racially endorsed, notions of familial honor, sexual purity, gyneolatry, and even white superiority and homogeneity are thus (paradoxically) reflected from the posited blackness or blankness of Bon's body.

What makes this portrayal of Bon's uncanny transformation so effective, providing one of the most powerful examples in Faulkner's canon of his unflinching gaze upon race, is the concomitant strategy of familiarity and otherness through which it is displayed. In the depiction of Bon, racial demarcation is offered through that which is both the same and different, or, more accurately, through that which distinctions between sameness and difference cannot be perceived or known, but only abstractly or imaginatively posited. Although Bon is thought to be white and then black, neither racial identity can be posited definitively. Yet, because of the dual injunction that Bon must both be racially signified at the same time as he can have no firm knowledge of any means of making that signification possible (beyond a kind of racial hysteria by the Sutpens and by Quentin and Shreve), his self-identity can only be described as uncanny. The uncanny, Daniel Chapelle notes, involves "a pivotal experience that has two coexisting aspects or faces, a familiar one and an unfamiliar one."[11] This is how the Sutpens come to experience Bon (another Sutpen, of course) and the concomitant fear and attraction (or fear because of attraction) that this experience induces. Murdering the familiar (and familial) in the name of the unfamiliar, in some sense, sets the world of *Absalom, Absalom!* temporarily right again, oddly insisting that the invisible was visible all along.

Perhaps even more importantly, through Faulkner's portrayal of Bon one can see that race itself is being thought to be uncanny. As Bon's depiction teaches us, in the world of *Absalom, Absalom!* and, indeed, in the extra-textual domain that the novel represents, race must exist as a binary opposition—black or white; for social categorization, there exists nothing in between. Yet this determination is based not on any clear bipartite division of phenotypically empirical qualities or characteristics, but on a continuum, ranging from the visible to the invisible, from the observable to the imaginary. And, as Bon's case clearly shows, the categorizing features within the continuum that produce the crucial racial determination may be decided by imperceptible biological transmission—that is, by blood inheritance. In this world, hereditary dissemination of characteristics, even if indiscernible, has the same status as observable traits for racial demarcation. It is this logic that underlies the so-called one-drop rule, the notorious "Virginia Act to Preserve Racial Integrity" of 1924, the infamous Rhinelander case, and various antimiscegenation laws and other legal decisions on racial distinction and civil rights.[12] (It is worth noting that the "Negro" of the famous *Plessy vs. Ferguson* Supreme Court case of 1896 that upheld the doctrine of "separate but equal" was, according to the decision, "seven-eights white" and could visually "pass" as white.)[13] This is also the same logic that posits race as uncanny—"the presence of what ought to be absent," the return of the repressed Other in the familiar.

Race is fundamentally a classification of difference, and since Charles Bon exhibits no discernable difference, in order to comply with the ideological underpinning of a racially constructed social world, particularly the Jim Crow world of Quentin and Shreve, his difference has to be posited not experienced.[14] The effect is uncanny—"the world seems not be the place we had taken it to be. We no longer 'know our way about' " (36). Toni Morrison noted that "Faulkner in *Absalom, Absalom!* spends the entire book tracing race, and you can't find it. No one can see it. . . . As a reader you have been forced to hunt for a drop of black blood that means everything and nothing."[15] The uncanny, according to Stanley Cavell, involves a "difference so perfect that there is no way or feature in which the difference consists."[16] This is the particular quality of the racialized uncanny, in some sense, perhaps the most perfect form of the uncanny, since, as Cavell puts it, it is, above all, "a difference in which everything and nothing differs" (166).

Thus, the withheld and then staggered revelations of Bon's specific "difference" that truly isn't a difference in *Absalom, Absalom!* goes beyond characterization and narrative, flouting both basic rationality and secure human identity. Once the uncanny "creeps into the tranquillity of reason itself," Julia Kristeva notes, "we know that we are foreigners to ourselves, and it is with the help of that sole support that we can attempt to live with others."[17] *Absalom, Absalom!*, as Faulkner said in an interview, is "a manifestation of a general racial system in the South which was condensed and concentrated . . . a constant general condition in the South."[18] That this system or condition should be articulated through the uncanny, through a mode of thinking and feeling that presents us as foreigners to ourselves, says something significant about the rational instability of that system or condition but also about their ideological purchase and community support.

This recognition that racial categorization functions by means of an uncanny logic of public and personal self-division runs deep within the social imaginary of Yoknapatawpha. *Light in August,* for example, some-times viewed as a companion piece to *Absalom, Absalom!,* is a text that fits very comfortably under the general rubric of "foreigners to ourselves." As in *Absalom, Absalom!,* the fundamental undecidability of the uncanny is writ large in *Light in August,* infecting and affecting "representations, motifs, themes and situations, which . . . always mean something other than what they are" (Weber, 1132). "The uncanny," Nicholas Royle reminds us,

> involves feelings of uncertainty, in particular regarding the reality of who one is and what is being experienced. Suddenly one's sense of oneself [or of another] seems strangely questionable. The uncanny is a crisis of the proper: it entails a critical disturbance of what is proper . . . a disturbance of the very idea of personal or private property including the properness of proper names. . . . It is a crisis of the natural, touching upon everything that one might have thought was "part of nature": one's own nature, human nature, the nature of reality and the world. But the uncanny is not simply an experience of strangeness or aliena-tion. More specifically, it is a peculiar commingling of the familiar and unfamil-iar. It can take the form of something familiar unexpectedly arising in a strange and unfamiliar context. It can consist in a sense of homeliness uprooted, the revelation of something unhomely at the heart of hearth and home.[19]

Light in August is replete with examples of the "peculiar commingling of the familiar and unfamiliar" and the "crisis of the natural and the proper." Although the novel is obsessed with issues of perception and identification, as James Snead notes, it ends up stressing misperception and misrecognition.[20] For example, the initial confusion (and anticipated fusion) of Lucas Burch and Byron Bunch that propels Lena towards Jefferson in her quest for self-identity and her child's father openly inter-rogates the purportedly "natural" connection between proper name and selfhood. Not only are Burch and Bunch linguistically confounded, but Lena, because of the social mores of her quite visible "condition," is pub-licly called "Miz Burch," despite her private revelation to Mrs. Armstid. Moreover, the expectations raised by Lena's search for Burch in chapter 1, opens up possibilities that the "unnamed" stranger the reader confronts in chapter 2, may indeed be the one she is looking for. However, the conspicuously unidentified man we meet in the beginning of the second chapter is, of course, not Burch, nor even Brown (as we later learn Burch has rechristened himself), but Christmas. He uncannily appears out of nowhere, abrupt and unannounced:

> Byron Bunch knows this: . . . the group of men at work in the planer shed looked up, and saw the stranger standing there, watching them. They did not know how long he had been there. He looked like a tramp, yet not like a tramp either. His shoes were dusty and his trousers were soiled too. But they were of decent serge, sharply creased, and his shirt was soiled but it was a white shirt, and he wore a tie and a stiffbrim straw hat that was quite new. . . . He did not look like a professional hobo in his professional rags, but there was something definitely rootless about him, as though no town nor city was his, no street, no walls, no square of earth his home.[21]

The introduction of Christmas is doubly mediated rather than narratively authoritative, filtered through Bunch's perception of the perspectives of the local mill workers. The men attempt to code Christmas, to interpellate him within the social matrix of Yoknapatawpha. Yet, as many critics have noted, Christmas defies their categorizations. He simply does not signify, at least not according to any local classificatory system. His economic class and social position are impossible to pin down: he appears shiftless, but, then again, not quite. His clothes are those of a city worker, not a country laborer. They are, however, untidy, but of a quality and age that suggests a certain status; his tie and hat connote respectability, yet he appears itinerant. At first glance, he exhibits features that would connect him with the community, but he remains ineluctably adrift. Above all, he participates in the uncanny, an Other, who is not entirely an outsider, but both an insider and outsider at the same time. Right from his introduction, he is described in terms of "a peculiar commingling of the familiar and unfamiliar . . . homeliness uprooted . . . something unhomely at the heart of hearth and home": "no town nor city was his, no street, no walls, no square of earth his home"; he is both figuratively and literally "*unheimlich.*"

What underlies and determines his uncannily indeterminate social signification is obliquely hinted at a page or so later, where the reader first encounters his name and learns categorically that he is not Lucas Burch, the object of Lena's quest, but a newcomer called Christmas. The conversation between the foreman and the mill workers that should aid in solidifying Joe's identity, at least linguistically, actually works antithetically, further confounding his social determination:

> "His name is what?" one [of the workers] said.
> "Christmas."
> "Is he a foreigner?"

"Did you ever hear of a white man named Christmas?" the foreman said.
"I never heard of nobody a-tall named it," the other said. (33)

A local worker initially sees the name as connoting something alien, outside of the community (consistent with the opening description). The foreman, however, changes the modality of otherness by backhandedly introducing the issue of race, while the next worker's response pushes a possible construal even further from the comfortable and known. Again, Christmas does not signify; according to their categories of verbal identification, he does not fit within the surrounding social world; he has lost the "natural" connection between body and nomination. Yet, Byron's knowing, retrospective narrative point of view provides a glimpse of the specific disjunction that causes Christmas's uncanny aura: "that was the first time Byron remembered that he had ever thought how a man's name, which is supposed to be just the sound for who he is, can be somehow an augur of what he will do, if other men can only read the meaning in time. It seemed to him that none of them had looked especially at the stranger until they heard his name. But as soon as they heard it, it was as though there was something in the sound of it that was trying to tell them what to expect. . . . Only none of them had sense enough to recognize it. They just thought he was a foreigner" (33). Not a foreigner, then, his otherness is both more at home, yet, at the same time, more distant. "Did you ever hear of a white man named Christmas?" resonates with other indirect descriptors that obliquely or negatively introduce racial denomination. To the mill workers attempting to affix a meaning on Christmas, he appears inscrutable and unsettled: "None of them knew then where Christmas lived and what he was actually doing behind the veil, the screen of his negro's job at the mill" (36); they "did not know that Christmas was actually living in a tumble down negro cabin on Miss Burden's place, and that he had been living in it for more than two years" (36). According to the community, Christmas has a nonwhite name, lives in a Negro cabin, and has a Negro job; all the outward signs are available for an inferred racial identification as black, yet, like Bon, his white skin (purportedly the sovereign marker) keeps him from being signified as such, at least until he crosses the boundaries of sex and desire and can be accused of committing a crime against white purity.

Christmas's real crime, like Bon's, involves publicly exposing the racial uncanny, blatantly housing an impossible difference within the body of the same. In both cases it takes the narrative form of transgressing the sexual taboo of amalgamation, threatening the gene pool, the supreme bastion of white hegemony. Just as Bon is not identified as black until the possibility of miscegenation arises, Christmas is not finally denominated as "nigger" until Brown uses him to shift the blame away from himself, and accuses Christmas of the murder of and cohabitation with Joanna Burden. Once Brown intimates to the sheriff that Christmas is black, "he knew he had them. . . . The folks in this town is so smart. Fooled for three years. Calling him foreigner for three years, when soon as I watched him three days I knew he wasn't no more a foreigner than I am. . . . I'm talking about Christmas . . . the man that killed that white woman after he had done lived with her in plain sight of this whole town. . . . He's got nigger blood in him" (98).

As important as Faulkner's presentation of Christmas's own tortured and ultimately futile quest for definitive racial subjectivity is—his hopeless attempt to try to come to terms with the impossibility of existing as he must in the no-man's-land in-between races—it is the performative drama of social and cultural interpellation that is imbued with all the disturbing and defining power of the uncanny. For himself, for Yoknapatawpha, and, indeed, for America, Christmas cannot truly exist simultaneously in both races (fundamental binary racial logic forbids it); neither, of course, can he have no race. By placing Christmas in this classic double bind, *Light in August*, like *Absalom, Absalom!*, mobilizes the disturbing energies of the racial uncanny, demonstrating both the impossibility of race as a subjective and social category and the impossibility of it not functioning in this way.

Exhibiting no observable racial markers, it is the imperceptibility of Christmas's and Bon's purported inheritance, their presumed invisible "black blood," that provokes the true fear and horror of the racial uncanny. In these texts, not being able to locate the outsider that is central to defining the insider, the threat to racial identification becomes exceedingly acute, and must be suppressed. The locus of necessary racial identification—the absolute determination of the racial binary—occurs at the point of sexual contact, the site of possible inheritance and amalgamation. Although Joanna Burden was murdered, the seemingly more important malefaction committed against her and white society is miscegenation, a racial crime; this is substantiated by the punishment that is used to mete the crime, Christmas's castration. Looking at her dead body, the white townspeople fall into a kind of communal racial hysteria: they "believed aloud that it was an anonymous negro crime committed not by a negro but by Negro and who knew, believed, and hoped that she had been ravished too: at least once before her throat was cut and at least once afterward" (288). What is doubly uncanny in the cases of Bon and Christmas is that the abstractly determined Negro who would commit the crime of producing "impure" racial inheritance is himself identified entirely by his own presumptive racial inheritance, resulting from the same purported "crime" (a racially invisible product of miscegenation).

In this way, their narratives give emphatic credence to the society's deeply repressed fear that the racial crime itself can never be absolutely determined or contained because racial distinction is fundamentally baseless and nonexistent. It is thus the impossibility of race itself that is the insuperable horror that Bon and Christmas display.

Potential mulattos, possible passers, murdered or lynched for inescapably challenging white homogeneity and supremacy, Faulkner's Bon and Christmas work at the edgy junction of race and heredity, an impossible site that cannot but deeply perturb the stability of America's hearth and home. In manuscript, both *Absalom, Absalom!* and *Light in August* were entitled "Dark House," an extraordinarily appropriate emblem of the racial uncanny. But, of course, in both cases, the title was discarded, repressed, and, interestingly, never used for any other text. What remains, however, undergirding all of Yoknapatawpha and its encompassing domains, never to be forgot (much like Christmas's apotheosis), is the image's estranged familiarity that, despite reason, law, and society, projects darkness in every house.

NOTES

1. Sigmund Freud, "The 'Uncanny,'" in *The Standard Edition of the Complete Psychological Works of Sigmund Freud*, ed. and trans. James Strachey, vol. 17 (London: The Hogarth Press, 1955), 219.

2. David Spurr, "Spectres of Modernity: Notes on the Uncanny in Modern Literature," *Rivista di Letterature moderne e comparate* 55.1 (2002): 68.

3. Gordon C. F. Bearn, "Wittgenstein and the Uncanny," *Soundings: An Interdisciplinary Journal* 76.1 (1993): 33.

4. Samuel Weber, "The Sideshow, Or: Remarks on a Canny Moment," *Modern Language Notes* 88.5 (1973): 1132.

5. William Faulkner, *Absalom, Absalom!* (1936; New York: Vintage International, 1990), 117–18.

6. See J. Hillis Miller, "The Two Relativisms: Point of View and Indeterminacy in the Novel *Absalom, Absalom!*," *Relativism in the Arts* 10 (1983): 160–62.

7. William Faulkner, *The Sound and the Fury* (1929; New York: Vintage International, 1984), 86.

8. W. E. B. DuBois, *The Souls of Black Folk* (New York: Modern Library, 1996).

9. Toni Morrison, *Playing in the Dark: Whiteness and the Literary Imagination* (Cambridge: Harvard University Press, 1992).

10. Judith Butler, *Bodies that Matter: On the Discursive Limits of "Sex"* (New York: Routledge, 1993); also see Mary Joanne Dondlinger, "Getting around the Body: The Matter of Race and Gender in Faulkner's *Light in August*," in *Faulkner and the Natural World: Faulkner and Yoknapatawpha, 1996*, ed. Donald M. Kartiganer and Ann J. Abadie (Jackson: University Press of Mississippi, 1999), 104.

11. Daniel Chapelle, *Nietzsche and Psychoanalysis* (Albany: State University of New York Press, 1993), 191.

12. See Werner Sollors, *Interracialism: Black-White Intermarriage in American History, Literature, and Law* (Oxford: Oxford University Press, 2000), 546.

13. Eric Sundquist, *Faulkner: The House Divided* (Baltimore: Johns Hopkins University Press, 1983), 68–69.

14. See Thadious Davis, "The Signifying Abstraction: Reading 'the Negro' in *Absalom, Absalom!*," in *William Faulkner's "Absalom, Absalom!*," ed. Fred Hobson (New York: Oxford University Press, 2003), 97–99.

15. Quoted in Elissa Schappell, "Toni Morrison: The Art of Fiction," *The Paris Review* 35.128 (1993): 101.

16. Stanley Cavell, *In Quest of the Ordinary: Lines of Skepticism and Romanticism* (Chicago: University of Chicago Press, 1988), 166.

17. Julia Kristeva, *Strangers to Ourselves*, trans. Leon S. Roudiez (New York: Columbia University Press, 1991), 170.

18. William Faulkner, *Faulkner in the University: Class Conferences at the University of Virginia, 1957–1958* (Charlottesville: University Press of Virginia, 1977), 94.

19. Nicholas Royle, *The Uncanny: An Introduction* (New York: Manchester University Press, 2002), 1.

20. James A. Snead, *Figures of Division: William Faulkner's Major Novels* (New York: Methuen, 1986), see, e.g., 86.

21. William Faulkner, *Light in August* (1932; New York: Vintage Books, 1985), 31.

A Mammy Callie Legacy

LAEL GOLD

"[T]he Bible is the great conjure book in the world."
—Zora Neale Hurston, "Paraphernalia of Conjure"

Faulkner's turn of phrase in a letter about his Mammy written just two weeks after her death ("She transferred to my father's family the wealth of a devotion and loyalty whose match I have never seen.")[1] suggests a value system similar to African cultures that measure wealth not only in material goods but in number and depth of human contacts as well. Along with the emotional sustenance described in this missive are other legacies passed on to Faulkner from his caretaker Caroline Barr and other blacks who populated his Mississippi childhood. What was African American in this white author's upbringing and surroundings indelibly marked and markedly enriched his writing as well as his life. For instance, the most fertile intertextual strand in Faulkner's fiction is also a chief part of this African inheritance; as we shall see, the persistence and perspicacity of Faulkner's allusions to the Hebrew Bible grew out of his relationship to the unlettered and unpropertied former slave whom he called Mammy Callie.

Unbuckling the Bible Belt

That Faulkner's fiction, set primarily in Yoknapatawpha County, alludes heavily to the Bible is hardly surprising. It is, after all, the only intertext knowledge of which Faulkner shared with nearly all of his fictional county's fictional inhabitants, and his representation of this book in their minds, living rooms, and churches is merely a matter of realist constraint. With perhaps the sole exceptions of the mentally deficient Benjy Compson and Jim Bond, even the most marginal and least literate of his characters are familiar, often intimately so, with the divinely inflected exploits recounted in the writings of the ancient Hebrews and earliest Christians. What's more, no other text played as crucial a role in the social climate and historical legacies Faulkner depicts. Historical documents as disparate as the constitution of the Confederate States of America and abolitionist tracts all had recourse to Scriptural justification of their opposing stances. The Bible, in other words, was not a book Faulkner first encountered at the Oxford

Public Library, nor one enthusiastically recommended by his friend and intellectual mentor Phil Stone; as it was for Twain, Melville, and so many other American authors, the Bible was the very stuff of Faulkner's world.

Fictional Yoknapatawpha, in other words, is located squarely within the region H. L. Mencken snidely dubbed the "Bible belt." Mencken's term, which has long since entered the American lexicon, was meant to deride the book's literalist readers—fundamentalists, mostly white Protestants— who held the Bible to be the inerrant word of God. A very different thinker than Mencken, Russian literary critic Mikhail Bakhtin, also bristled at the idea of a final and inerrant word. In Bakhtin's argot, the Bible is "dialogi- cal," a text, that is, that by objectifying discourse relativizes its own utter- ance.[2] However, this highly dialogical text, in cultural contexts like the one of Faulkner's upbringing, is often misread as the quintessence of the "monological," conscripted, in other words, into "the service of the estab- lished, dogmatic worldviews of . . . religious doctrines," and "transformed into a simple form for expounding already found, ready-made irrefutable truth."[3] When not open to debate, the Bible can hardly richly express the sort of dynamic responsiveness celebrated by Bakhtin, for whom "[e]very word is directed toward an answer and cannot escape the profound influ- ence of the answering word that it anticipates."[4]

However commonplace, there is a perverse quality to a monological treatment of the Bible, a text that presents exactly the sort of interrela- tion of utterances variously described by Bakhtin in terms of "polyphony," "heteroglossia," and "carnival."[5] Unable to perceive a nuanced middle ground, Mencken's fundamentalists read the Bible in literalist black and white. Faulkner's experience of Scripture, on the other hand, was marked, not by the high contrast of religious absolutism, but by the moral inde- terminacy of another black and white—the culturally constructed racial binaries of his time and place.

Faulkner's depiction of the Bible in his fiction is indeed heavily linked to race. Careful attention to his representation of this book, as a material object and in the consciousness of his European American and African American characters, can inform reading of its wider creative incorpora- tion into his fiction.[6] In *Playing in the Dark: Whiteness and the Literary Imagination*, Faulkner's literary descendant, Toni Morrison, invites explo- ration of the way "black people ignite critical moments of change or dis- covery or emphasis in literature not written by them." She also encourages readers of American literature to consider the effects of what she terms its "Africanist" presences. [7] The chiaroscuro pattern that emerges when we examine the Bible's physical and psychical presence in Faulkner's charac- ters' lives yields a way of reading the broader relation between his fiction and the Bible by providing clues to the dynamic force of these allusions and to the impulse behind them. What's more, attention to this racialized pattern will move us in the direction indicated by Morrison.

Two Bibles

Absalom, Absalom!, If I Forget Thee, Jerusalem (née *The Wild Palms*), and *Go Down, Moses* all bear titles that allude to the Hebrew Bible via snippets of direct address from II Samuel, Psalms, and Exodus, respectively. Faulkner slightly but significantly alters the King James Version's renderings of all three eponymous phrases. In the case of *Go Down, Moses*, there is little mystery but much meaning in the change. For the title alludes to the Bible by way of a slave song of the same name. In this instance, then, Faulkner only follows the lead of the anonymous composer of this spiritual, a song of enormous power that roused slaves to resist captivity and flee their bonds.

It is fitting that the novel's central allusion to the Bible be mediated by this oral and indeed musical text of African American origin. This peculiarity introduces, at the outset, a racial doubleness that will inform our discussion. To some degree, two Bibles, one white and one black, are represented and cited throughout *Go Down, Moses* and in the earlier *The Sound and the Fury* as well.

Faulkner, like most Americans, experienced the Bible, an ancient Near Eastern text, via a European linguistic, literary, and liturgical filter. This Europeanized Bible was in turn Africanized by African slaves and their North American descendants who incorporated the West's central sacred text into indigenous magical and spiritual ritual.[8] These complications of biblical reception and transmission left their marks on Faulkner's fiction. The duality of Faulkner's African and European spiritual and cultural heritage is recapitulated in the twofold nature of his biblical allusions in *Go Down, Moses*. "[T]he Book" over which Ike McCaslin and Cass Edmonds debate differs distinctly from the Bible to which Rider's Aunt and Mollie Beauchamp refer. Notably, both of these latter maternal, African American characters, like Dilsey in *The Sound and the Fury*, share as their prototype Faulkner's other mother, his beloved Mammy Callie.[9]

In *The Book of God*, Gabriel Josipovici notes the disjunction between our childhood experience as auditors of Bible stories and our adult experience as readers of those same tales.[10] A delightful trace of this first encounter with biblical lore persists in the first section of *Absalom, Absalom!*: "the *Be Sutpen's Hundred* like the oldentime *Be Light*."[11] The charming understatement "the oldentime" captures the fairy-tale quality the Bible first held for Faulkner and underscores the role of Mammy Callie in the transmission of these tales that Faulkner probably heard intermingled with her "fund of stories about old times before the war, and the days afterward too, when the riders of the Ku Klux Klan appeared claiming they were dead Confederates momentarily escaping the flames of hell to ride the night."[12] Indeed, orality is the distinguishing and fundamental aspect of the black or African American Bible represented in Faulkner's fiction. What's more, time and again the novels demonstrate a keen understanding that "[f]or such an oral awareness, to explain is not to present a set of finished reasons, but to tell a story."[13]

Just as orality distinguishes the black Bible represented in Faulkner's fiction, writing distinguishes its white counterpart. Not surprisingly, this white Bible veers away from the simple storytelling that characterizes the black Bible into less illuminating theological entanglements. For instance, Ike McCaslin and Cass Edmonds encounter the Bible in section four of "The Bear" in a highly logocentric manner. In this section, Ike may give lip service to "the heart's truth," but he does so in an interaction that takes the form of reasoned argument.[14] Just as the prose of this section is fragmented and disjointed, so these characters' relation to the Bible is tortured and full of contradiction. As Cass protests, "you have taken to proving your points and disproving mine by the same text" (GDM 250). The cousins' debate reminds readers that the Bible was used to oppress and enslave Africans and their American descendants. Cass mentions the so-called curse of Ham during this extended discussion with his cousin Ike concerning the latter's decision to renounce the tainted legacy passed down to him from slaveholding ancestors. The biblical passage at issue was used rhetorically to justify the enslavement of Africans. It recounts Noah's curse of his youngest son and of that son's descendants who are identified with various African peoples.[15]

In *Playing in the Dark*, Toni Morrison alerts readers to "the pattern of thinking about racialism in terms of its consequences on the victim—of always defining it asymmetrically from the perspective of its impact on the object of racist policy and attitudes." She exhorts literary studies to an investigation of "the impact of racism on those who perpetuate it."[16] A comparison between the relation to the Bible of white Yoknapatawphans and their black, formerly enslaved neighbors suggests that one such impact is the alienation of whites from this book used by their people to oppress and subjugate another.

For one, the moral imperatives of this sacred text had to be overlooked by those who used it to justify slavery. Furthermore, some degree of alienation may be rooted in literacy itself, when, as on the Southern plantation, some are excluded from the precincts of letters. Some could write, others could not. Such was the feudal predicament on Southern plantations that perpetuated illiteracy among their slaves. Of course, the act of excluding inevitably excludes the excluders; stratification isolates those at the top. Several of Faulkner's novels poignantly depict this isolation.

Ike and Cass merely speak *about* "the Book," whereas several African American characters in *Go Down, Moses* could be said to *speak* it. These characters have a wholly different relation to the sacred text about which Ike and Cass debate. Just as, in their particular circumstances, alienation was a concomitant of literacy, intimacy may have been a concomitant of orality. Indeed, in several scenes in *Go Down, Moses* and *The Sound and the Fury*, Faulkner seems to share Walter Ong's perception that "since sound is indicative of here-and-now activity, the word as sound establishes here-and-now personal presence." As Ong claims, "the spoken word does have more power than the written to do what the word is meant to do, to communicate."[17] And significantly for our consideration of the Bible, a text meant to somehow contain or convey the divine, this communication is not merely interpersonal but extra-personal as well: "Enacted primarily in song, prayer, and story, among oral peoples language functions not simply to dialogue with other humans but also to converse with the more-than-human cosmos, to renew reciprocity with the surrounding powers of earth and sky, to invoke kinship even with those entities which, to the civilized mind, are utterly insentient and inert."[18] More than anywhere else in his corpus, in *Go Down, Moses* Faulkner expressed his keen awareness of this primal function of language. With his invocation, "Oleh, Chief, . . . Grandfather," Sam Fathers, whom we'd never imagine in a church, initiates Ike into this sort of orality that is more communing than communication (GDM 177).

Rider's aunt in "Pantaloon in Black" was mentioned earlier, but, for startling immediacy, nothing surpasses Mollie Beauchamp's near oracular insistence, "Roth Edmonds sold my Benjamin, sold him in Egypt. Pharaoh got him" (GDM 362). Caught up in grief over her wayward nephew's execution, the elderly black woman seamlessly weaves her neighbors and family into the biblical narrative. Ike McCaslin hinged many of his abstract speculations on Scripture. Mollie experiences the sacred stories she cites as an immediate reality rather than as objects of analysis.

Conjure and Scripture

This sort of intensely vivid biblical citation is a phenomenon detailed by the scholar of African American religion and culture Theophus Smith. In *Conjuring Culture: Biblical Formations of Black America*, Smith describes how the Bible in concert with African magical and religious practice gains potency and efficacy: "(T)he sacred text of Western culture, the Bible, comes to view as a magical formulary for African Americans; a book of ritual prescriptions for reenvisioning and therein transforming history and culture."[19] "Pantaloon in Black" contains a trace of the practice of conjure and of its illegibility to the white community: Mannie's grave surrounded "by shards of pottery and broken bottles and old brick and other objects insignificant to sight but actually of profound meaning and fatal to touch, which no white man could have read" (GDM, 132). In "Go Down, Moses," Mollie's allusion to Jacob's lament becomes a kind of vehicle for her grief.[20] Along with her brother and sister-in-law, Mollie expresses her sorrow by voicing the biblical tale that corresponds to their loss.

> "Oh yes, Lord," Worsham said. "Pharaoh got him."
> "Done sold my Benjamin," the old Negress said. "Sold him in Egypt." She began to sway faintly back and forth in the chair.
> "Oh yes, Lord," Worsham said. (GDM 362)

These mourners' "conjurational employment of biblical figures" with therapeutic (and in other cases socially transformative) effect is just the sort of syncretic singsong described by Smith.[21]

Faulkner reinforces the contrast between black and white experiences of the Bible by providing a white foil in close proximity to Mollie, her brother, and his wife.[22] Like Ike and Faulkner himself, Gavin Stevens is transfixed by the Bible. However genuine Stevens's fascination with this book, his highly intellectual engagement with it ultimately proves wrongheaded and befuddled. "Gavin Stevens, Phi Beta Kappa, Harvard, Ph.D., Heidelberg, whose office was his hobby, although it made his living for him, and whose serious vocation was a twenty-two-year-old unfinished translation of the Old Testament back into classic Greek" (GDM 353). Ironically, this long-term project bespeaks distance from rather than proximity to the text. The Septuagint is already at one linguistic remove from the Bible's original Hebrew, and Stevens's patently crazy project of backward translation from some English version, most probably the King James, into Greek only compounds that distance.

Mollie, by contrast, has never read the Bible in any language. We learn expressly of her illiteracy at the chapter's end. Faulkner reinforces her habitation in a world without print by not fixing the spelling of her name, so that "Molly" in "The Fire and the Hearth" becomes "Aunt Mollie" in "Go Down, Moses." Nonetheless, the Bible is available to this illiterate, elderly former slave in a way it is not to Stevens.[23] This is dramatized by Stevens's abrupt flight from the site of Mollie and her relations' biblically enabled mourning. For all his philological fine-tuning of Scripture, Stevens is uncomfortable with the Bible in incantatory form.

From one angle, Faulkner's dichotomy between whiteness and logocentricity, on the one hand, and blackness and the conjurational, on the other, reinforces racist stereotypes. Assumptions about African irrationality and intellectual inferiority are, after all, a mainstay of racist rhetoric and ideology.[24] However, if these associations break down, for the most part, along racial lines, so, for the most part, does the massive cultural divide of literacy. One exception, Fonsiba's carpetbagger husband, is absorbed in the world of books in a way that seems to absent him from reality and severely curtail his effectiveness in the world of people and things. And the book's only intellectually inferior character is a childlike white man, Boon Hoggenbeck.

What's more, what is extrarational, such as emotion and faith, need not be irrational. While Mollie's biblical citations may sound like so much ignorant mumbo jumbo to her white auditors, the alert reader detects their critical content. Her application of biblical narrative to her own situation not only aids her grieving, it also contains a scathing hidden polemic against the white power structure. Borrowing from Henry Louis Gates, we might say that Mollie is "signifying." In other words, by inserting Roth Edmonds into the biblical scenario, Mollie repeats the story in Genesis "with a signal difference."[25]

> "Roth Edmonds sold him," the old Negress said. She swayed back and forth in the chair. "Sold my Benjamin."
> "Hush," Miss Worsham said. "Hush, Mollie. Hush now."
> "No," Stevens said. "No he didn't, Aunt Mollie. It wasn't Mr Edmonds. Mr Edmonds didn't—" (GDM 362)

Notably, though neither Stevens nor Miss Worsham senses at a conscious level the import of Mollie's statement, both seek instantly to deny its accuracy and silence her. Neither can hear nor wishes to hear what the elderly woman's words indicate: Roth Edmonds's and, by extension, their own complicity and even culpability (as willing participants in the racist status quo) in the demise of Samuel Worsham Beauchamp.[26]

Primitive Moderns

Cultural and literary critic Marianna Torgovnick's examination of the modernist fascination with the primitive provides another angle on Faulkner's racialized Bible.[27] Both in its scenes of communion with nature and in its depiction of an Africanized, oral Bible, *Go Down, Moses* presents a textbook example of a preoccupation and idealizing impulse common among Faulkner's contemporaries.[28] Indeed, the textual coincidence of these thematic elements may well arise from the unity of the impulse behind them.

Torgovnick's work calls into question and contextualizes the dichotomous perception underlying Faulkner's representation of a dual Bible. At
the same time, it attunes us to an implied Faulknerian critique, akin to
Martin Buber's, of the antioceanic modernist bias prevalent in Freud and
others. Finally, Faulkner's perhaps unconscious link between the Bible and
primitivism provides an especially telling and ironically charged expression of this "utopian desire to go back and uncover irreducible features of
the psyche, body, land and community—to reinhabit core experiences."[29]

We need neither affirm nor deny the validity of Faulkner's representation to consider the larger cultural pattern of which it is a part.[30]
Faulkner's idealized depiction of African American spirituality has all the
earmarks of an attraction felt by many moderns. As it turns out, Mollie
and Gavin Stevens are but one iteration of a widely accepted polarity
described by Torgovnick: "Views of primitives were based on perceived,
repeated oppositions between the primitive and civilization, in which the
primitive was coded metaphorically as feminine, collective and ecstatic,
and civilization was coded as masculine, individualistic, and devoted to
the quotidian business of the family, city, or state."[31] The primitive excited
a double-edged interest; Mollie and her young, dead nephew each might
elicit one of the "two broad kinds of reactions . . . : fear and horror at the
primitives' paganism, licentiousness and violence; admiration for their
communal life and idyllic closeness to nature." In other words, primitivism tends to express itself both "negatively—for example, as fear of
the primitive or as a detour into violence; and positively—as admiration
for the primitive, conceived to be the conduit of spiritual emotions."[32]
Both oppositions, between civilized and primitive culture and between
the exalted and the demonized primitive, are readily found in the pages
of Faulkner.

Modernist ambivalence toward the primitive is also embodied in contradictory theories of the oceanic put forward by Faulkner's European
contemporaries Martin Buber and Sigmund Freud. The oceanic—"best
defined as a dissolution of subject-object divisions so radical that one experiences the sensation of merging with the universe"—is, for Torgovnick,
the starting point of the fascination with the primitive, which "begins
with the discontinuities separating human bodies, animals, and inanimate
things—and seeks to bridge the gap."[33] While Freud associated this desire
with the death wish, for Buber it marked the successful abrogation of
dehumanizing, hierarchized relationships. Buber focused upon "relationships of mastery—human beings over other human beings and humans
over other categories of existence, such as animals and rocks—as the root
cause of Western malaise."[34] This emphasis—implicitly critical, according

to Torgovnick, of both Nietzschean and Hegelian theories of master/slave relations—is especially suggestive for our reading of Faulkner, an author whose personal experience and fiction alike are pervaded by the interpersonal legacies of slavery.[35] Although Faulkner's prose often highlights the frailty of language and the fractured nature of human interaction, like Buber, he prized the oceanic. Although occasionally some ambivalence seeps through, Faulkner represented the oceanic in a mostly positive light—for instance, as Sam Fathers saluting an ancestral buck or as that same wild buck "looking not like a ghost but as if all of light were condensed in him and he were the source of it" (GDM 157).

Faulkner's depiction of the woods and eponymous bear in the middle sections of *Go Down, Moses* along with his mythic characterization of the Native and African American Sam Fathers have long been recognized as the baldest expressions of primitivism in his corpus. Amid the oceanic greenery of the woods, young Ike must relinquish all the gadgets with which civilization has provided him—gun, pocket watch, and compass—in order to encounter the bear, the "epitome and apotheosis of the old wild life" (GDM 185). Books too are gadgets, and, in the same novel, their absence a boon to those deprived of them. Like Ike without his compass, often only those Yoknapatawphans who are ignorant of the Bible in printed form can connect with what is essential and enduring.

Torgovnick's ideas allow us to question the assumptions behind Faulkner's portrayal while remaining sympathetic to a probable yearning from which it sprang. She hazards the following explanation of ingrained misperceptions of the primitive: "[A]s Africa and the Americas were being 'discovered' or 'opened' by the West, Europeans were increasingly ghettoizing and repressing at home feelings and practices comparable to what they believed they saw among primitives—including feelings of kinship with animals and with nature and what is usually called mysticism. . . . So [these patterns of feeling] were projected abroad in a complicated process by which an aspect of the self was displaced onto the Other."[36] The spiritually other and contemporaneous primitive can be found elsewhere in Faulkner's corpus than *Go Down, Moses*. Most striking is its presence in *The Sound and the Fury*, the novel in which he also first represents both a black oral Bible and a white written one. Notably, the groundbreaking anthropological studies by Margaret Mead, Franz Boas, Marcel Mauss, and others that contributed to the modern fascination with the primitive, all the while fostering misperceptions of tribal, non-Western peoples, were published during and just prior to its composition.[37] Indeed, as Faulkner penned Dilsey, Benjy, Caddie, and the rest of the Compson family's tale, this cultural phenomenon was at its zenith.

The Sounded and the Fury

Of Faulkner's three biblically titled novels—*Absalom, Absalom!*, *If I Forget Thee, Jerusalem*, and *Go Down, Moses*—only the last represents the Bible in a twofold, racially inflected manner. As mentioned above, the primary and preliminary sign of this duality is the title itself, borrowed from a Negro spiritual. By contrast, the earlier novels' titles allude to the Bible by way of direct citation.[38] What's more, whereas the earlier titles reproduce the anguished cries of a mourning father and a dispossessed people, respectively, "Go Down, Moses" in its original context is a divine command to liberating action. This departure accords with a tonal and ideological shift at play in the novel proper. For, while the former two titles anticipate a bleakness in tone and outlook, the latter tempers nihilism and disillusionment with hope. That Faulkner's overt depiction of an African American Bible coincides with this shift is no accident; this escape from futility and despair is effected by African American characters who, again, serve the healing function and play the imagined role of contemporary primitives.

Go Down, Moses is neither the first nor the only instance of this fuller representation of the Bible creating a happy rupture, a respite from unmitigated bleakness. *The Sound and the Fury* neatly anticipates this relation between a racially doubled Bible and palpable emotional relief. First, this sort of shift is embodied by Reverend Shegog, who, in the Easter section of the novel, begins his sermon, we are told, sounding "like a white man": "His voice was level and cold. It sounded too big to have come from him and they listened at first through curiosity, as they would have to a monkey talking."[39] Undoubtedly, speaking "like a white man" involves speaking like one who primarily experiences the Bible via reading. Further along in his sermonizing, Shegog speaks as a black man, in other words, as, among other things, an auditor and speaker, and therefore as one who penetrates his audience.[40]

Initially, however virtuosic, Shegog's mere performance, labeled white, leaves his listeners unmoved. Inexplicably, when he speaks again, it is in a voice "as different as day and dark from his former tone, with a sad, timbrous quality like an alto horn, sinking into their hearts and speaking there again when it had ceased in fading and cumulate echoes" (SATF 183). Rather than theological expatiation, Shegog's sermon, after this transformation, combines image and incident from Revelation, John, Genesis, Luke, Matthew, Romans, and Corinthians to conjure an affecting biblical tableau.

No longer a thing apart, the Bible, thus Africanized, pierces the very being of those congregated: "They did not mark just when his intonation, his pronunciation, became negroid, they just sat swaying a little in their seats as the voice took them into itself" (SATF 184). With the racial shift in intonation, the speakers' immediacy contrasts sharply with his earlier remove. Shegog speaks of witnessing at firsthand the scene he recounts. What's more, as Faulkner represents it, Shegog's auditors are themselves absorbed, not merely in the preacher's words, but into the very scene depicted by his sermon: "'I sees, O Jesus! Oh I sees!' and still another, without words, like bubbles rising in water" (SATF 184). As the aqueous simile indicates, these rapt parishioners are so overcome as to be submerged; they drown beneath the flow of Shegog's words. This watery imagery is entirely apt; for, if not the ocean, certainly the oceanic carries this congregation away.

The immediacy of the preacher's cadences transports him and them beyond language: "He was like a worn small rock whelmed by the successive waves of his voice. With his body he seemed to feed the voice that, succubus like, had fleshed its teeth in him. And the congregation seemed to watch with its own eyes while the voice consumed him, until he was nothing and they were nothing and there was not even a voice but instead their hearts were speaking to one another in chanting measures beyond the need for words" (SATF 183). Thus breaking both internal and external bounds, Faulkner's careful representation of the heightened power of black orality evokes the oceanic.

The simultaneous appeal and threat of the primitive is also conveyed by these images. Their suggestion, first of suffocation and then of possession, betrays in their author and inspires in the reader a nagging sense of ambivalence. Even as it provides vicarious emotional relief for the reader, this Easter Sunday scene presents these eerie, ominous elements. In this scene at least, absolute connection has an air of menace about it.

Faulkner's physical characterization of Shegog also conveys an undercurrent of revulsion beneath the attractiveness of this episode. With reference to the preacher's appearance, Faulkner repeatedly deploys racist simian tropes. He describes this figure, for instance, as having a "monkey body" and "monkey face" (SATF 183). This distressing imagery suggests Faulkner's internalization of certain negative physical stereotypes about blacks, while the narrative proximity between primate features and primitive effect carries racist, evolutionist implications as well. Interestingly, the monkey metaphor is most prevalent before Shegog undergoes his mysterious racial and vocal transformation. With one exception, it is only when speaking as a white man with a voice described as a "cold inflectionless wire" that his audience perceives him and the narrator describes him in this way (SATF 183). While not mitigating the passage's racism, this may complicate it in ways that anticipate the studied destabilization

of racial categories featured in later novels such as *Light in August* and
Absalom, Absalom!

Absalom, Absalom! and *If I Forget Thee, Jerusalem* lack any sense of
the Bible as something powerfully active in the world. Rather, it is an
overarching presence, a text evoked by global allusions with markers—
the novels' titles—external to their narratives. The Bible, in other words,
seems to hover over these works. Rather than involving and actuating
Faulkner's characters, it remains removed. Along these same lines, as literary allusions, these biblical titles carry the aura of destiny or doom—not
of something that effects change but of something that seals fate.

Both *Go Down, Moses* and *The Sound and the Fury* include this bleak
perspective as well. Indeed, *The Sound and the Fury* bears its own allusive title that augurs despair even more powerfully than the titles of the
later novels. Nonetheless, the Bible's lively presence in these narratives
and its biracial fullness counterbalance this outlook. As an intertext, the
Bible moves from the abstract to the active. And, in both novels, there's
a political as well as a spiritual cast to this activity. From a worldly point
of view, the latter alone, the purely spiritual, is seen to be stifling or para-
lyzing; such a perspective considers inertial the manner of those with an
otherworldly frame of reference. However, as depicted here by Faulkner,
those engaged with this African American Bible are transported by it both
out of this world altogether and more deeply into the world as well. The
racial doubleness of Faulkner's representation of the Bible breaks open
the intertext ideologically by adding praxis to theory. The political and the
religious power of Shegog's words are by no means at odds. Like Exodus,
his sermon conveys both a spiritual and a social call to freedom. The spiritual efficacy of the black preacher's words only reinforce the urgency of
his social message; for he clearly identifies the cross with a lynching tree
and Roman soldiers with Southern police.[41] "I hears de boastin en de
braggin: Ef you be Jesus, lif up yo tree en walk! I hears de weepin en de
cryin en de turnt-away face of God: dey done kilt Jesus; dey done kilt my
Son!" (SATF 184). In Smith's sense of the term, the conjurational power
of Shegog's retelling of the Passion narrative is unmistakable.

An encounter between Dilsey and Mrs. Compson that follows fast upon
the heels of Shegog's sermon provides an externalized illustration of this
same racially dichotomous Bible.

> "You might hand me my bible."
> "I give it to you dis mawnin, befo I left."
> "You laid it on the edge of the bed. How long did you expect it to stay
> there?"
>
> Dilsey crossed to the bed and groped among the shadows beneath the edge
> of it and found the bible, face down. She smoothed the bent pages and laid the

book on the bed again. Mrs Compson didn't open her eyes. (SATF 187)

This ironic interaction highlights the roles of orality and literacy in this split. Because, for Mrs. Compson, the Bible is experienced by means of a physical object rather than living voice and active memory, it literally remains closed to her and neither alters her thinking nor affects her spirit.

Dilsey, on the other hand, for whom the Bible is an oral text, is connected with it intimately and inescapably. The next words out of her mouth are the same reference to Revelation that Shegog inspired her to utter earlier. With reference to her intimate and emotionally devastating connection with successive generations of Compsons, the old servant mutters, "Ise seed de first en de last. . . I seed de first en de last" (SATF 187). Because it resides inside of her rather than on a printed page, Dilsey's oral and conjurational Bible immediately spills forth and invades her experience.

The narrative proximity of this scene to the scene in which Dilsey, and the novel along with her, is broken open by Shegog's witnessing words highlights the ironic disjunction between the divergent biblical experiences of white mistress and black servant. While, in celebration of the risen Christ, Dilsey and her community gain emotional entry into the Passion narrative, Mrs. Compson resists rising from her own bed on Easter Sunday. This scene of habitual convalescence, of slackness of body and spirit, suggests once more the more profound and personal engagement of those who experience the Bible via oral rather than written transmission. As does *Go Down, Moses*, *The Sound and the Fury* contains unmistakable traces of the paradoxical alienation of those with access to the written word from that word itself.

Doubling and Dialogism

If Mrs. Compson's connection to the Bible is minimal, this is not so of all of Faulkner's white characters. Cora Tull in *As I Lay Dying* epitomizes the other sort of white relationship to Christianity depicted by Faulkner. When not passively disregarding Scripture or actively over-intellectualizing it, white Yoknapatawphans tend to apply its precepts to their neighbors in highly hypocritical, sometimes downright cruel ways. Many of these characters read the Bible in a literalist manner. In Bakhtinian language, they read it monologically.

Faulkner, who treasured the Bible's "scoundrels and blackguards . . . doing the best they could, just like people do now," had a fuller, more dialogical perception of Scripture.[42] Which is to say that, for him, it was too multifarious to present a master narrative, its characterizations too complex to reduce to any uniform moral vision. Along with his own sensitivity as a reader, his multiple and incongruous experiences of the Bible enriched and complicated Faulkner's experience of this already dialogical text.

Mischievous happenstance spared the young Faulkner from the institutional indoctrination of Sunday school. At least a lengthy reprieve from early and no doubt reductive schooling in Scripture was inadvertently won by eight-year-old Bill and his brother John one Sunday morning. When the two boys dirtied their white suits, their exasperated and relatively impious mother gave up on their church education altogether.[43] What some might have called a hazard to the child's soul probably proved a boon to his imagination. Certainly, received notions of biblical character and narrative are rarely to be found in his fiction, and then generally only in the mouths of the aforementioned hypocrites. For Faulkner during childhood, ancient Hebrew stories were brought to life not on the pages of a Sunday school primer but via the voice and imagination of Mammy Callie and others.

When he did perforce encounter the Bible in print, it was surely the King James Version. From the quotidian utterance of the evening storyteller to the exalted prose of this archaic translation, Faulkner's linguistic experiences of the Bible were richly divergent. Heterogeneity distinguishes Faulkner's own creations as well. A master literary modulator—in novels such as *Go Down, Moses, Light in August,* and *As I Lay Dying*— he shifted fluidly from tragic to comic registers. Bakhtin pinpoints the origin of all "seriocomical genres," as "the living present, often even the very day. For the first time in ancient literature the subject of serious (to be sure, at the same time comical) representation is presented without any epic or tragic distance, presented not in the absolute past of myth and legend but on the plane of the present day, in a zone of immediate and even crudely familiar contact with living contemporaries."[44] We may well imagine that his black Bible's oral transmission in a pungently immediate vernacular eased its effective absorption into the "seriocomic" world of Faulkner's novels. What's more, this vocalized Bible—partaking in the living world of Bakhtin's dialogic—moved an already so disposed Faulkner still further in a dialogical direction.

Faulkner's allusive or intertextual play with the Bible, his various incorporations of it into his fiction, all tend away from its monological reading and toward an increasingly dialogical one. Indeed, as the origin of the term "intertextuality" demonstrates, we here skirt tautology; originally coined by Julia Kristeva to translate Bakhtin's notion of the dialogic, "intertextuality" denotes the coincidence, within a literary work, of intersecting texts that mutually relativize one another.[45] Because of its kinship with the oral word, Faulkner's biblical intertextuality, rich with sometimes ironic historical overtones, may nudge the term away from the Lacanian and Derridean influence that led Kristeva to provide "text" as an alternative for "word" in her translation of Bakhtin. Though the poststructuralists ultimately collapse the oral and written into this single category, "text," it is unlikely that Bakhtin himself would have done so. Faulkner, famed scribe of interminable sentences that only a reader could love, highlighted orality in his fiction to enlivening effect.

The humble roots and subversive role of Faulkner's African American Bible would have heightened its interest for Bakhtin; as a slave appropriation and adaptation of the normative text of the master's culture, it is the quintessence of the topsy-turvy element of language and culture that he termed "carnival." As Kristeva explains, "The poetic word, polyvalent and multi-determined, adheres to a logic exceeding that of codified discourse and fully comes into being only in the margins of recognized culture. Bakhtin was the first to study this logic, and he looked for its roots in carnival. Carnivalesque discourse breaks through the laws of a language censored by grammar and semantics and, at the same time, is a social and political protest."[46] Her discussion of Bakhtinian carnival suggests some formal effect of the oral Bible on Faulkner's prose. Surely, Faulkner's main permissions to break grammatical and syntactical laws were gained from his modernist cohort and various of their stylistic forebears. Beyond this literary lineage, however, his ongoing encounter with a vernacular potent enough to carnivalize the Bible also had a freeing effect on his language.

No avid reader and writer like Faulkner could but wish to share the experience of the printed word. In passing, the Joseph Blotner biography mentions a strikingly pertinent moment in Faulkner's relationship with his beloved Mammy. The then world-renowned man of letters chose to use some of his Nobel Prize monies to benefit "the poor folk of Lafayette County," many of whom were black and one of whom he had once engaged to teach Caroline Barr how to read and write.[47] None of the biographies elaborate on whether these lessons were initiated or how the pupil fared. In any case, the poignancy of the gesture remains. Mammy Callie had brought Bill Faulkner into her world of stories; now he wished to bring her into his.

NOTES

1. "A Letter to Bishop Robert E. Jones," *Georgia Review* 55, 3 (2001): 530.

2. This is not to imply that Bakhtin anywhere in his writings recognizes the Bible's rampant dialogism. Somewhat perplexingly, this sensitive critic seems little attuned to this aspect of Scripture. In "Bakhtin's Misreadings of the Bible," *Hebrew University Studies in Literature and the Arts*, 16 (1988): 132), Harold Fisch notes the Russian theorist's tendency merely to "treat the biblical material as that which is satirized." Nearly always the ideological antagonist in Bakhtin's drama of literary evolution and production, the Bible is repeatedly

and unfairly typecast, so to speak, as the heavy, the conservative, and the simpleton. See Fisch for a detailed reading of Bakhtin's failure to recognize the Bible's positively formative (rather than solely oppositional) role in the origin of the novel, as well.

3. Mikhail Bakhtin, *Problems of Dostoevsky's Poetics*, ed. and trans. Caryl Emerson (Minneapolis: Minnesota University Press, 1984), 110.

4. Mikhail Bakhtin, "Discourse in the Novel," in *The Dialogic Imagination: Four Essays*, ed. Michael Holquist (Austin: Texas University Press, 1981), 280.

5. James P. Zappen, "Mikhail Bakhtin," in *Twentieth-Century Rhetoric and Rhetoricians: Critical Studies and Sources*, ed. Michael G. Moran and Michelle Ballif (Westport, Conn.: Greenwood Press, 2000), 7–20. For biblical criticism that celebrates and elucidates the Bible as an exemplar of Bakhtinian dialogism, see Ilana Pardes, *Countertraditions in the Bible: A Feminist Approach* and Walter L. Reed, *Dialogues of the Word: The Bible as Literature according to Bakhtin*.

6. All evoked texts are creatively incorporated, via varieties of allusive play or stylistic and thematic influence, into the alluding texts to which they are linked. Due to its singular role in extra-literary Western culture, however, the Bible, more than any other evoked text, is likely to be represented in its materiality as well. Evocation via material representation is a subcategory of literary allusion in which the evoked text not only works musically, linguistically and thematically on the imagination of author and reader, but is also a narrative datum, a piece of the scenery, so to speak, about which that author's characters maneuver. Another subcategory of allusion, one that subsumes material representation and is also most frequently biblical, might be termed representation of consciousness. Whether or not it is represented as a material object, the Bible is apt to weigh heavily in the consciousness, and sometimes, indeed, on the conscience, of literary characters and creators alike.

7. Toni Morrison, *Playing in the Dark: Whiteness and the Literary Imagination* (New York: Vintage Books, 1992), VIII, 6.

8. Theophus H. Smith, *Conjuring Culture: Biblical Formations of Black America* (New York: Oxford University Press, 1994), 3.

9. However loving, the emotional bonds linking a black caretaker—especially a former slave such as Caroline Barr—with her white, privileged charges are undeniably complex. As much has been discussed by a variety of Faulkner's critics, including Minrose Gwin, "Her Shape, His Hand: The Spaces of African American Women in *Go Down, Moses*," and Judith Sensibar, "Who Wears the Mask? Memory, Race, and Desire in *Go Down, Moses*," both in *New Essays on "Go Down, Moses*," ed. Linda Wagner-Martin (New York: Cambridge University Press, 1996). Both note a distressing concomitant of these sorts of arrangements, the disrupted connection of a mammy to her own biological family. However, while for Gwin, Faulkner's characterization of the Mammy Callie-like Mollie in *Go Down, Moses* both "reflects and deflects" "certain expectations of blackness and femaleness" (92), for Sensibar, Faulkner's invocation "of Barr's eulogy," with reference to Mollie, "is a reactionary move" (115) and his characterization of this figure merely "sentimentalized and stereotyped" (116). Much closer to Gwin's interpretation is my own presented in my dissertation's second chapter (Lael Judith Gold, "Next Year in Yoknapatawpha: The Biracial Bible of William Faulkner" [PhD dissertation, University of California, Berkeley, 2004], 30–73), which treats at length the Faulkner–Caroline Barr relationship and its echoes in *Go Down, Moses* and reads a telling divide between Faulkner's sentimentalizing public statements and the interrogation of such sentimentality in his fiction. Gwin speaks of Mollie's remarkable "motion" that has "the effect of creating an alternative narrative space . . . which contains both female and Africanist stories" (920). Likewise, my reading emphasizes this figure's moral freedom. Like Sensibar, on the other hand, Thadious Davis in *Faulkner's "Negro": Art and the Southern Context* (Baton Rouge: Louisiana State University Press, 1983) tends to collapse Faulkner and his fictional character Roth: "Roth's tribute echoes Faulkner's dedication to Callie Barr, as well as the dominant characteristic of the Negro in *Soldiers' Pay*, *Flags in the Dust*, and *The Sound and the Fury*. While these characteristics stress the humanity of blacks, they are nonetheless reductive" (242). With less reference to the fiction and more to the biography, Bart H. Welling, in "In Praise of the Black Mother: An Unpublished Faulkner Letter on

'Mammy' Caroline Barr," *Georgia Review*, 55, 3 (2001): 536–542, also treats the complexities of Faulkner's hybrid identity and emotional ties to Caroline Barr.

10. Gabriel Josipovici, *The Book of God* (New Haven: Yale University Press, 1988), 8.

11. William Faulkner, *Absalom, Absalom!* (New York: Modern Library, 1936), 9. Further references will be cited in the text as AA.

12. Joseph Blotner, *Faulkner: A Biography* (New York: Vintage Books, 1974), 13.

13. David Abram, *The Spell of the Sensuous: Perception and Language in a More-Than-Human World* (New York: Pantheon Books, 1996), 265.

14. William Faulkner, *Go Down, Moses* (New York: Random House, 1942), 249. Further references will be cited in the text as GDM.

15. This specious interpretation of Genesis 9: 20–27 has been widely and convincingly refuted, most notably by the celebrated Puritan Chief Justice Samuel Sewall in "The Selling of Joseph: A Memorial," in *A House Divided: The Antebellum Slavery Debates in America, 1776–1865*, ed. Mason I. Lowance Jr. (Princeton: Princeton University Press, 2003), who observed that Canaan rather than Ham is cursed three times. A more apt criticism of the widely held proslavery reading also accords in a highly literal way with Ike's immediate objection to Cass's reference to Ham: "There are some things He said in the Book, and some things reported of Him that He did not say" (GDM, 249). In fact, nowhere does God curse Ham. Rather, it is the hungover father, Noah, who curses his youngest son. The reader is not privy to God's perspective on either Noah's venom or the older sons' scrupulous filial piety. There is no reason to attribute any efficacy to Noah's words. Fascinatingly, in light of Cass's defense of hunting and land ownership, this incident follows God's express authorization of these same activities. Also, the occasion of Noah's curse of Ham—a son's gaze upon his stupefied father's nakedness—is an apt analogue of Ike's quest to lay bare his grandfather's crimes.

16. Morrison, 11.

17. Walter Ong, *The Presence of the Word: Some Prolegomena for Cultural and Religious History* (New York: Simon & Schuster, 1967), 113, 15.

18. Abram, 70–71.

19. Smith, 3.

20. *Go Down, Moses*, 353–54, 361–63. Genesis 37: 33–35 recounts Jacob's intense grief at what he understands to be the loss of his son Joseph. Joseph, in fact, is not killed by a wild beast, as misreported by his treacherous brothers, but instead sold by them into slavery in Egypt. As will be discussed, Faulkner's conflation of Joseph with his younger brother Benjamin in Mollie's lament is an "error" laden with meaning.

21. Smith, 3.

22. In *Faulkner's "Negro,"* Thadious Davis traces this sort of race-based contrast in Faulkner as far back as his first novel: "the conclusion of *Soldiers' Pay* depends directly upon the felt presence of the Negro as a community of faith and feeling. In the final chapter the earthy, religious blacks stand in thematic counterpoint to the post–World War I despair and disillusionment at the center of the novel" (34). Davis notes its broader prevalence in Faulkner's fiction as well: "Black life remains a foil to emptiness, the loss of value and meaning, in white southern life" (126).

23. Faulkner's doubled Bible implies a denigration of the written word and celebration of the spoken word consistent with a Western philosophical bias highlighted and countered by Jacques Derrida, who expressly collapses the opposition between alienated writing and harmonious speech. As Derrida sees it, both are texts dependent for meaning on an infinite process of division and difference. Faulkner's representation of an oral African American Bible also reinforces a link between phonocentricity ("the living voice") and logocentricity (a "transcendental signifier," in this case, the Judeo-Christian Lord of biblical fame). Derrida's poststructuralist theory of deconstruction would deny both sides of this equation. Jacques Derrida, *Of Grammatology*, trans. Gayatri Chakravorty Spivak (Baltimore: Johns Hopkins University Press, 1976), 50, 90, and Terry Eagleton, *Literary Theory: An Introduction* (Minneapolis: University of Minnesota Press, 1983), 130–31.

24. "So, while the Enlightenment is famous for establishing its existence upon man's ability to reason, it simultaneously used the absence and presence of reason to delimit and

circumscribe the very humanity of the cultures and people of color which Europeans had been 'discovering' since the Renaissance." Henry Louis Gates Jr., *The Signifying Monkey* (Oxford: Oxford University Press, 1988), 130.

25. Ibid., 110.

26. A second and subtler signal difference is Mollie's conflation of Benjamin and Joseph. That the Joseph believed by his father to be dead and by his brothers to be enslaved actually attained a place of great importance in Pharaoh's court renders paradoxical this particular instance of signifying. According to Mollie's lament, it is the boy Benjamin, whom the brothers are loath to endanger, who has been destroyed. Among other possible meanings, the elderly aunt's words suggest a keen awareness of the ongoing vulnerabilities post-emancipation of black males, such as her beloved nephew, despite their migration to supposedly freer urban centers in the North.

27. Marianna Torgovnick, *Primitive Passions: Men, Women, and the Search for Ecstasy* (New York: Knopf, 1997). Torgovnick pointedly avoids the social evolutionist and derogatory use of "primitive" as synonymous with "simple" or "crude" (4). Her employment of the term instead encompasses wider-ranging, nonpatronizing associations. "Primitivism inhabits thinking about origins and pure states; it informs desires for known beginnings and, by extension, for predictable ends" (5).

28. Thadious Davis, in *Faulkner's "Negro,"* situates the primitive bent of Faulkner's African American characterizations geographically rather than generationally. Before discussing their appeal and effect (below), she begins by enumerating "the pervasive, superficial generalizations about the Negro's personality: his love of rhetoric, his ability to tell a good story, his enjoyment of life, his capacity for love and laughter, his harmony with the natural rhythms of life, his instinct for survival, his faith in God and belief in the supernatural. Various combinations of these stereotypes attracted white authors of the transitional South to the black experience. These same stereotypes led to gross distortions of blacks (primarily as amoral primitives) that cannot be overlooked in a consideration of the literary background affecting Faulkner and contributed to by him" (28).

29. Ibid., 5. Not surprisingly, this same sort of yearning can also be attributed to Ike McCaslin; as James Snead puts it in *Figures of Division* (New York: Methuen, 1986), *Go Down, Moses* "explores Ike McCaslin's desire for a pre-exchange state of things, an origin before the need for articulation, division, difference, and domination" (181).

30. In *Go Down, Moses*, Faulkner implicitly acknowledges and pointedly inscribes—by means of parallels to similarly situated myopic, white male characters—the probability of his own storytelling's shortcomings in this regard. Indeed, the impaired perception of those who bear witness across racial lines is a recurring theme of the novel. Of special note, in this particular context, is the poignant figure of Roth Edmonds, in "The Fire and the Hearth," who sentimentalizes and likely misattributes maternal feelings and motivations to the black woman, Mollie Beauchamp, who was "the only mother he ever knew" (GDM, 97). Not surprisingly, Mollie bears a more than marked resemblance to Caroline Barr.

31. Torgovnick, 14.

32. Ibid., 7.

33. Ibid., 5.

34. Ibid., 11.

35. Ibid., 223, note 20.

36. Ibid., 114.

37. Ibid., 9–10.

38. Though direct, these citations are slightly and significantly inaccurate.

39. William Faulkner, *The Sound and the Fury*, 2nd ed. (New York: W. W. Norton, 1994), 183. Further references will be cited in the text as SATF.

40. By stark contrast, one example of how a white man speaks is provided by this novel's allusive title taken from the leading light of the Western canon, William Shakespeare. The original tragic context in Macbeth of the phrase "sound and fury" is perhaps the most powerful statement of utter nihilism ever articulated, the very antithesis of hope:

To-morrow, and to-morrow, and to-morrow,

Creeps in this petty pace from day to day
To the last syllable of recorded time,
And all our yesterdays have lighted fools
The way to dusty death. Out, out, brief candle!
Life's but a walking shadow, a poor player
That struts and frets his hour upon the stage
And then is heard no more: it is a tale
Told by an idiot, full of sound and fury,
Signifying nothing. (*Macbeth* V.v)

41. James Snead offers the following sobering counterclaim: "Without time, there is not separation and frustration, but also, no articulation; 'the language of the heart' can alter nothing—particularly not Southern apartheid. The ahistorical timelessness in which Dilsey and Benjy—to name only two—exist has for far too long received the title 'redemptive.' If the oppressed tolerate outrages past and present, and the threat of future outrages, then they have no choice but to 'endure' into eternity. Their 'redemption,' by this measure, is eternal damnation. The sermon by Reverend Shegog may be a structural and even ethical highpoint in the novel, but its futility becomes clear as soon as Dilsey leaves the all-black church for the Compson household" (39). While Benjy's stasis and Dilsey's long-suffering disposition may seem to corroborate this bleak view, the role in the civil rights movement of the stirring oratory of the African American church suggests a possible efficacious joining of time and eternity, one perhaps anticipated by the outsider Shegog.

42. Frederick L. Gwynn and Joseph Blotner, eds., *Faulkner in the University: Class Conferences at the University of Virginia, 1957–1958* (Charlottesville: University of Virginia Press, 1959), 286.

43. John Faulkner, *My Brother Bill* (Athens, Ga.: Hill Street Press, 1998), 16–18.

44. Bakhtin, *Problems*, 108.

45. As Kristeva puts it *in Desire in Language: Semiotic Approach to Literature and Art*, ed. Leon S. Roudiez (New York: Columbia University Press, 1980), "Bakhtinian dialogism identifies writing as both subjectivity and communication, or better, as intertextuality" (68). As presented by Robert Stam in *Reflexivity in Film and Literature from Don Quixote to Jean-Luc Godard* (New York: Columbia University Press, 1992), her notion of intertextuality, that every text presents "an intersection of textual surfaces where other texts may be read" (20), derives from Bakhtinian formulations, such as "The literary word is aware of the presence of another literary word alongside it" (quoted in Stam, 20). For Kristeva, "any text is constructed as a mosaic of quotations; any text is the absorption and transformation of another. The notion of intertextuality replaces that of intersubjectivity, and poetic language is read as at least double" (66). Faulkner's fiction continues to transform the already transformed and doubled Bible. An originally Near Eastern text, the Bible was first Europeanized and then Americanized and Africanized long before its absorption into novels like *Go Down, Moses* and *The Sound and the Fury*.

46. Kristeva, 65.

47. Blotner, 535.

Afterword: In the House of Faulkner

Jay Parini

I will examine inheritance in the broadest sense of that term, meditating on what it means to take something from the past, about how the past informs—quite literally—the present and future, and especially about what it means for a biographer to enter another life-house, so to speak, even though the owner of that house doesn't especially want visitors.

Let's begin with the word itself, "inheritance." It derives from the Latin *heres* (*haero*), meaning "to grasp"; *herus* is the master of a house, in that he has come to possess the land upon which the house sits. It also means that he has grasped the importance of his possession, that he values it. An "heir apparent" is one who succeeds to the property, from the Latin *apparens*, meaning "manifest." And so the heir makes himself apparent, manifests himself, by his presence on the scene. There is a literalness here that seems worth considering, which is why I'm dwelling on the roots of words.

Faulkner, of course, was fascinated, if not obsessed, by ideas of inheritance, of heritage, of what—again quite literally—*inheres*: the indwelling mystery of the *genius loci*. This obsession takes the form in some of Faulkner's writing ("The Bear," for example) of a highly developed sense of ecology, from the Greek root *eco* (*oikos*) meaning "house." One enters a holy place when one stands on sacred ground, which in Faulkner often means the wilderness, the house of the Lord in a larger sense—a house which has no specific heir, in that nobody has a right to own this wild land, the space inhabited by Sam Fathers in "The Bear," the "unaxed wilderness as of old."[1]

I will return to "The Bear" at the end of this essay, but for the moment, let's keep in mind the estimable and legendary figure of Sam Fathers, who is a kind of father to Ike, the boy and the man, whose own obsession with his inheritance is, indeed, the fulcrum of that story. It turns on what he will make of his literal inheritance, and how he thinks about this property, and how he regards the larger "house" of the environment, the wilderness that has been receding year by year, as civilization absorbs what was wild, takes away a resource of inspiration, a habitat for the bear and other wild creatures, absorbs and dissolves even those narratives so treasured by young Ike as he comes to the hunting camp and sits around the campfire and listens, again and again, to tales that are told and revised, remade, reshaped into legend—a parallel process, perhaps, for the work of fiction-making that absorbed Faulkner himself for so many decades.

In Faulkner's fiction, special attention is paid to houses, as Noel Polk has explained in *Children of the Dark House*.[2] Polk notes that both *Absalom, Absalom!* and *Light in August* were both, in early drafts, called "Dark House." There is the echo here, as he suggests, of *Bleak House*, which was Dickens's great novel of succession, of inheritance. This was also Dickens's systematic attack on the labyrinthine legal system, which had failed to understand what it really meant to inherit anything. But Faulkner moves beyond Dickens here. In both "Dark House" novels, he summons a bleak image of a burning house, an antebellum mansion, and the purgative fires that destroy them erase, at least partially, the sins of a particular family and a historical era. Secrets in need of expiation lie buried in each of these houses. In Faulkner, these sins often entail racism, slavery, miscegenation, and a confusion over inheritance.

The haunted landscape of Faulkner's fiction teems with houses, many of them in a collapsed condition, a physical decay that seems redolent of moral rot, as in *Sanctuary*, where Faulkner opens with an unforgettable image of the Old Frenchman Place:

> The house was a gutted ruin rising gaunt and stark out of a grove of unpruned cedar trees. It was a landmark, known as the Old Frenchman Place, built before the Civil War; a plantation house set in the middle of a tract of land; of cotton fields and gardens and lawns long since gone back to jungle, which the people of the neighborhood had been pulling down piecemeal for firewood for fifty years or digging with secret and sporadic optimism for the gold which the builder was reputed to have buried somewhere about the place when Grant came through the county on his Vicksburg campaign.[3]

This gutted ruin recurs in Faulkner, and in many ways it remains at the center of his work, as much symbol as literal dwelling. To an extent, the ruined house becomes an elegiac symbol of the plantation system itself, with its destructive class structure, its violence (against slaves), its endless closets full of dangling skeletons, which dance in the mind of Faulkner's characters, giving them pause, making them frantic or cautious or reckless. Of course, every ruin was, at some point, a remarkable place, a Big House, as Faulkner might have said, referring to his grandfather's house in Oxford. Even Rowan Oak was, in his own life, a symbolic residence, rescued by Faulkner and the royalties from his books from the always threatening wilderness around it. While it may never have been as pristine as the house of Major de Spain, and could not hold a candle to the mansion summoned from the ooze and muck itself by Thomas Sutpen,

Rowan Oak was a house of his own re-creation, a place where he sat for decades, telling and retelling the same stories, refashioning himself.

Faulkner's characters often dream of houses. They are frequently seen looking out of them, through the framing device of a window, into the landscape and beyond. Freud once said that dreams of houses are usually about the dreamer's own soul; a ruined house is, therefore, a distressed soul. A house is a dwelling place, but it is also a family story, a tale of many souls, some of them in conflict, and not occasionally ruled over—and ultimately ruined—by a father who (for various reasons) cannot accept the responsibility of his house, cannot accept the authority (or authorship) that his position demands of him. In this sense, the author is the builder of a house, a "maker" in the old Scottish sense of the poet as one who makes (indeed, the Greek root of "poem" is the word "to make.")

Again, Noel Polk has been here before me, tracing the genealogy of houses in his book, looking in particular at the ruins of the House of Compson and the House of Snopes. As a biographer, I'm going to move outside these texts and take the life of Faulkner itself as a text—a sin committed by every biographer, I'm afraid—and examine the House of Faulkner, looking at the ecology of this house subjectively, with the understanding that no take on a life is ever complete or definitive.

I feel somewhat rebuked by Faulkner himself, who wanted no biographer coming along to attempt to rebuild the house he had himself deconstructed nicely over many decades. He wrote in frustration to Malcolm Cowley, who in editing *The Portable Faulkner* (1946) probed for biographical details: "It is my ambition to be, as a private individual, abolished and voided from history, leaving it markless, no refuse save the printed books; I wish I had had enough sense to see ahead thirty years ago and, like some of the Elizabethans, not signed them. It is my aim, and every effort bent, that the sum and history of my life, which in the same sentence is my obit and epitaph too, shall be them both: He made the books and he died."[4] Faulkner made the books, and he died—it's a predictable course—but the story didn't end there. Biographers began to gather around the House of Faulkner in earnest in the fifties, with several early attempts to refashion or reconstrue the structure itself, such as Robert Coughlan's two-part biographical profile appearing in *Life*. Further profiles, at book-length, came along soon after his death from deep inside the House itself. Faulkner's two surviving brothers, John and Murry, weighed in with gossipy memoirs: *My Brother Bill* (1963) and *The Falkners of Mississippi* (1967). These were attempts to right, if not write, the record, to set things straight before the rebuilding fell to outsiders, such as Joseph Blotner, David Minter, Stephen Oakes, Frederick R. Karl, and (alas) me—and this only skims the surface, as a fair number of books exist that, to one degree or another, might be called biographical studies, such as Judith B. Wittenberg's *Faulkner: The Transfiguration of Biography* (1979), Joel Williamson's *William Faulkner and Southern History* (1993), or the more recent study by James G. Watson, *William Faulkner: Self-Presentation and Performance* (2000).

These memoirs, biographies, and biographical studies all participate in the rebuilding project, erecting the House of Faulkner, and anyone who comes along cannot simply pretend that nobody was there before. Faulkner, I think, has been lucky in the quality and quantity of attention he has received. Most centrally, of course, there is Joseph Blotner's massive two-volume biography of 1974, with its 1984 condensation and revision. The vast labor of these volumes cannot be denied or gainsaid, as Blotner was in contact with many of those in Faulkner's immediate circle, most of whom are now beyond conversation. He did yeoman's work in reconstructing the author's history and personal *mythos*, shaping and bending the material to fit a certain pattern, against which all subsequent biographers must work, either as augmenters or resisters.

Of course the very notion of a definitive biography is a myth that belongs to earlier times, dating back to the age of philology. As I have always argued, biography is fiction, as in the root meaning of the term *fictio*, meaning "to shape," to make a selection, an arrangement of the agreed-upon facts. The figure drawn in a biography is never the man himself; art and life intermingle in complex ways, but they should not be confused. As a work of art, a biography is a species of narrative; like a novelist, a biographer must tell a story, which means that foreshadowing is important. There must be a narrative build toward a climax, or several climaxes. There is always, alas, the final climax of death, and the denouement of the funeral and what happens to the family afterwards. There is, more importantly perhaps, the prologue: the events and characters leading up to the heir apparent, the accomplished author—the author on horseback, so to speak.

There is, in other words, the inheritance: all of those elements—historical, cultural, and familial—that lead up to the advent of the author. An author may try to ignore his or her past, or use it with various degrees of delicacy or fidelity. Faulkner was ruthless in his use of history, willing and able to ransack this material for his own purposes, willing to sacrifice "truth," in its somewhat tedious and literal sense, to Truth in a larger sense, as the word moves toward the Word—what in the Gospel of John is described as the *logos* at the center of meaning. James Watson describes this process rather well: "Breaking into his own life experience, and breaking that, in turn, into diverse, often divergent segments counterposed against one another, [Faulkner] created a world of controlled chaos, made in his own protean image and reflective of his own multiple sense of self."[5]

A good deal of Faulkner's fiction is about the work of memory, about what Coleridge shrewdly described as the activity of the Secondary Imagination, which involves a breaking apart of reality as first perceived by the Primary Imagination. It involves breaking up and rebuilding: the work of the artist, which is also the work of the critic and biographer, who must look for motives, discern patterns, construe meanings, and—at times—deliver judgments. And so the House of Faulkner was built by many hands, beginning with the author's own, then aided and abetted by countless hands to follow, as the same core material is sifted, analyzed, selected, reshaped.

In perhaps the finest example of the Secondary Imagination at work, there is the retelling of the South by Quentin Compson to his roommate, Shreve, in *Absalom, Absalom!* The retelling becomes a collaborative venture, as the young men try to get at the core of the story, as it remains elusive in the retelling, made up of "rag-tag and bob-end" as Faulkner says. Shreve in this novel stands in for the audience of all of Faulkner's fiction when he says, *"Tell about the South."* This imperative falls to Quentin, who in turn stands in for the artist himself, shaping and reshaping the materials of history and myth, such as the story of Sutpen's return from the Civil War, his seduction of Milly, how Wash killed him, and how Judith lived in succeeding years at Sutpen's Hundred.

This tale was already told before by Faulkner in "Wash," a short story written in 1933 and published a year later, in *Harper's*. It was published again in *Doctor Martino and Other Stories* in April of 1934, by which time Faulkner was writing *Absalom*. He gathers elements of the story, with added or expanded details, not once but twice, as in chapter 6, where the context is dramatically expanded, and in chapter 7, where Quentin breaks into Shreve's attempts to frame this material and retells the story as his father told it to him, further expanding the historical context, reformulating, rebuilding the narrative—much as Faulkner himself revisits his own past, again and again, remaking stories, turning twice-told tales into thrice-told tales, as in the example of the story of Wash Jones.

This work of fiction-making may contain "paradox and inconsistency," as Faulkner says in *Absalom*, "but nothing fault nor false." Indeed, Faulkner had a great tolerance for inconsistency, and it has driven many a scholar to his or her grave—those scholars who wish for an ideal order, that is. There are, for instance, many inconsistencies between the text of *Absalom* completed in 1936 and the genealogy and chronology that he later appended to the novel. Faulkner's famous map of Yoknapatawpha County itself has several mistakes in it, as when Tull's farm appears on

the wrong side of the river from where, in *As I Lay Dying*, it was supposed to lie, nearer the Bundren place. On the other hand, Faulkner
was a fanatic about the details of his manuscripts, keen on the specifics
of punctuation and spelling, and he wanted his own inconsistencies and
irrelevancies; they expressed the chaos of his cosmos in ways that seemed,
to the artist in him, appropriate. Indeed, he could be extremely testy with
editors who dared to mess with his confusions and contradictions.

An artist is, necessarily, his own father; but he has fathers himself, literally and figuratively. Faulkner's own lineage on his father's side traces back,
again and again, to his idealized vision of W. C. Falkner, Faulkner's name-
sake, the Old Colonel, who stands in for one view of patrimony, of what
one inherits from one's fathers. As we know, the Old Colonel was a legend
in his own time, one of those swashbuckling men who lit out for the territory, an American Adam who built himself and his own house, increasing
his lands, breaking the wilderness, bending it to his will and whim.

Born in 1825, in Tennessee, the Old Colonel came to Mississippi as a
boy of fifteen. Without a penny to his name, he wandered from town to
town, meeting a seven-year-old girl, Lizzie Vance, whom he would marry
in later life, after the death of his first wife. All sorts of legends swirl
around this meeting, most of them probably fictitious; in any case, he
fathered eight children by Lizzie, and made himself a fortune by hook
and by crook. He owned a violent streak, and lost three fingers in 1846,
in a fight over a woman. He may well, as Joel Williamson has suggested,
have fathered a mulatto daughter, thus committing the act of miscegenation that so preoccupies various characters in Faulkner's fiction, such as
Charles Bon or Joe Christmas. He became a Civil War hero in dubious
circumstances, leading a reckless charge at the Battle of First Manassas
that led to his being voted out of his regiment a year later, although he
retained the rank of colonel, which he seems to have passed on to his son,
the Young Colonel.

The Old Colonel invested in railroads and real estate, he farmed, was a
banker, and wrote books, including *The White Rose of Memphis*, a popular novel of 1880, about a motley group heading south to New Orleans
on a party boat: a book that his grandson, William, would refashion in his
second novel, *Mosquitoes*. By 1879, the Old Colonel was worth fifty thousand dollars, making him a wealthy man, the owner of a big house, a *pater
familias* with long coattails. He died in a violent scene, shot to death at
point-blank range in the town square of Ripley by a business associate.

This was, of course, the wild west, a frontier society. The man who
killed the Old Colonel got off with a slap on the hand, charged only with
aggravated manslaughter. But the legend of W. C. Falkner lived on,
largely in his grandson's head. That grandson transformed his grandfather

in his fiction time and again, most vividly in the figure of John Sartoris, in his eponymous novel. Just as the Old Colonel was commemorated with a statue that stood eight feet high, so was John Sartoris. In the Sartoris statue, writes Faulkner, "His head was lifted a little in that gesture of haughty pride which repeated itself generation after generation with a fateful fidelity, his back to the world and his carven eyes gazing out across the valley where his railroad ran, and the blue changeless hills beyond, and beyond that the ramparts of infinity itself."[6]

One can find traces of W. C. and his son, J. W. T. Falkner, the Young Colonel, in so many figures in Faulkner's fiction, from Sartoris to Thomas Sutpen and beyond. What I suggest in my own biography, *One Matchless Time*, is that Faulkner unconsciously set himself the task of reclaiming his inheritance, which had been squandered by his own father, Murry. Indeed, the three generations of Falkners—the Old Colonel, the Young Colonel, and Murry—represent a fierce decline in family fortunes and reputation. Billy Falkner and his three brothers grew up in the shadow of two great men, the Old Colonel and the Young Colonel, rebuked by the image of their own father, a hard-drinking man who lived on the largess of his father, invited to the Big House for Sunday dinner, perpetually outshone.

Faulkner set his lands in order. By making large sums of money in Hollywood, and by writing novels that attracted worldwide attention, including the Nobel Prize for Literature, he managed to rebuild the House of Faulkner, to purchase and restore his own Big House, to buy one of the actual farms, Greenfield Farm, that had once belonged to the family. He may have been called Count No 'Count by his neighbors in Oxford, who mocked his pretensions, but by the end of his life nobody could reasonably doubt his reputation.

Faulkner's work was not visionary but revisionary, as he told and retold tales, describing the decline of the South in terms familiar from his own family history. He understood the racial tensions of the region and realized that slavery was the Original Sin for which generations must pay a price. He also understood, and meditated in deeply nuanced terms, that the relationship between the human community and the land around it, the soil itself, was troubled. Civilization, as Freud reminds us, is based on repression; this has an ecological dimension as well, as played out so memorably in "The Bear," one of Faulkner's central achievements.

At least on some elemental level, it's a simple story, although mythic in its dimensions and profound in its ramifications. "There was a man and a dog too this time. Two beasts, counting Old Ben, the bear, and two men, counting Boon Hogganbeck, in whom some of the same blood ran which ran in Sam Fathers, even though Boon's was a plebeian strain of it and only Sam and Old Ben and the mongrel Lion were taintless and incorruptible."[7]

The main narrative centers on the yearly hunt for the bear, a valued ritual, itself a valued inheritance as well as a rite of passage. Old Ben represents "the apotheosis of the old wildlife which the little puny humans swarmed and hacked," and the hunters, like readers, who must reconstruct any great text in the hard work of interpretation, returning to the scene of the hunt in a ritual fashion. Interestingly, Ike McCaslin, the boy, mistrusts all written texts, including his family ledgers, which contain his dark inheritance, the secrets that plague him, that he must repress, and that in the end repress him. As Richard Godden and Noel Polk have shown, in their article "Reading the Ledgers," this document offers clues to the past that bears so heavily on the present.[8]

Faulkner quotes the ledgers only in passing, offering all that the present really ever has of the past: partial inscriptions, manifestations that occur in a piecemeal way and require not deconstruction but imaginative reconstruction. As Godden and Polk argue, it is more than miscegenation in the past that plagues this family, that is part of Ike's inheritance. There is the hint of homosexuality as well, between Buck and Buddy, and in the possibility that Buck has purchased the slave Percival Brownlee for sexual reasons. All of this remains speculative, requiring a piecing together of narrative strands that dangle in provocative ways; but it is enough to say that Ike is worried about what may have happened. He is so worried, in fact, and so disgusted, that he renounces his inheritance.

In a larger sense, "The Bear" is about Ike's gradual realization that his family bears a special burden acquired by its participation in slavery, and its transgression of various boundaries—between the races and between men. As always, a Faulkner text concerns itself with problems of meaning and interpretation; this seems especially true of a story that buries a cryptic text within the larger narrative. The reader identifies with Ike as he attempts to uncover his own past, weaving a text of sorts from the various strands. He has learned that his legendary ancestor, Carothers McCaslin, perhaps another refraction of the Old Colonel, raped his own daughter, whom he had fathered with a slave girl called Eunice. We may even share Ike's need to repress the truth about Buck and Buddy and the slave, Brownlee, assuming that he does understand that such truths may exist.

Whatever the specificity of Ike's knowledge, he rejects his inheritance because he cannot accept the sins of his fathers. He must, instead, transfer his gaze to Sam Fathers, so aptly named. As Richard Gray has said, "The illusions of power over nature and ownership are clearly being dismissed: Ike has come to learn that nobody owns the land. Now he is casting aside a past and a patrimony that claimed to possess both land and people, and that still seems to proclaim, 'They're mine!'—in other words, that nature and human nature are available for use and profit."[9]

Ike cannot, of course, completely free himself from what inheres; he takes the Original Sins of his fathers with him into the wilderness. He merely steps out from under literal responsibilities, passing the family estate on to his cousin, who will no doubt abuse the land and people he acquires. In acting as he does, Ike ruins his own marriage and turns himself into a fairly pathetic figure, a pale version of Sam Fathers, without the mystical aura. Once again, we encounter a tale of generations in decline, a story about lost energies, of succession that leads nowhere.

Faulkner's symbolism works on many fronts, which is part of its attraction for readers. The death of the bear, Old Ben, is soon followed by the destruction of the hunting camp and its tradition of storytelling. Soon enough, the railroad comes, destroying the wilderness, bringing with it the ruins of modern industrial life. Faulkner describes the train in primitive terms as it "shrieked and began to move: a rapid churning of exhaust, a lethargic deliberate clashing of slack couplings traveling backward along the train, the exhaust changing to the deep slow clapping bites of power as the caboose too began to move and from the cupola he watched the train's head complete the first and only curve in the entire line's length and vanish into the wilderness, dragging its length of train behind it so that it resembled a small dingy harmless snake vanishing into the weeds."[10]

The wilderness must die, having been violated in such a fashion. The virile bear, Old Ben, gives way to the sterile life of Ike McCaslin, unfathered, himself incapable of fathering. He becomes, in effect, the last McCaslin, without inheritance.

In a peculiar way, one can read "The Bear" as a cautionary tale about reading the past, about using the past without agility, or without a keen sense of irony, without "sublimating the actual into the apocryphal," as Faulkner himself put it. Truth is not always beauty, and without beauty—which here I will identify with imagined truth, with the fullest possible application of the Secondary Imagination—there is certainly no hope to inherit everything from the past that belongs to us, so that we—the heirs apparent of the House of Faulkner—can live fully in the rich and perpetual present of his language.

NOTES

1. William Faulkner, *Go Down, Moses* (New York: Random House, 1942), 319.

2. Noel Polk, *Children of the Dark House: Text and Context in Faulkner* (Jackson: University Press of Mississippi, 1996).

3. William Faulkner, *Sanctuary* (New York: Cape and Smith, 1931), 4.

4. Malcolm Cowley, ed., *The Faulkner-Cowley File: Letters and Memories, 1944–1962* (New York: Viking, 1966), 126.

5. James G. Watson, *William Faulkner: Self-Presentation and Performance* (Austin: University of Texas Press, 2000), 2.

6. William Faulkner, *Sartoris* (New York: Harcourt, Brace, 1929), 229.

7. *Go Down, Moses*, 155.

8. Richard Godden and Noel Polk, "Reading the Ledgers," *Mississippi Quarterly* (Summer 2002).

9. Richard Gray, *The Life of William Faulkner: A Critical Biography* (Oxford: Blackwell, 1994), 282.

10. *Go Down, Moses*, 318.

Contributors

Susan V. Donaldson, professor of English at the College of William and Mary, is the author of *Competing Voices: The American Novel, 1865–1914* and coeditor of *Haunted Bodies: Gender and Southern Texts*. The author of over thirty articles, primarily on Southern literature, she is currently working on a book-length study, "The Politics of Storytelling in the American South."

Lael Gold is a lecturer in Comparative Literature at the University of California at Berkeley. She received her PhD at Berkeley in 2004, with a dissertation entitled "Next Year in Yoknapatawpha: The Biracial Bible of William Faulkner."

Adam Gussow, assistant professor of English and Southern Studies at the University of Mississippi, is the author of *Mister Satan's Apprentice: A Blues Memoir* and *Seems Like Murder Here: Southern Violence and the Blues Tradition*, winner of the C. Hugh Holman Award for the best book of literary scholarship or criticism in Southern literature published in 2002.

Martin Kreiswirth is associate provost (Graduate Education), dean of Graduate and Postdoctoral studies, and professor of English at McGill University in Montreal, Canada. He is the author of *William Faulkner: The Making of a Novelist* and coeditor of three volumes, including *The Johns Hopkins Guide to Literary Theory and Criticism*, as well as editor of the *Mississippi Quarterly*'s special issue on Faulkner's Yoknapatawpha.

Jay Parini is the Axinn Professor of English at Middlebury College. He has published four volumes of poetry, six novels, and three biographies, most recently the widely praised *One Matchless Time: A Life of William Faulkner*. He has also edited several volumes, including *The Oxford Encyclopedia of American Literature*.

Noel Polk, professor of English at Mississippi State University, is the author or editor of over a dozen volumes, including *Outside the Southern Myth*, *Children of the Dark House*, *Eudora Welty: A Bibliography of Her Work*, and *Reading Faulkner: The Sound and the Fury*. He is editor of the *Mississippi Quarterly*.

Judith L. Sensibar is professor emerita of English at Arizona State University. She is the author of *The Origins of Faulkner's Art* and *Faulkner's Poetry: A Bibliographical Guide to Texts and Criticism* and editor of Faulkner's *Vision in Spring*. Her current project is the completion of "'We Have Waited Long Enough': The Story of William Faulkner, His Black and White Mothers, and His Wife," forthcoming from Yale University Press.

Jon Smith, assistant professor of English at the University of Montevallo, is coeditor of *Look Away! The U.S. South in New World Studies* and author of "Southern Culture on the Skids: Narcissism, Branding, and the Burden of Southern History," forthcoming from the University Press of Mississippi.

Joseph R. Urgo, former chair of the Department of English at the University of Mississippi, is dean of the faculty at Hamilton College. He is the author of *Faulkner's Apocrypha: "A Fable," Snopes, and the Spirit of Human Rebellion*; *Willa Cather and the Myth of American Migration*; *Novel Frames: Literature as Guide to Race, Sex, and History in America Culture*; and, most recently, *In the Age of Distraction*.

Priscilla Wald, associate professor at Duke University, is the author of *Constituting Americans: Cultural Anxiety and Narrative Form* and is currently completing a book-length study, "Cultures and Carriers: From 'Typhoid Mary' to 'Patient Zero.'" She is also associate editor of the journal *American Literature*.

Index

References to illustrations appear in *italics*.